Revolution and Counter-Revolution in Ancient India

Revolution and Counter-Revolution in Ancient India

Dr. B.R. Ambedkar

NAMASKAR
BOOKS
happy reading to you

Published by
NAMASKAR BOOKS
Building No. 2/42 (Second Floor)
Ansari Road, Daryaganj
New Delhi-110002
e-mail: namaskarbooks@gmail.com
Website: www.namaskarbooks.com

ISBN: 978-93-94871-34-2
Revolution and Counter-Revolution in Ancient India
By Dr. B. R. Ambedkar

Edition 2025

Price
₹ 650.00 (Rupees Six Hundred Fifty only)

Printed at Sita Fine Arts, Delhi

Editor's Note or Editorial Note

Editorial Note in the manuscript published in Dr. Babasaheb Ambedkar: *Writings and Speeches, Vol. 3* by the Government of Maharashtra:

Dr. B.R. Ambedkar had proposed to write a treatise titled 'Revolution and Counter-Revolution in Ancient India.' The table of contents has been printed in the chapter of schemes. He had originally planned to write seven books under this broad title. The Committee was able to find some pages and though the few chapters in his collection, the chapters are also incomplete. After careful scrutiny, the Committee came to a decision that 'Revolution and Counter-Revolution in Ancient India' is to be presented in this volume with the available material, though incompleteness. Despite its Dr. Ambedkar considered the rise of Buddhism as a revolution. The Counter-Revolution pioneered by Brahmins resulted in the decline and fall of Buddhism.

As such, the following chapters are included under this title:

1. *Ancient India on Exhumation*
2. *The Ancient Regime : The State of the Aryan Society*
3. *A Sunken Priesthood*
4. *Reformers and Their Fate*
5. *The Decline and Fall of Buddhism*
6. *The Literature of Brahmanism*
7. *The Triumph of Brahmanism*
8. *The Morals of the House—Manusmruti or the Gospel of Counter-Revolution*
9. *Philosophic Defence of Counter-Revolution (Krishna and His Gita)*

10. Analysis of Virata Parva and Udyoga Parva

11. Brahmins vs. Kshatriyas

12. The Shudras and the Counter-Revolution

13. The Women and the Counter-Revolution

The readers may compare these chapters with the proposed plan provided in the last chapters of Schemes.

– **Editors**

Contents

Part I

Chapter I
Ancient India on Exhumation

There are two typed copies of this chapter. Both contain additions and corrections in the handwriting of Dr. Babasaheb Ambedkar. After careful consideration, we decided that the latter version should be included here. This essay, consisting of three pages only, seems to be an introduction to a larger subject Dr. Ambedkar probably had in his mind.

– Editors

Much of the ancient history of India is no history at all. It is note that ancient India has no history. On the contrary, it has plenty of it. But it has lost its character. It has been transformed into mythology to amuse women and children. This seems to have been done deliberately by the Brahminical writers. Take the word *Deva.* What does it mean? Does the word Jana Vishesh represent a member of the human family? It has been made to appear as a superhuman agency. By this, the pith of history contained in it is squeezed out.

Along with the word Deva occur the names of Yaksha, Gana, Gandharva, and Kinnars. Who were they? The impression one gets from reading the *Mahabharata* and *Ramayana* is that they were imaginary beings who filled the horizon but did not exist.

But the Yaksha, Gana, Gandharva, and Kinnaras were also members of the human family. They were in the service of the Devas. The Yakshas were guarding the palaces. The Ganas were guarding the Devas. The Gandharvas were amusing the Devas with music and dancing. The Kinnaras were also in the service of the Devas. The descendants of the Kinnaras are even now living in Himachal Pradesh.

Take the name *Asura*. The descriptions of Asuras given in the Mahabharata and Ramayana make it seem as though they belonged to a non-human world. An Asura is described as eating ten cartloads of food. They are monsters in size. They sleep for six months. They have ten mouths. Who is a Rakshasa? He too is described as a non-human creature. In size, in his capacity for eating, and in his habits of life, he resembled the Asura.

There are plenty of references to the Nagas. But who is a Naga? A Naga is represented as a serpent or a snake. Can this be true? Whether true or not, it is so, and Hindus believe it. Ancient Indian history must be exhumed. Without its exhumation, Ancient India will go without history. Fortunately, with the help of the Buddhist literature, Ancient Indian history can be dug out of the debris that the Brahmin writers have heaped upon it in a fit of madness.

The Buddhist literature helps a great deal to remove the debris and see the underlying substance quite clearly and distinctly.

The Buddhist literature shows that the Devas were a community of human beings. There are so many Devas who come to the Buddha to have their doubts and difficulties removed. How could this be unless the Devas were human beings?

Again, the Buddhist canonical literature throws a flood of light on the puzzling question of the Nagas. It makes a distinction between womb-born Nagas and egg-born Nagas, thereby making it clear that the word Naga has a twofold meaning. In its original sense, it stood for the name of a human community.

The Asuras, again, are not monsters. They too are Jan-Vishesh—human beings. According to *Satapatha Bramhana*, the *Asuras* are the descendants of Prajapati, the Lord of the Creation. How they became evil spirits is not known. But the fact is recorded that they fought against the Devas for the possession of the earth, that they were overcome by the Devas, and that they finally succumbed. The point is clear that the Asuras were members of the human family and not monsters.

With this exhumation of debris, we can see Ancient Indian history in a new light.

❑

Chapter 2

The Ancient Regime: The State of the Aryan Society

This essay consists of II typed foolscap pages tagged into a file. From the last sentence, it appears that the chapter is incomplete.

–Editors

Buddhism was a revolution. It was as great a revolution as the French Revolution. Though it began as a religious revolution, it became more than religious revolution. It became a social and political revolution. To be able to realise how profound was the character of this revolution, it is necessary to know the state of the society before the revolution began its course. To use the language of the French Revolution, it is necessary to have a picture of the ancient regime in India.

To understand the great reform, which he brought about by his teaching, it is necessary to have some idea of the degraded condition of the Aryan civilisation at the time when Buddha started on the mission of his life.

The Aryan Community of his time was steeped in the worst kind of debauchery: social, religious and spiritual.

To mention only a few of the social evils, attention may be drawn to gambling. Gambling had become as widespread among the Aryans as drinking.

Every king had a hall of gambling attached to his palace. Every king had an expert gambler in his employment as a companion to play with. King *Virat* had in his employment *Kanka* as an expert gambler. Gambling was not merely a pastime with kings. They played with heavy stakes. They staked kingdoms, dependants, relatives, slaves, servants. King Nala staked everything in gambling with his brother *Paskkar* and lost everything. The only thing he did not stake was himself and his wife Damayanti. Nala had to go and live in the forest as a beggar. There were kings who went beyond Nala. The Mahabharata[f[2]] tells how Yudhishthira the eldest of the Pandavas, gambled and staked everything: his brothers and also his and their wife, Draupadi. Gambling was a matter of honour with the Aryans, and any invitation to gamble was regarded as an injury to one's honour and dignity. Yudhishthira gambled with such disastrous consequences although he was warned beforehand. His excuse was that he was invited to gamble and that, as a man of honour, he could not decline such an invitation.

This vice of gambling was not confined to kings. It had infected even the common folk. The *Rig Veda* contains lamentations of a poor Aryan ruined by gambling. The habit of gambling had become so common in Kautilya's time that there were gambling houses licensed by the king, from which the king derived considerable revenue.

Drinking was another evil which was rampant among the Aryans. Liquors were of two sorts: *Soma* and *Sura.* Soma was a sacrificial wine. The drinking of the Soma was, in the beginning, permitted only to Brahmins, Kshatriyas and Vaishyas. Subsequently, it was permitted only to Brahmins and Kshatriyas. The Vaishyas were excluded from it, and the Shudras were never permitted to taste it. Its manufacture was a secret known only to the Brahmins. *Sura* was open to all and was drunk by all. The Brahmins also drank Sura. Shukracharya, the priest to the Asuras, drank so heavily that, in his drunken state, he gave the life–giving *Mantra*—known only to him and with which he used to revive the *Asuras* killed by the Devas—to *Kach,* the son of Brihaspati, who was the priest of the Devas. The Mahabharata mentions an occasion when both Krishna and Arjuna were dead drunk. That shows that the best in the Aryan Society were not only not free from the drinking habit but that they drank heavily. The most shameful part of it was that even the Aryan women were addicted to drinking. For instance, *Sudeshna,* the wife of King Virat, tells her maid Sairandhri to go to Kichaka's palace and bring Sura, as she is dying to have a drink. It is not to be supposed that only queens indulged themselves in drinking. The habit of drinking was common among women of all classes and even Brahmin women were not free from it. The fact that liquor and dancing were indulged in by the Aryan women is clear from the *Kaushitaki Grihya Sutra* 1.11-12, which says: "Four or eight women who are not widowed, after having been regaled with wine and food, are to dance for four times on the night previous to the wedding ceremony."

That the drinking of intoxicating liquor was indulged in by Brahmin women, not to speak of women of the lower Varnas, as late as the seventh and eighth centuries A.D. in the Central region of Aryavarta, is again evident from Kumarila Bhatta's *Tantravarttika* I (iii). 4, which states, "Among the people of modern days, we find the Brahmin women of the countries of Ahichchhatra and Mathura to be addicted to drinking." Kumarila condemned the drinking practice in the case of Brahmins only, but not of Kshatriyas and Vaishyas, men and women, if the liquor was distilled from fruits or flowers (Madhavi), and molasses (Gaudi) and not from grains (Sura).

The sexual immorality of the Aryan Society must shock their present-day descendants. The Aryans of pre-Buddhist days had no such rule of prohibited degrees as we have today to govern their sexual or martial relationships.

According to the Aryan Mythology, Brahma is the creator. Brahma had three sons and a daughter. His one son, Daksha, married his sister. The daughters born of this marriage between brother and sister were married, some to Kashyapa, the son of Marichi (the son of Brahma), and some to Dharma, the third son of Brahma.

In the Rig-Veda, there is an episode related of Yama and Yami, brother and sister. According to this episode, Yami, the sister, invites her brother Yama to cohabit with her and becomes angry when he refuses to do so.

A father could marry his daughter. Vashishta married his own daughter, Shatrupa, when she came of age (16).-Manu married his daughter Ilaf. Janhu married his daughter, Janhavi. Surya married his daughter, Usha.

There was polyandry, not of the ordinary type. The polyandry prevalent among the Aryans was a polyandry where kinsmen cohabited with one woman. Dhahaprachetani and his son Soma cohabited with Marisha, the daughter of Soma.

There are numerous instances of grandfather marrying his granddaughter. Daksha married his daughter to his father Brahma, and from that marriage was born the famous Narada. Dauhitra married his 27 daughters to his father, Soma, for cohabitation and procreation. The Aryans did not mind cohabiting with women in the open and within sight of people. The Rishis used to perform certain religious rites called *Vamdevya vrata.* These rites used to be performed on the *Yagna Bhumi.* If any woman came there, expressed a desire for sexual intercourse, and asked the sage to satisfy her, the sage would cohabit with her then and there in the open on the *Yagna Bhumi.* Instances of this may be mentioned. The case of the sage Parashara having sexual intercourse with Satyavati, and also of Dirghatapa. That such a custom was common is shown by the existence of the word *Ayoni*. The word Ayoni is understood to mean 'immaculate conception'. That is not, however, the original meaning of the word. The original meaning of the word *Yoni* is 'house'. Ayoni means conceived out of the house i.e., in the open. That there was nothing deemed to be wrong in this is clear from the fact that both Sita and Draupadi were Ayonija. That this was very common is clear from the fact that religious injunctions had to be issued against such a practice.

The practice of renting out their women to others for a time was prevalent among the Aryans. As an illustration, the story of Madhavi mentioned. Yayati gave his daughter Madhavi as an offering to his Guru Galav. Galav rented out the girl Madhavi to three kings, each for a period. Thereafter, he gave her in marriage to Vishwamitra. She remained with him until a son was born to her. Later, Galav took away the girl and returned to her father, Yayati.

Besides the practice of letting out women to others temporarily at a rent, there was prevalent among the Aryans another practice, namely allowing procreation by the best among them. Raising a family was treated by them as though it was akin to breeding or stock-raising. Among the Aryas, there was a class of people called *Devas* who were Aryans but of superior status and prowess. The Aryans allowed their women to have sexual intercourse with any one of the classes of Devas in the interest of good breeding. This practice prevailed so extensively that the Devas came to regard prelibation concerning the Aryan women as their prescriptive right. No Aryan woman could be married unless this right of prelibation had been redeemed and the woman released from the control of the Devas by offering what was technically called *Avadan.* The *Laja Homa,* which is performed in every Hindu marriage and the details of which are given in the *Ashwalayan Grahya Sutra* is a relic of this act of the redemption of the Aryan woman from the right of prelibation of the Devas. The *Avadan* in the *Laja Homa* is nothing but the price for the extinguishing of the right of the Devas over the bride. The *Saptapadi,* performed in all Hindu marriages and regarded as the most essential ceremony—without which there is no lawful marriage—has an integral connection with this right of prelibation of the Devas. Saptapadi means the bridegroom walking seven steps with the bride. Why is this essential? The answer is that the Devas if they were dissatisfied with the compensation, could claim the woman before the seventh step was taken. After the seventh step was taken, the right of the Devas was extinguished, and the bridegroom could take away the bride and live as husband and wife without being obstructed or molested by the Devas.

There was no rule of chastity for maidens. A girl could have sexual intercourse with and also progeny from anybody without contracting marriage. It is evident from the root meaning of the word *Kanya,* which means a girl. Kanya comes from the root *Kam,* which means a girl free to offer herself to any man. That they did offer themselves to any man and had children without contracting regular marriage is illustrated by the case of Kunti and Matsyagandha. Kunti had children from different men before she was married to Pandu and Matsyagandha had sexual intercourse with the sage Parashara before she married to Shantanu, the father of Bhishma.

Bestiality was also prevalent among the Aryans. The story of the sage Kindama having sexual intercourse with a female dear is well known. Another instance is of Surya cohabiting with a mare. But the most hideous instance is of a woman having sexual intercourse with the horse in the *Ashvamedha Yagna.*

(INCOMPLETE)

❑

Chapter 3
A Sunken Priesthood

This essay is numbered Chapter III in the file of the 'Ancient Regime' and contains 16 foolscap-typed pages. This Chapter also seems to be left incomplete.

—Editors.

The priestly profession in the ancient Aryan society was monopolised by the Brahmins. None except a Brahmin could become a priest. As custodians of religion, the Brahmins were the guides of the people in moral and spiritual matters. They were to set the standard for people to follow. Did the Brahmins act up to the standard? Unfortunately, all the evidence we have shows that the Brahmins had fallen to the utmost depth of moral degradation.

A Shrotriya Brahmin was not supposed to keep with him a store of provisions lasting for more than a week. But they had systematically trampled upon this rule and were addicted to the use of stored-up items namely: foods, drinks, clothing, equipage, bedding, perfumes, and currystuffs. The Brahmins were addicted to visiting shows such as:—

(1) Nautch dances (*Nakkam*).

(2) Singing of songs (*Gitam*).

(3) Instrumental music (*Vaditam*).

(4) Shows at fairs (*Pekham*).

(5) Ballad recitations (*Akkhanam*).

(6) Hand music (*Paniseram*).

(7) The chanting of bards (*Vetala*).

(8) Tam-tam playing (*Kumbhathunam*).

(9) Fair scenes (*Sobhanagarkam*).

(10) Acrobatic feats by Kandalas (Kandala-vamsa-dhopanam).

(11) Combats of elephants, horses, buffaloes, bulls, goats, rams, cocks, and quails.

(12) Bouts at quarterstaff, boxing, wrestling.

(13) Sham-fights, roll-calls, manoeuvres, reviews.

They were addicted to games and recreation; that is to say:

(1) Games on boards with eight or ten rows of squares.

(2) The same games are played by imagining such boards in the air.

(3) Going over diagrams drawn on the ground so that one steps only where one ought to go.

(4) Either removing the pieces or men from a help with one's nail or putting them into a heap, in each case without shaking it. He who shakes the heap loses.

(5) Throwing dice.

(6) Hitting a short stick with a long one.

(7) Dipping the hand with the fingers stretched out in lac, red dye, or flour water, and striking the wet hand on the ground or a wall, calling out 'What shall it be?' and showing the form required—elephants, horses, etc .

(8) Games with balls.

(9) Blowing through toy pipes made of leaves.

(10) Ploughing with toy ploughs.

(11) Turning somersaults.

(12) Playing with toy windmills made of palm leaves.

(13) Playing with toy measures made of palm leaves.

(14) Playing with toy carts or toy bows.

(15) Guessing at letters traced in the air, or on a playfellow's back.

(16) Guessing the playfellow's thoughts.

(17) Mimicry of deformities.

They were addicted to the use of high and large couches; that is to say:

(1) Moveable settees, high and six feet long (*Asandi*).

(2) Divans with animal figures carved on the supports (*Pallanko*).

(3) Goat's hair coverings with very long fleece (*Gonako*).

(4) Patchwork counterpanes of many colours (*Kittaka*).

(5) White blankets (*Patika*).

(6) Woollen coverlets embroidered with flowers (*Patalika*).

(7) Quilts stuffed with cotton wool (*Tulika*).

(8) Coverlets embroidered with figures of lions, tigers, etc. (*Vikatika*).

(9) Rugs with fur on both sides (*Uddalom*).

(10) Rugs with fur on one side (*Ekantalomi*).

(11) Coverlets embroidered with gems (*Katthissam*).

(12) Silk coverlets (*Koseyyam*).

(13) Carpets large enough for sixteen dancers (*Kittakam*).

(14) Elephant, horse, and chariot rugs.

(15) Rugs of antelope skins sewn together (*Aginepaveni*).

(16) Rugs made of the plantain leaves.

(17) Carpets with awnings above them (*Sauttarakkhadam*).

(18) Sofas with red pillows for the head and feet.

The Brahmins were addicted to the use of means for adorning and beautifying themselves; that is to say: rubbing in scented powders on one's body, shampooing it, and bathing it; patting the limbs with clubs after the manner of wrestlers; the use of mirrors, eye-ointments, garlands, rouge, cosmetics, bracelets, necklaces, walking sticks, reed cases for drugs, rapiers, sunshades, embroidered slippers, turbans, diadems, whisks of the yak's tail, and long-fringed white robes.

The Brahmins were addicted to such low conversation as these:

Tales of kings, robbers, and ministers of state; tales of war, terrors, and battles; talk about foods and drinks, clothes, beds, garlands, and perfumes; talks about relationships, equipages, villages, towns, cities, and countries; tales about women and heroes; gossip at street corners, or places where water is fetched; ghost stories; desultory talk; speculations about the creation of the land or sea, or about existence and non-existence. The Brahmins were addicted to the use of wrangling phrases, such as:

"You do not understand this doctrine and discipline, but I do." "How should you know about this doctrine and discipline?" "You have fallen into wrong views. It is I who is in the right." "I am speaking to the point but you are not." "You are putting last what ought to come first and first what ought to come last."

"What you have excoriated so long is all quite upsetting." "You are proved to be wrong." " Set to work to clear your views." "Disentangle yourself if you can."

The Brahmins were addicted to taking messages, going on errands, and acting as go-betweens— whether for kings, ministers of state, Kshatriyas, Brahmins, or young men— saying: 'Go there, come hither, take this with you, bring that from there.'

The Brahmins were tricksters, droners of holy words in prayers, diviners, and exorcists, ever hungering to add gain to gain.

The Brahmins earned their living by wrong means of livelihood, by low arts, such as these:

(1) Palmistry—prophesying long life, prosperity, etc. (or the reverse) from marks on a child's hands, feet, etc.

(2) Divining using omens and signs.

(3) Auguries drawn from thunderbolts and other celestial portents.

(4) Prognostication by interpreting dreams.

(5) Fortune-telling from marks on the body.

(6) Auguries from the marks on cloth gnawed by mice.

(7) Sacrificing to Agni.

(8) Offering oblations from a spoon.

(9) Making offerings to gods of husks, of the red powder between the grain and the husk, of husked grain ready for boiling, or of ghee and oil.

(10) Sacrificing by spewing mustard seeds, etc., into the fire from one's mouth.

(11) Drawing blood from one's right knee as a sacrifice to the gods.

(12) Looking at the knuckles, etc., and, after muttering a charm, divining whether a man is well-born lucky or not.

(13) Determining whether the site for a proposed house or pleasance, is lucky or not.

(14) Advising on customary law.

(15) Laying demons in a cemetery.

(16) Laying ghosts.

(17) Knowledge of the charms to be used when lodging in an earthhouse.

(18) Snake charming.

(19) The poison craft.

(20) The scorpion craft.

(21) The mouse craft.

(22) The bird craft.

(23) The crow craft.

(24) Foretelling the number of years a man has yet to live.

(25) Giving charms to ward off arrows.

(26) The animal wheel.

The Brahmins earned their living by wrong means of livelihood, by low arts, such as these:

Knowledge of the signs of good and bad qualities in the following things, and of the marks in them denoting the health or luck of their owners: to wit, gems, staves, garments, swords, arrows, bows, other weapons, women, men, boys, girls, slaves, slave-girls, elephants, horses, buffaloes, bulls, oxen, goats, sheep, fowls, quails, iguanas, herrings, tortoises, and other animals.

The Brahmins earned their living by wrong means of livelihood, by low arts such as soothsaying, to the effect that:

(1) The chiefs will march out.

(2) The home chiefs will attack and the enemies retreat.

(3) The enemies' chiefs will attack, and ours will retreat.

(4) The home chiefs will gain the victory, and ours will suffer defeat.

(5) The foreign chiefs will gain the victory on this side, and ours will suffer defeat.

Thus, there will be victory on this side and defeat on that. The Brahmins, while living on food provided by the faithful, earned their living by wrong means of livelihood, by such low arts as fore-telling:

(1) There will be an eclipse of the Moon.

(2) There will be an eclipse of the Sun.

(3) There will be an eclipse of a star (Nakshatra).

(4) There will be aberration of the Sun or the Moon.

(5) The Sun or the Moon will return to its usual path.

(6) There will be aberrations of the stars.

(7) The stars will return to their usual course.

(8) There will be a jungle fire.

(9) There will be a fall of meteors.

(10) There will be an earthquake.

(11) The god will thunder.

(12) There will be rising and setting, clearness and dimness of the Sun, the Moon, or the stars, or foretelling of each of these twelve phenomena that they will betoken such and such a result.

The Brahmins earned their living by wrong means of the livelihood, by low arts, such as these:

(1) Foretelling an abundant rainfall.

(2) Foretelling a deficient rainfall.

(3) Foretelling a good harvest.

(4) Foretelling scarcity of food.

(5) Foretelling tranquillity.

(6) Foretelling disturbances.

(7) Foretelling a pestilence.

(8) Foretelling a healthy season.

(9) Counting on the fingers.

(10) Counting without using the fingers.

(11) Summing up large totals.

(12) Composing ballads, poetising.

(13) Casuistry, sophistry.

The Brahmins, while living on food provided by the faithful, earned their living by wrong means of livelihood, by low arts, such as:

(1) Selecting an auspicious day for marriages when the bride or bridegroom is brought home.

(2) Selecting an auspicious day for marriages when the bride or bridegroom is sent forth.

(3) Fixing create time for the conclusion of treaties of peace (or using charms to procure harmony).

(4) Fixing create time for the outbreak of hostilities (or using charms to create discord).

(5) Fixing an auspicious time for the calling in of debts (or charms for success in throwing dice).

(6) Fixing an auspicious time time for the expenditure of money (or charms to bring ill luck to an opponent throwing dice).

(7) Using charms to make people lucky.

(8) Using charms to make people unlucky.

(9) Using charms to procure abortion.

(10) Incantations to keep a man's jaws fixed.

(11) Incantations to bring on dumbness.

(12) Incantations to make a man throw up his hands.

(13) Incantations to bring on deafness.

(14) Obtaining oracular answers using the magic mirror.

(15) Obtaining oracular answers through a girl possessed.

(16) Obtaining oracular answers from a god.

(17) The worship of the Sun.

(18) The worship of the Great One.

(19) Bringing forth flames from one's mouth.

(20) Invoking Siri, the Goddess of Luck.

The Brahmins earned their living by wrong means of livelihood, by low arts, such as these:

(1) Vowing gifts to a god if a certain benefit is granted.

(2) Paying such vows.

(3) Repeating charms while lodging in an earthhouse.

(4) Causing virility.

(5) Making a man impotent.

(6) Fixing lucky sites for dwellings.

(7) Consecrating sites.

(8) Ceremonial rinsing of the mouth.

(9) Ceremonial bathing.

(10) Offering sacrifices.

(11) Administering emetics and purgatives.

(12) Purging people to relieve the head (that is, by giving drugs to make people sneeze).

(13) Oiling people's ears (either to make them grow or to heal sores on them).

(14) Satisfying people's eyes (soothing them by dropping medicinal oils into them).

(15) Administering drugs through the nose.

(16) Applying collyrium to the eyes.

(17) Giving medicinal ointment for the eyes.

(18) Practising as an oculist.

(19) Practising as a surgeon.

(20) Practising as a doctor for children.

(21) Administering roots and drugs.

(22) Administering medicines in rotation.

(INCOMPLETE)

❑

Chapter 4
Reformers and Their Fate

This is a typed bound copy consisting of 87 pages. The Ambatta Sutta starts at page 69 of the manuscript, and after page 70, pages are numbered from A to Z. The beginning of page 71 starts with Lohicca Sutta.

– Editors

I. Aryan Society.

II. Buddha and Reform.

III. I

It was Sir T. Madhava Raw who, speaking of Hindu society in his time, said:

"The longer one lives, observes, and thinks, the more deeply does he feel that there is no community on the face of the earth which suffers less from political evils and more from self-inflicted, self-accepted, or self-created, and therefore avoidable evils, than the Hindu Community."

This view expresses quite accurately and without exaggeration the necessity of social reform in Hindu society.

The first social reformer, and the greatest of them all, is Gautama Buddha. Any history of social reform must begin with him, and no history of social reform in India will be complete, which omits to take account of his great achievements.

Siddhartha, surname Gautama, was born in the Sakya clan at Kapilvastu in Northern India, on the borders of Nepal, in 563 B.C. Tradition says he was a prince. He received an education fit for a prince, was married, and had a son. Oppressed by the evils and misery then prevalent in Aryan society, he renounced the world at the age of twenty-nine and left his home in search of truth and deliverance. He became a mendicant and studied with two distinguished teachers, but finding that their teachings did not satisfy him, he left them and became an ascetic. He gave up that as well, finding it futile. Through deep contemplation, he gained insight into things, and as a result of this insight, he formulated his own *Dhamma.* This was at the age of thirty-five. The remainder of his eighty years was spent spreading his Dhamma and founding and administering an order of monks. He died around the year 483 B.C. at Kusinara, surrounded by his devoted followers.

To carry out his mission, the Buddha devoted all his days to the achievement of enlightenment. His time was divided between feeding the lamp of his own spiritual life by solitary meditation—just as Jesus spent hours in lonely prayer—and active preaching to large audiences of his monks, instructing the more advanced in the subtle points of inner development, directing the affairs of the Order, rebuking breaches of discipline, confirming the faithful in their virtue, receiving deputation, carrying on discussions with learned opponents, comforting the sorrowful, visiting kings and peasants, Brahmins and outcasts, rich and poor. He was a friend of publicans and sinners, and many public harlots, finding themselves understood and pitied, gave up their evil ways to take refuge in the "Blessed One." Such a life demanded a variety of moral qualities and social gifts, among then a combination of democratic sentiments with an aristocratic *savoir faire* which is seldom met. In reading the dialogues, one can never forget that gautama had the birth and upbringing of an aristocrat. He converses not only with Brahmins and pundits but with princes, ministers, and kings on easy and equal terms. He is a good diner-out, with a fund of anecdotes and a real sense of humour, and is a welcome quest at every house. A distinguished Brahmin is pictured as describing him thus:

"The venerable Gautama is well born on both sides, of pure descent...is handsome, pleasant to look upon, inspiring trust, gifted with great beauty of complexion, fair in colour, fine in presence, stately to behold, virtuous with the virtue of the Arhats, gifted with goodness and virtue, and with a pleasant voice and polite address, with no passion of lust left in him nor any fickleness of mind. He bids all men welcome, is congenial, conciliatory, not supercilious, accessible to all, not backwards in conversation". But what appealed most to the India of his time, and has appealed most to India through the ages, is expressed by the Brahmin in these words:

"The monk gautama has gone forth into the religious life, giving up the great clan of his relatives, giving up much money and gold, treasure both buried and above ground. Truly, while he was still a young man, without a grey hair on his head, in the beauty of his early manhood, he went forth from the household life into the homeless state."

"Such a life as his demanded not only pleasant manners, sympathy, and kindness but also firmness and courage. When the occasion required it, he could be calmly severe with those who worked evil against the Order. He bore physical pain not only with equanimity but with no diminution of his inner joy. Courage was also needed and was found; for example, in the Buddha's calm attitude during Devadatta's various attempts to assassinate him, facing threats of murder, and the conversion of the famous bandit in the Kingdom of Kosala, whom all the countryside feared, The Buddha visited him alone and unarmed in his lair, transforming him from a scourge of the kingdom to a peaceful member of the Order. Neither pain, danger, nor insults marred his spiritual peace. When he was reviled he reviled not again. Nor was he lacking tender thoughtfulness for those who needed his comfort and support."

He was beloved of all. Repeatedly, he is described, or describes himself, as one born into the world for the good of the many, for the happiness of the many, for the advantage, the good, and the happiness of gods and men, out of compassion for the world.

He left an indelible mark on Aryan society, and although his name has largely disappeared from India, the impression of his teaching remains.

His religion spread like wild fire. It soon became the religion of the whole of India. But it did not remain confined to India. It reached every corner of the then-known world. All races accepted it. Even the Afghans were once Buddhists. It did not remain confined to Asia. There is evidence to show that Buddhism was the religion of Celtic Britain.What was the cause of this rapid spread of Buddhism? On this point, what Prof. Hopkins has said is worth quoting. This is what he says:

"The cause, then, of the rapid spread of Buddhism at the beginning of its career lies only in the conditions of its teaching and the influential backing of its founder. It was the individual Buddha that captivated men; it was the teaching that emanated from him that fired enthusiasm; it was his position as an aristocrat that made him acceptable to the aristocracy and his magnetism that made him the idol of the people. From every page, stands out the strong, attractive personality of this teacher, and winner of hearts. No man ever lived so godless yet so godlike. Arrogating to himself no divinity, despairing of future bliss, but without fear as without hope, leader of thought but lovingly despising the folly of the world, exalted but adored, the universal brother, he wandered among men simply, serenely, with gentle irony subduing those that opposed him. From congregation to congregation, speaking with majestic sweetness, he was the master to each, and the friend of all. His voice was singularly vibrant and eloquent; his very tones convinced the hearer and his looks inspired awe. From tradition, it appears that he must have been one of those whose personality alone suffices to make a man not only a leader but also a god to the hearts of his fellows. When such a one speaks, he obtains hearers.

It matters little what he says, for he influences the emotions, and bends whoever listens to his will. But if added to this personality, there is the feeling in the minds of others that what this man teaches is not only a novelty, but also the very hope of their salvation. If for the first time, they recognise in his words the truth that makes slaves into free men, of classes a brotherhood—then it is not difficult to see wherein lies the lightning-like speed with which the electric current passes from heart to heart. Such a man was Buddha, such was the essence of his teaching, and such was the inevitable rapidity of Buddhistic expansion and the profound influence of the shock that was produced by the new faith upon the moral consciousness of Buddha's people."

To understand the great reform which he brought about through his teaching, it is necessary to have some idea of the degraded condition of Aryan civilisation at the time when Buddha embarked on the mission of his life.

The Aryan community of his time was steeped in the worst kind of debauchery: social, religious, and spiritual.

To mention only a few social evils, attention may be drawn to gambling. Gambling had become as widespread among the Aryans as drinking.

Every king had a gambling hall attached to his palace and each had an expert gambler employed as a companion to play with. King Virat, for example, had employed Kanka as his expert gambler. Gambling was not merely a pastime with kings; they played with heavy stakes, wagering kingdoms, dependents, relatives, slaves, and servants. King Nala staked everything in a gambling with Pushkara and lost it all. The only things he did not stake were himself and his wife, Damayanti. As a result, Nala had to live in the forest as a beggar. There were kings who went beyond Nala. The Mahabharata tells how Yudhishthira, the eldest of the Pandavas, gambled and staked everything—his brothers and even their wife, Draupadi. Gambling was a matter of honour among the *Aryans,* and any invitation to gamble was regraded as an injury to one's honour and dignity. Yudhishthira gambled with such disastrous consequences –despite being warned beforehand. His excuse was that he had been invited to gamble, and as a man of honour, he could not decline such an invitation.

This vice of gambling was not confined to kings. It had infected even the common folk. The Rig Veda contains lamentations of poor *Aryans* ruined by gambling. The habit of gambling had become so widespread by Kautilya's time that there were gambling houses licensed by the king, from which the king derived considerable revenue.

Drinking was another rampant evil among the Aryans. Liquors were of two sorts: *Soma* and *Sura. Soma* was a sacrificial wine. The drinking of the Soma was in the beginning permitted only to Brahmins, Kshatriyas, and Vaishyas. Subsequently, it was restricted to Brahmins and Kshatriyas. The Vaishyas were excluded from it, and the Shudras were never permitted to taste it. Its manufacture was a secret known only to the Brahmins. *Sura,* on the other hand was open to all and drunk by everyone. Brahmins Shukracharya, the priest to the *Asuras,* drank so heavily that in a drunken state, he gave the life-giving *mantras*—known to him only and used to revive the Asuras killed by the —Devas to Kaccha the son of Brihaspati, the priest of the Devas. The *Mahabharata* also mentions an occasion when both Krishna and Arjuna were dead drunk, showing that the best in the Aryan society was, not only unfree from the drinking habit but drank heavily. The most shameful part of it was that even the Aryan women were addicted to drinking. For instance, Sudeshna, the wife of King Virat, tells her maid Sairandhri to go to Kichakas palace and bring *Sura,* as she was dying for a drink. It is not to be supposed that only queens indulged in drinking. —drinking was common among women of all classes, including Brahmin women. That liquor and dancing was indulged in by the Aryan women is evident from the *Kausitaki Grihya Sutra* (1. 11-12), which says, "Four or eight women who are not widowed, after having been regaled with wine and food, are to dance for four times on the night before the wedding ceremony."

Turning to the Aryan society, it was marked by class war and class degradation. Aryan society recognised four classes: the Brahmins, Kshatriyas, Vaishyas, and Shudras. These divisions were not merely horizontal, where each class was par on with the others in terms of social relationships. These divisions had become vertical, with one class above the other. Being placed above or below, there was both jealousy and rivalry among the four classes. This jealousy and rivalry gave rise to enmity. This enmity was particularly noticeable between the two highest classes, namely, the Brahmins and the Kshatriyas. There was a regular class war between them, so intense that it would delight the heart of any Marxist to read the descriptions. Unfortunately, there is no detailed history of this class war between the Brahmins and the Kshatriyas—only a few instances have been recorded. Vena, Pururavas, Nahusha, Sudas, Sumukh, and Nimi were some of the Kshatriya kings who came into conflict with the Brahmins. The issues in these conflicts were different.

The issue between Vena and the Brahmins was whether a King could command the Brahmins to worship him and offer sacrifices to him instead of the gods. The issue between Pururavas and the Brahmins was whether a Kshatriya king could confiscate the property of the Brahmin. The issue between Nahusha and the Brahmins was whether a Kshatriya king could order a Brahmin to do a servile job. The issue between Nimi and the Brahmins was whether the king was bound to employ only his family priest at the sacrificial ceremonies. The issue between Sudas and the Brahmins was whether the king was bound to employ only a Brahmin as a priest.

It shows how significiant the issues were between the two classes. No wonder the struggle between them was also the bitterest. The wars between them were not merely occasional riots. They were wars of extermination. It is stated that Parashurama, a Brahmin, fought against the Kshatriyas twenty-one times and killed every Kshatriya.

While the two classes were fighting among themselves for supremacy, they both combined to suppress the Vaishyas and the Shudras. The Vaishya was seen as a milch cow, living only to pay taxes, while the Shudra was treated as a general beast of burden. These two classes existed solely to make the lives of the Brahmins and Kshatriyas glorious and comfortable. They had no right to live for themselves. They lived to make the lives of their betters possible.

Below these two classes, there were others. They were the Chandalas and Shvapakas. They were not untouchables, but they were degraded. They were outside the pale of society and outside the pale of law. They had no rights and no opportunities. They were the rejects of Aryan society.

The religion of the Aryan consisted of the *Yagna* or sacrifice. The sacrifice was a means to enter into the godhead of the gods and even to control the gods. The traditional sacrifices were twenty-one in number, divided into three classes of seven each. The first class included sacrifices of butter, milk, corn, etc. The second class covered *Soma* sacrifices, and third was animal sacrifices. The sacrifice could be of short duration or could last for a year or more, the latter being called a *Sattra.* The argument in favour of the sacrifice was that eternal holiness was won by the one offering the sacrifice. Not only did the individual benefits but also their Manes who would reduce pleasure with the offering, and their estate would be elavated to a higher world.

The sacrifice was by no means meant as an aid for the acquisition of heavenly bliss alone. Many of the great sacrifices were to gain material benefits on earth. The idea of sacrificing without the ulterior motive of gain was unknown. Brahmanic India did not have a concept of thank offerings. Ordinarily, the gain was represented as a compensatory gift from the divinity to whom the sacrifice was made. The sacrifice began with the recitation: "He offers the sacrifice to the god with this text: 'Do thou give to me, and I will give to thee; do thou bestow on me, and I will bestow on thee'."

The ceremony of the sacrifice was awe-inspiring. Every word was pregnant with consequences and even the pronunciation of the word or accent was considered fateful. There are indications, however, that the priest themselves understood that much the ceremony was pure hocus-pocus and not as much importance as it was made out to be.

Every sacrifice meant a fee to the priest. As for the fee, the rules were precise, and their proposers were unblushing. The priest performed the sacrifice solely for the fee, which had to consist of valuable garments, kine, horses, or gold—each given according to specific instruction. The priests had developed a great complex set of forms where, at every turn, fees were demanded. The whole expense, falling on the individual for whose benefit the sacrifice was performed, must have been enormous. How costly it became can be seen from the fact that, in one instance, the fee for the sacrifice is mentioned as one thousand cows. For this greed, which extended so far as to proclaim that he who gives a thousand cows obtains all things of heaven. The priest had a good precedent. The gods of heaven, in all tales told of them, also demanded a reward from each other when they help their fellow gods. If the gods sought rewards, the priest felt justified in doing the same.

The principal sacrifice was the animal sacrifice. It was both costly and barbaric. In the Aryan religion, five sacrificial animals are mentioned. In this list of sacrificial animals, man came first. The sacrifice of a man was the costliest. The rules of sacrifice required that the individual to be slaughtered must be neither a priest nor a slave. He must be a Kshatriya or Vaishya. According to the valuation of those times, the cost of buying a man for sacrifice was one thousand cows. Besides being costly and barbaric, the sacrifice was revolting, as the sacrificers were required not only to kill the man but also to eat him. Next to the man came the horse. It, also, was a costly sacrifice as the horse was a rare and necessary animal for the Aryans during their conquest of India. The Aryans could hardly afford to sacrifice such a potent instrument of military domination. The sacrifice was revolting particularly as one of the rituals in the horse sacrifice involved the copulation of the horse with the wife of the sacrificer before it was slaughtered.

The animals most commonly offered for sacrifice were, of course, the cattle, which were used by the people for their agricultural purposes. They were mostly cows and bullocks.

The Yagnas were costly, and they would have died out due to the sheer Yagna expense involved. But they did not. The reason is that the stoppage of Yagna raised the issue of the loss of the Brahmin's fees. There could be no fees if the Yagna ceased to be performed, and the Brahmin would starve. The Brahmin, therefore, found a substitute for the costly sacrificial animals—a man made of straw, metal or earth. However, they did not altogether give up human sacrifice, fearing that if the Yagna stopped, they would lose their fees. When human sacrifice became rare, animal sacrifice came in as a substitute. Animal sacrifice was also a financial burden for the laity. Once again, rather than let the sacrifice fall out of practice, the Brahmins allowed smaller animals to replace cattle, just as cattle had replaced the man and the horse. All of this was to maintain the *Yagna* so that the Brahmin would not lose his fees, which were his maintenance. The Brahmins were so complitted to the continuation of the Yagna that they were satisfied with rice as an offering.

However, it must not assumed that the institution of substitutes of the Yagnas of the Aryans had become less horrid. The introduction of substitutes did not completely replace the more expensive and ghastly sacrifices with less expensive and more innocent ones. All it meant was that the offering would be according to the capacity of the sacrificer. If he was poor, his offering may be rice. If he was well-to-do, it might be a goat. If he was rich, it might be a man, horse, cow, or bull. The effect of the substitutes was that the Yagna was made affordable for all allowing the Brahmin to reap a larger harvest of total fees. It did not stop animal sacrifice. Animals continued to be sacrificed by the thousands.

The Yagna often became a regular carnage of cattle, with the Brahmins acting butchers. One can get some idea of the extent of this carnage of innocent animals from references to the Yagnas found in Buddhist literature. In the Suttanipata, description of a Yagna performed by Pasenadi, king of Kosala. It is stated that there were tied to the poles for slaughter at the Yagna: five hundred oxen, five hundred bulls, five hundred cows, five hundred goats, and five hundred lambs. The servants of the king, who were assigned to carry out the tasks according to the orders given to them by the officiating Brahmin priests, did so with tears in their eyes.

The Yagna, besides involving a terrible carnage, was a kind of carnival. In addition to roast meat, there was drink. The Brahmins had Soma as well as Sura. The others had Sura in abundance. Almost every Yagna was followed by gambling, and most extraordinarily, sexual intercourse in the open. The Yagna had become debauchery, and there was no religion left in it. The Aryan religion was just a series of observances. However, behind these observances, there was no yearning for a good and virtuous life. There was no hunger or thirst for righteousness. Their religion was without any spiritual content. The hymns of the Rig Veda furnish very good evidence of the absence of any spiritual basis in

Aryan religion. The hymns are prayers addressed by the Aryans to their gods. What do they ask for in these prayers? Do they ask to be kept away from temptation? Do they ask for deliverance from evil? Do they ask for forgiveness of sins? No. Most of the hymns are in praise of Indra.

They praise him for having brought destruction to the enemies of the Aryans. They praise him because he killed all the pregnant wives of Krishna, an Asura. They praise him because he destroyed hundreds of villages of the Asuras. They praise him because he killed lakhs of Dasyus. The Aryans pray to Indra to carry on greater destruction among the Anaryas, hoping to secure the food supplies and wealth of the Anaryas. Far from being spiritual and elevating, the hymns of the Rig Veda are saturated with wicked thoughts and wicked purposes. The Aryan religion never concerned itself with what is called a righteous life.

II

Such was the state of the Aryan society when Buddha was born. Two pertinent questions arise regarding Buddha as a reformer who laboured to reform the Aryan society: What were the chief planks in his reform? To what extent did he succeed in his reform movement?

To take up the first question, Buddha felt that for the inculcation of a good and pure life, an example was better than a precept. The most important thing he did was to lead a good and pure life so that it might serve as a model to all. How unblemished a life he led can be gathered from the *Brahmajāla Sutta.* It is reproduced below because it not only gives an idea of the pure life that Buddha led, but it also gives an idea of how impure a life the Brahmins, the best among the Aryans, led.

Brahmajāla Sutta

1. Thus have I heard. The Blessed One was once going along the high road between Rajagaha and Nalanda with a great company of brethren, about five hundred in number. Suppiya, the mendicant, was also along the high road between Rajagaha and Nalanda with his disciple, the young Brahmadatta. At that time, Suppiya, the mendicant, spoke in many ways and dispraise of the Buddha, the Doctrine, and the Order. However, young Brahmadatta, his pupil, expressed praise, in many ways, for the Buddha, and the Doctrine, the Order. Thus, these two, teacher and pupil, holding opinions in direct contradiction of each other, followed, step by step after the Blessed one and the company of the brethren.

2. The Blessed One stopped to pass the night at the royal rest house in the Ambalatthika pleasance, alongwith the company of brethren. Suppiya, the mendicant, and his young disciple Brahmadatta, also stayed there. At the rest houses, these two continued their discussion as before.

3. In the early dawn, a number of the brethren assembled as they rose in the pavilion. This was the trend of the talk that arose among them as they sat there: "How wonderful a thing is it, brethren, and how strange that the Blessed One, he who knows and sees, the Arahat the Buddha Supreme, should so clearly have perceived how various are the inclination of men! For see how, while Suppiya, the mendicant, speaks in many ways in dispraise of the Buddha, the Doctrine, and the Order, his disciple, young Brahmadatta, speaks in as many ways in praise of them. So do these two, teacher and pupil, follow step by step after the Blessed One and the company of the brethren, giving utterance to views in direct contradiction of one another."

4. Now, the Blessed One, on realising what was the drift of their talk, went to the pavilion and took his seat on the mat spread out for him. And when he had sat down, he said: "What is the talk on which you are engaged while sitting here, and what is the subject of the conversation between you?" And they told him all. And he said:

5. "Brethren, if outsiders should speak against me, the Doctrine, or the Order, you should not on that account either bear malice, suffer heart burn, or feel ill will. If you, on that account, should be angry and hurt, that would stand in the way of your own self-conquest. If, when others speak against us, you feel angry and displeased, would you then be able to judge how far that speech of theirs is well said or ill?" "That would not be so, Sir."

   But when outsiders speak in dispraise of me, the Doctrine, or the Order, you should unravel what is false and point it out as wrong, saying, "For this or that reason, this is not the fact, that is not so, such a thing is not found among us, is not in us."

6. But also, brethren, if outsiders should speak in praise of me, the Doctrine, on the Order, you should not, on that account, be filled with pleasure or happiness, or be lifted in heart. Were you to be so, that also would stand in the way of your self-conquest. When outsiders speak in praise of me, the Doctrine, or the Order, you should acknowledge what is right to be the fact, saying: "For this or that reason, this is the fact, that is so, such a thing is found among us, is in us."

7. It is in respect only of trifling things, matters of little value, and mere morality, that an unconverted man, when praising the Tathagata, would speak. And what are such trifling, minor details of mere morality that he would praise?
   (4) (The Moralities. Part 1).

8. "Putting away the killings of living things, Gautama, the recluse holds aloof from the destruction of life. He has laid the cudgel and the sword aside, and, ashamed of roughness and full of mercy, he dwells compassionate and kind to all creatures that have life." It is thus that the unconverted man when speaking in praise of the Tathagata, might speak.

   Or he might say: "Putting, away the taking of what has not been given, Gautama, the recluse lives aloof from grasping what is not his own. He takes only what is given, and, expecting that gifts will come, he passes his life in honesty and purity of heart."

   Or he might say: "Putting away in-chastity, Gautama, the recluse is chaste. He holds himself aloof, far from the vulgar practice, from the sexual act."

9. Or he might say: "Putting away lying words, Gautama, the recluse holds himself aloof from falsehood. He speaks the truth; from the truth, he never swerves. Faithful and trustworthy, he breaks not his word to the world."

   Or he might say: "Putting away slander, Gautama, the recluse holds himself aloof from calumny. What he hears here, he repeats not elsewhere, to raise a quarrel against the people here; what he hears elsewhere he repeats not here to raise a quarrel against the people there. Thus does he live as a binder together of those who are divided, an encourager of those who are friends, a peacemaker, a lover of peace, impassioned for peace, a speaker of words that make for peace?"

   Or he might say: "Putting away rudeness of speech, Gautama, the recluse holds himself aloof from harsh language. Whatsoever word is blameless, pleasant to the ear, lovely, reaching to the heart, urbane, pleasing to the people, beloved of the people – such are the words he speaks."

Or he might say: "Putting away frivolous talk, Gautama, the recluse holds himself aloof from vain conversation. In season, he speaks, by the facts, words full of meaning, on religion, on the discipline of the Order. He speaks, at the right time, words worthy to be laid up in one's heart, fitly illustrated, clearly divided, to the point."

10. Or he might say: "Gautama, the recluse holds himself aloof from causing injury to seeds or plants.

He eats only one meal a day, does not eat at night, and refrain from food after hours (after midday).

He refrains from being a spectator at shows or fairs with nautch dances, singing, and music.

He abstains from wearing, adorning, or ornamenting himself with garlands, scents, and unguents.

He abstains from the use of the large and lofty beds.

He abstains from accepting silver or gold.

He abstains from accepting uncooked grain.

He abstains from accepting raw meat.

He abstains from accepting women or girls.

He abstains from accepting bondmen or bondwomen.

He abstains from accepting sheep or goats.

He abstains from accepting fowls or swine.

He abstains from accepting elephants, cattle, horses, or mares.

He abstains from accepting cultivated fields or wasteland.

He abstains from the acting as a go-between or messenger.

He abstains from buying and selling.

He abstains from cheating with scales, bronzes, or measures.

He abstains from the crooked ways of bribery, cheating, and fraud.

He abstains from maiming, murder, putting in bonds, highway robbery, dacoity, and violence."

Such are the things, brethren, which an unconverted man, when speaking in praise of the Tathagata might say.

Here ends the Kulashila (the Short Paragraphs on Conduct).

11. Or he might say: "Whereas some recluses and Brahmins, while living on food provided by the faithful, continue being addicted to the injury of seedlings and growing plants, whether propagated from roots, cuttings, joints, buddings, or seeds—Gautama, the recluse, holds aloof from such injury to seedlings and growing plants."

12. Or he might say: "Whereas some recluses and Brahmins, while living on food provided by the faithful, continue being addicted to the use of things stored up – stores, to wit, of foods, drinks, clothing, equipages, bedding, perfumes, and curry-stuffs—Gautama, the recluse, holds aloof from such use of things stored up."

13. Or he might say: "Whereas some recluses and Brahmins, while living on food provided by the faithful, continue being addicted to visiting shows, that is to say:

    (1) Nautch dances (*Nakkarn*),

    (2) Singing of songs (*Gitam*),

    (3) Instrumental music (*Vaditam*),

    (4) Shows at fairs (*Pekham*),

    (5) Ballad recitations (*Akkhanam*),

    (6) Hand music (*Paniseram*),

(7) The chanting of bards (*Vetala*),

(8) Tam-tam playing (*Kumbhathunam*) ,

(9) Fair scences (*Sobhanagarkarn*),

(10) Acrobatic feats by Kandalas (*Kandala-vamsa-dhopanam*),

(11) Combats of elephants, horses, buffaloes, bulls, goats, rams, cocks and quails,

(12) Bouts at quarterstaff, boxing, wrestling,

(13) Sham-fights, roll-calls, manoeuvres, reviews. Gautama, the recluse, holds aloof from visiting such shows."

14. Or he might say: "Whereas some recluses and Brahmins, while living on food provided by the faithful, continue being addicted to games and recreations, that is to say:

(1) Games on boards with eight or ten rows of squares.

(2) The same games played by imagining such boards in the air.

(3) Keep going over diagrams drawn on the ground so that onesteps only where one ought to go.

(4) Either removing the pieces or men from a heap with one's nail or putting them into a heap, in each case without shaking it. He who shakes the heap loses.

(5) Throwing dice.

(6) Hitting a short stick with a long one.

(7) Dipping the hand with the fingers stretched out in lac, red dye, or flour water, and striking the wet hand on the ground or a wall calling out, 'What shall it be?' and showing the form require—elephants, horses, etc.

(8) Games with balls.

(9) Blowing through toy pipes made of leaves.

(10) Ploughing with toy ploughs.

(11) Turning somersaults.

(12) Playing with toy windmills made of palm leaves.

(13) Playing with toy measures made of palm leaves.

(14) Playing with toy carts or toy bows.

(15) Guessing letters traced in the air or on a playfellow's back.

(16) Guessing the playfellow's thoughts.

(17) Mimicry of deformities. Gautama the recluse, holds aloof from such games and recreations."

15. Or he might say: "Whereas some recluses and Brahmins, while living on food provided by the faithful, continue addicted to the use of high and large couches; that is to say:

(1) Moveable settees, high and six feet long (*Asandi*).

(2) Divans with animal figures carved on the supports (*Pallanko*).

(3) Goats' hair coverings with very long fleece (*Ganako*).

(4) Patchwork counterpanes of many colours (*Kittaka*).

(5) White blankets (*Patika*).

(6) Woollen coverlets embroidered with flowers (*Patalika*).

(7) Quilts stuffed with cottonwood (*Tulika*).

(8) Coverlets embroidered with figures of lions, tigers, etc., (*Vikatika*).

(9) Rugs with fur on both sides (*Uddalomi*).

(10) Rugs with fur on one side (*Ekantalomi*).

(11) Coverlets embroidered with gems (*Katthissam*).

(12) Silk coverlets (*Koseyyam*).

(13) Carpets large enough for sixteen dancers (*Kuttakam*).

(14) Elephant, horse, and chariot rugs.

(15) Rugs of antelope skins sewn together (*Aginapaveni*).

(16) Rugs made of the plantain leaves.

(17) Carpets with awnings above them (*Sauttarakkhadam*).

(18) Sofas with red pillows for the head and feet."

16. Or he might say: "Whereas some recluses and Brahmins, while living on food provided by the faithful, continue being addicted to the use of means for adorning and beautifying themselves; that is to say:

Rubbing in scented powders on one's body, shampooing it, and bathing it, and patting the limbs with clubs after the manner of wrestlers. The use of mirrors, eye-ointments, garlands, rouge, cosmetics, bracelets, necklaces, walking sticks, reed cases for drugs, rapiers, sunshades, embroidered slippers, turbans, diadems, whisks of the yak's tail, and long-fringed white robes. Gautama, the recluse, holds aloof from such means of adorning and beautifying the person."

17. Or he might say: "Whereas some recluses and Brahmins, while living on food provided by the faithful, continue being addicted to such low conversation as these:

Tales of kings, robbers, and ministers of state; tales of war, terrors and battles; talk about foods and drinks, clothes, beds, garlands and perfumes; talks about relationships, equipages, villages, towns, cities, and countries. Tales about women and heroes; gossip at street corners or places where water is fetched; ghost stories; desultory talk; speculations about the creation of the land or sea, or about existence and non-existence.

Gautama, the recluse, holds aloof from such low conversation."

18. Or he might say: "Whereas some recluses and Brahmins, while living on food provided by the faithful, continue being addicted to the use of wrangling phrases, such as:

'You do not understand this doctrine and discipline, but I do.'

'How should you know about this doctrine and discipline?'

'You have fallen into wrong views. It is I who is in the right.'

'I am speaking to the point, but you are not.'

'You are putting last what ought to come first, and first what ought to come last.'

'What you have excoriated so long is all quite upsetting.'

'Your challenge has been taken up.'

'You are proved to be wrong.'

'Set to work to clear your views.'

'Disentangle yourself if you can.'

'Gautama the recluse, holds aloof from such wrangling phrases.'

19. Or he might say: "Whereas some recluses and Brahmins, while living on food provided by the faithful, continue being addicted to taking messages, going on errands, and

acting as go-betweens; whether for kings, ministers of state, Kshatriyas, Brahmins, or young men, saying, 'Go there, comehither, take this with you, bring that from thence.'

Gautama, the recluse, abstains from such servile duties."

20. Or he might say: "Whereas some recluses and Brahmins, while living on food provided by the faithful, are tricksters, droners of holy words prayers in diviners, and exorcists, ever hungering to add gain to gain.

    Gautama the recluse holds aloof from such deception and patter." Here ends the Majjhima-Sila (the Longer Paragraphs on Conduct).

21. Or he might say: "Whereas some recluses and Brahmins, while living on food provided by the faithful, earn their living by wrong means of livelihood, by low arts, such as these:

    (1) Palmistry—prophesying long life, prosperity, etc. (or the reverse), from marks on a child's hands, feet, etc.

    (2) Divining using of omens and signs.

    (3) Auguries had drawn from thunderbolts and other celestial portents.

    (4) Prognostication by interpreting dreams.

    (5) Fortune telling from marks on the body.

    (6) Auguries from the marks on cloth gnawed by mice.

    (7) Sacrificing to Agni.

    (8) Offering oblations from a spoon.

    (9) Making offerings to gods of husks, the red powder between the grain and the husk, husked grain ready for boiling, ghee, and oil.

(10) Sacrificing by spewing mustard seeds, etc., into the fire out of one's mouth.

(11) Drawing blood from one's right knee as a sacrifice to the gods.

(12) Looking at the knuckles, and, after muttering a charm, divining whether a man is well-born and lucky or not.

(13) Determining whether the site for a proposed house or pleasance is lucky or not.

(14) Advising on customary law.

(15) Laying demons in a cemetery.

(16) Laying ghosts.

(17) Knowledge of the charms to be used when lodging in an earthhouse.

(18) Snake charming.

(19) The poison craft.

(20) The scorpion craft.

(21) The mouse craft.

(22) The bird craft.

(23) The crow craft.

(24) Foretelling the number of years man has yet to live.

(25) Giving charms to ward off arrows.

(26) The animal wheel.

Gautama the recluse, holds aloof from such low arts."

22. Or he might say: "Whereas some recluses and Brahmins while living on food provided by the faithful, earn their living by wrong means of livelihood, by low arts, such as these:

Knowledge of the signs of good and bad qualities in the following things, and of the marks in them denoting the health or luck of their owners, to wit: gems, staves, garments, swords, arrows, bows, other weapons, women, men, boys, girls, slaves, slave-girls, elephants, horses, buffaloes, bulls, oxen, goats, sheep, fowls, quails, iguanas, herrings, tortoises, and other animals.

Gautama the recluse, holds aloof from such low arts."

23. Or he might say: "Whereas some recluses and Brahmins, while living on food provided by the faithful, earn their living by wrong means of livelihood, by low arts, such as soothsaying to the effect that:

The chiefs will march out.

The home chiefs will attack, and the enemies will retreat.

The enemies' chiefs will attack, and ours will retreat.

The home chiefs will gain the victory, and ours will suffer defeat.

The foreign chiefs will gain the victory on this side, and ours will suffer defeat.

Thus, there will be victory on this side and defeat on that.

Gautama, the recluse, holds aloof from such low arts."

24. Or he might say: "Whereas some recluses and Brahmins, while living on food provided by the faithful, earn their living by wrong means of livelihood, by such low arts as foretelling:

(1) There will be an eclipse of the Moon.

(2) There will be an eclipse of the Sun.

(3) There will be an eclipse of a Star (*Nakshatra*).

(4) There will be an aberration the Sun or the Moon.

(5) The Sun or the Moon will return to its usual path.

(6) There will be aberrations of the Stars.

(7) The Stars will return to their usual course.

(8) There will be a fall of meteors.

(9) There will be a jungle fire.

(10) There will be an earthquake.

(11) The God will thunder.

(12) There will be rising and setting, clearness and dimness of the Sun, the Moon, or the stars, or foretelling of each of these twelve phenomena that they will betoken such a result.

Gautama, the recluse holds aloof from such low arts.

25. Or he might say: "Whereas some recluses and Brahmins, while living on food provided by the faithful, earn their living by wrong means of the livelihood, by low arts, such as these:

(1) Foretelling an abundant rainfall.

(2) Foretelling a deficient rainfall.

(3) Foretelling a good harvest.

(4) Foretelling scarcity of food.

(5) Foretelling tranquillity.

(6) Foretelling disturbances.

(7) Foretelling a pestilence.

(8) Foretelling a healthy season.

(9) Counting on the fingers.

(10) Counting without using the fingers.

(11) Summing up large totals.

(12) Composing ballads, poetising, casuistry, and sophistry.

Gautama, the recluse, holds aloof from such low arts."

26. Or he might say: "Whereas some recluses and Brahmins, while living on food provided by the faithful, earn their living by wrong means of livelihood, by low arts, such as:

(1) Arranging a lucky day for marriages when the bride or bridegroom is brought home.

(2) Arranging a lucky day for marriages when the bride or bridegroom is sent forth.

(3) Fixing an auspicious time for the conclusion of treaties of peace (or using charms to procure harmony).

(4) Fixing an auspicious time for the outbreak of hostilities (or using charms to make discord).

(5) Fixing an auspicious time for the calling in of debts (or charms for success in throwing dice).

(6) Fixing an auspicious time for the expenditure of money (or charms to bring ill fortune to an opponent while throwing dice).

(7) Using charms to make people fortunate.

(8) Using charms to make people unfortunate.

(9) Using charms to procure abortion.

(10) Incantations to keep a man's jaws fixed.

(11) Incantations to bring on dumbness.

(12) Incantations to make a man throw up his hands.

(13) Incantations to bring on deafness.

(14) Obtaining oracular answers using the magic mirror.

(15) Obtaining oracular answers through a girl possessed.

(16) Obtaining oracular answers from a god.

(17) The worship of the Sun.

(18) The worship of the Great One.

(19) Bringing forth flames from one's mouth.

(20) Invoking Siri, the Goddess of Luck.

Gautama the recluse, holds aloof from such low arts."

27. Or he might say: "Whereas some recluses and Brahmins, while living on food provided by the faithful, earn their living by wrong means of livelihood, by low arts, such as these:

(1) Vowing gifts to a god if a certain benefit is granted.

(2) Praying for such vows.

(3) Reciting charms while lodging in an earthhouse.

(4) Causing virility.

(5) Making a man impotent.

(6) Fixing on lucky sites for dwellings.

(7) Consecrating sites.

(8) Ceremonial rinsing of the mouth.

(9) Ceremonial bathing.

(10) Offering sacrifices.

(11) Administering emetics and purgatives.

(12) Purging people to relieve the head (that is, by giving drugs to make people sneeze).

(13) Oiling people's ears (either to make them grow or to heal sores on them).

(14) Satisfying people's eyes (soothing them by dropping medicinal oils into them).

(15) Administering drugs through the nose.

(16) Applying collyrium to the eyes.

(17) Giving medical ointment for the eyes.

(18) Practising as an oculist.

(19) Practising as a surgeon.

(20) Practising as a doctor for children.

(21) Administering roots and drugs.

(22) Administering medicines in rotation.

Gautama, the recluse, holds aloof from such low arts."

These, brethren, are the trifling matters, the minor details of morality, of which the unconverted man, when praising the Tathagata, might speak.

Here, end the Long Paragraphs on Conduct.

III

This was indeed the highest standard for a moral life for an individual to follow. So high a standard of moral life was quite unknown to the Aryan society of his day.

He did not stop merely by setting an example by leading a life of purity. He also wanted to mould the character of the ordinary men and women in society. For their guidance, he devised a form of baptism which was quite unknown to Aryan society. The baptism consisted of the convert to Buddhism undertaking to observe certain moral precepts laid down by Buddha. These precepts are known as Pancha Sila or the five precepts. They are:

(1) Not to kill,

(2) Not to steal,

(3) Not to lie,

(4) Not to be unchaste, and

(5) Not to drink intoxicants.

These five precepts were for the laity.

For the Monks, there were five additional precepts:

(6) Not to eat at forbidden times,

(7) Not to dance, sing, or attend theatrical or other spectacles,

(8) To abstain from the use of garlands, scents, and ornaments,

(9) To abstain from the use of high or broad beds, and

(10) Never to receive money.

These *Silas* or precepts formed the moral code, intending to regulate the thoughts and actions of men and women.

Of these, the most important one was the precept 'not to kill'. Buddha took care to make it clear that the precept did not merely mean abstention from taking life. He insisted that the precept must be understood to mean positive sympathy, goodwill, and love for everything that breathes.

He gave the same positive and extended content to other precepts. One of the Buddha's lay followers once reported to him the teaching of a non-Buddhist ascetic, to the effect that the highest ideal consisted in the absence of evil deeds, evil words, evil thoughts, and evil life. The Buddha's comment upon this is significant. "If," said he, "this were true, then every suckling child would have attained the ideal of life. Life is the knowledge of good and evil and after that, the exchange of evil deeds, words, thoughts, and life for good ones. It is to be brought about only by a long and determined effort of the will."

Buddha's teachings were not merely negative. They are positive and constructive. Buddha was not satisfied with a man following his precepts. He insisted upon encouraging others to follow them. For example in the *Aṅguttara Nikāya,* the Buddha is quoted as distinguishing between a good man and a very good man by saying that one who abstains from killing, stealing, unchastity, lying, and drunkenness may be called good. But only he deserves to be called very good who abstains from these evil things himself and also instigates others to do the same.

As has been well mentioned, the two cardinal virtues of Buddhism are love and wisdom.

How deeply he inculcated the practice of love as a virtue is evident from his own words: "As a mother, at the risk of her life, watches over her child, her only child, so also let every one cultivate a boundless loving mind towards all beings. And let him cultivate goodwill towards the entire world, a boundless (loving) mind above and below and across, unobstructed, without hatred, and without enmity. This way of living is the best in the world." So taught Buddha.

"Universal pity, sympathy for all suffering beings, goodwill to every form of sentient life -- these things characterised the Tathagata (Buddha) as they have few others of the sons of men, and he succeeded in a most surprising degree in handing on his point of view to his followers."

Buddha held to the doctrine of wisdom as firmly as he did to the doctrine of love. He believed that moral life began with knowledge and ended with wisdom. He came to save the world, and his method for the accomplishment of this end was the destruction of ignorance and the dissemination of knowledge as to the true values of life and the wise way to live. Buddha did not arrogate to himself the power to save people. People had to do that for themselves. And the way to save lay through knowledge. So much insistence did he place upon the knowledge that he did not think morality without knowledge was a virtue.

There are three things against which Buddha carried a great campaign.

He repudiated the authority of the Vedas. Secondly, he denounced the *Yagna* as a form of religion. The attitude of Buddha towards Yagna is well stated in the Jātakamālā in the form of a story. The story runs thus:

The Story of the Sacrifice

Those hearts that are pure do not act upon the enticement of the wicked. Knowing this pure-heartedness is to be striven after. It will be taught by the following:

Long ago the Bodhisattva. it is said, was a king who had obtained his kingdom though hereditary succession. He had reached this state as the effect of his merit and ruled his realm in peace, undisturbed by any rival, his sovereignty universally acknowledged. His country was free from any kind of annoyance, vexation, or disaster. Both his domestic affairs and foreign relations were quite stable in every respect, and all his vassals obeyed his commands.

1. This monarch, having subdued the passions his enemies, felt no inclination for such profits as are to be blamed when enjoyed but was, with his whole heart, intent on promoting the happiness of his subjects. Holding virtuous practice (Dharma) as the only purpose of his actions, he behaved like a Muni.

2. For he knew the nature of humankind, that people set a high value on imitating the behaviour of the highest. For this reason, desirous of bringing salvation to his subjects, he was particularly attached to the due performance of his religious duties.

3. He practised almsgiving, kept strictly to the precepts of moral conduct (sila), cultivated forbearance, and strove for the benefit of all beings. His mild countenance, being in accordance with his thoughts devoted to the happiness of his subjects, made him appear like the embodied Dharma.

Now, it once happened that although protected by his rule, his realm—the faulty actions of its inhabitants and inadvertence on the part of the angels charged with the care of rain—was afflicted in several districts by drought and the troublesome effects of such a disaster. The king, fully convinced that this plague had been brought about by the violation of righteousness by himself or his subjects and deeply concerned about the distress of his people (whose welfare was the constant object of his thoughts and cares), sought advice from men of acknowledged competence, reputed for their knowledge in matters of religion. So, keeping counsel with the elders among the Brahmins, headed by his family priest (purohit) and his ministers, he asked them for a means to put an end to the calamity. They, believing that a solemn sacrifice as enjoined by the Veda would cause abundant rain, explained to him that he must perform such a sacrifice, which was frightful, as it require the massacre of many hundreds of living beings. But, after being informed of everything concerning the slaughter prescribed for the sacrifice, his innate compassion forbade him from approving of their advice in his heart. Yet, out of civility, unwilling to offend them by harsh words of refusal, he evaded the topic, turning the conversation to other topics.

The Brahmins, however, upon finding the opportunity to discuss with the king the matters of religion, once again admonished him to perform the sacrifice, as they did not understand his deeply hidden reluctance.

4. "You constantly take care not to neglect the proper time of performing your different royal duties, established for the sake of obtaining and ruling the land. The order of these actions is in agreement with the precepts of righteousness (Dharma)."

5. "How is it, then, that you, who are so clever in the observance of the triad (Dharma, Artha, and Kama), bearing your bow to defend the good of your people, are so careless and almost sluggish regarding that bridge to the world of the Devas, the name of which is 'sacrifice'?"

6. "Like servants, the kings (your vassals) revere your commands, thinking them to be the surest Gauge of success. Now the time has come, O destroyer of your foes, to gather superior blessings through sacrifice, which will to procure for you a shining glory."

7. "Certainly, that holiness requisite for a *dikshita* is already yours, because of your habitual practice of charity and your strictness in observing the restraint (of good conduct). Nevertheless, it would be fitting for you to discharge your debt to the Devas by such sacrifices as are the subject matter of the Veda. The deities, satisfied by duly and faultlessly performed sacrifice, honour all beings in return by sending rain. Thus considering, take to mind the welfare of your subjects and your own, and consent to the performance of a regular sacrifice, which will enhance your glory."

8. Thereupon, he entered upon this thought: "Very badly guarded is my poor person indeed, being to such leaders. While faithfully believing in and loving the law, I should

uproot my virtue of tender heartiness by relaying on the words of others. For, truly:

9. 'Those who are reputed among men to be the best refuge are the very people who intend to harm, borrowing their arguments from the law. Alas! Such a man, who follows the wrong path shown by them, will soon find himself driven to straits, for he will be surrounded by evils."

10. "What connection, forsooth, may there be, between righteousness and injuring animals? How can my residence in the world of the Devas or the propitiation of the deities have anything to do with the murder of victims?"

11. "The animal, slaughtered according to the rites with the prescribed prayers—as if those sacred formulas were so many darts to wound it goes to heaven, they say, and with this object, it is killed. In this way, that action is interpreted being done according to the law. Yet it is a lie."

12. "For how is it possible that in the next world, one should reap the fruits of what has been done by others? And by what reason will the sacrificial animal mount to heaven, though it has not abstained from wicked actions, nor devoted itself to the practice of good ones, simply because it has been killed in sacrifice, and not on the ground of its actions?"

13. "And should the victim killed in sacrifice go to heaven, should we not expect the Brahmins to offer themselves to be immolated in sacrifice? A similar practice, however, is not seen among them. Who, then, may take to heart the advice proffered by these counsellors?"

14. "As for the Celestials beings, should we believe that they, who are wont to enjoy the fair ambrosia of incomparable scent, flavour, magnificence, and effective power served to them by the beautiful *Apsaras*, would abandon it to delight

in the slaughter of a pitiable victim, that they might feast on the omentum and other parts of its body offered to them in sacrifice?

Therefore, it is the proper time to act so and so. "Having thus made up his mind, the king feigned eagerness to undertake the sacrifice, and in approval of their words, he spoke to them in this manner: "Verily, I am well protected, well gratified, having such counsellors as Your Lordships, thus bent on securing my happiness! Therefore, I will have a human sacrifice (*purushamedha*) of a thousand victims performed. Let my officials, each in his sphere of business, be ordered to gather the requisites necessary for that purpose. Let also an inquiry be made for the most fitting ground on which to raise the tents and other buildings for the *sattra*. Further, the proper time for the sacrifice must be fixed by the astrologers, examining the auspicious lunar days, *karanas*, *muhurtas*, and constellations." The purohit answered: "To succeed in your enterprise, Your Majesty ought to take the *Avabhritha* (final bath) at the end of one sacrifice, after which you may successively undertake the others. For if the thousand human victims were to be seized at once, your subjects, to be sure, would blame you and be stirred up to great agitation on their account." These words of the purohit having been approved by the other Brahmins, the king replied: Do not fear the wrath of the people, Reverands. I shall take measures to prevent any agitation among my subjects."

15. After this, the king convoked an assembly of the townsmen and the landsmen, and said: "I intend to perform a human sacrifice of a thousand victims. But nobody behaving honestly is fit to be designated for immolation on my part. With this in mind, I give you this advice: Whomsoever

of you I shall henceforward perceive transgressing the boundaries of moral conduct, despising my royal will, him I order to be caught to be a victim at my sacrifice, thinking such an individual is a stain on his family and a danger to my country. With the object of carrying this resolution into effect, I shall cause you to be observed by faultless and sharp-sighted emissaries, who have shaken off sleepy carelessness and will report to me concerning your conduct."

16. Then the foremost of the assembly, folding their hands and bringing them to their foreheads, spoke:

"Your Majesty, all your actions tend to the happiness of your subjects; what reason can there be to despise you on that account? Even (God) Brahma cannot but sanction your behaviour. Your Majesty, who is the authority of the virtuous, be our highest authority. For this reason, anything which pleases Your Majesty must please us too. Indeed, you are pleased with nothing else but our enjoyment and our good."

After this, notables of the town and the country accepted his command in this manner. The king dispersed throughout his towns and all over his country, officers notified as such by their outward appearance to the people with the charge of laying hold of the evildoers, and everywhere he ordered proclamations to be made by beat of drum day after day, of this kind:

17. "The King, a granter of security as he is, warrants safety to everyone who constantly cultivates honesty and good conduct, in short, to the virtuous. Yet, intending to perform a human sacrifice for the benefit of his subjects, he wants thousand human victims to be taken from those who delight in misconduct.

18. "Therefore, whosoever henceforward, licentiously indulging in misbehaviour, shall disregard the command of our monarch, which is even observed by the kings' vassals, shall be brought to the state as a sacrificial victim by the very force of his actions, and people shall witness his miserable suffering when he shall pine with pain, his body being fastened to the sacrificial post."

When the inhabitants of that realms became aware of their king's careful search for evildoers to destine them to be victims at his sacrifice—for they heard the most frightful royal proclamation day after day and saw the king's servants, who were appointed to look out for wicked people and seize them, appearing everywhere—they abandoned their attachment to bad conduct and became intent on strictly observing the moral precepts and self-control. They avoided every occasion of hatred and enmity and, settling their quarrels and differences, cherished mutual love and esteem. Obedience to the words of parents and teachers, a general spirit of liberality and sharing with others, hospitality, good manners, and modesty prevailed among them. In short, they lived as it was in the Krita Yuga (*Satya Yuga*).

19. The fear of death had awakened in their thoughts of the next world; the risk of tarnishing the honour of their families had stirred their care of guarding their reputation; and the great purity of their hearts had strengthened their sense of shame. With these factors at work, people were soon distinguished by their spotless behaviour.

20. Even though everyone became more than ever intent on keeping righteous conduct, still the king's servants did not diminish their watchfulness in the pursuit of the evildoers.

It also contributed to preventing people from falling short of righteousness.

21. The king, learning from his emissaries of this state of things in his realm, felt extremely rejoiced. He bestowed rich presents on those messengers as a reward for the good news they brought him and enjoined his ministers, speaking something like this:

22. "The protection of my subjects is my highest desire, you know. Now, they have become worthy to be recipients of sacrificial gifts, and it is for my sacrifice that I have provided this wealth. Well, I intend to accomplish my sacrifice in the manner that I have considered to be the proper once. Let everyone know who wishes for money, that it may be fuel for his happiness, come and accept it from my hand to hearts' content. In this way, the distress and poverty, vexing our country may soon be driven out. Indeed, whenever I consider my strong determination to protect my subjects and the great assistance I derive from you, my excellent companions in this task, it often seems to me as though these sufferings of my people, by exciting my anger, were burning in my mind like a blazing fire."

23. The ministers accepted the royal command and immediately went to execute it. They ordered alms-halls to be established in all villages, towns, and markets, as well as at all stations on the roads. This being done, they caused all who begged to satisfy their wants to be provided day after day with gifts of those objects, just as had been ordered by the king.

24. Thus, poverty disappeared, and the people, having received wealth from the king, dressed and adorned with manifold and fine garments and ornaments, exhibiting the splendour of festival days.

25. The glory of the king, magnified by the eulogies of the rejoiced recipients of his gifts, spread like in all directions in the flower dust of the lotuses carried forth by the small waves of a lake, extending over a larger and larger surface.

26. After all the people, due to the wise measures taken by their ruler, had become intent on virtuous behaviour, the plagues and calamities, overpowered by the growth of qualities conducive to prosperity, faded away, having lost their hold.

28. The seasons succeeded each other in due course, rejoicing everybody by their regularity and, like newly established kings, complying with the lawful order of things. Consequently, the earth produced various kinds of corn in abundance, and there was abundance of pure, blue water and lotuses in all water basins.

28. No epidemics afflicted humankind; the medicinal herbs possessed their efficacious virtues more than ever; the monsoons blew in due time and regularly; the planets moved along in auspicious paths.

29. There was no danger to be feared, either from abroad, or within, dangerous derangement of the elements. Continuing in righteousness and self-control, cultivating good behaviour and modesty, the people of the country enjoyed the prerogatives of the Krita Yuga. By the power of the king performing his sacrifice the precepts of the law, the sufferings of the indigent were put ended, along with the plagues and calamities, and the country abounded in a prosperous and thriving population offering the pleasing aspect of felicity. Accordingly, people never wearied of repeating benedictions on their king and extending his renown in all directions.

One day, one of the highest royal officials, whose heart had been inclined to the True Belief, spoke thus to the king:

30. This is a true saying, in truth. "Monarchs, because they always deal with all kinds of business—the highest, the lowest, and the intermediate—by far surpass in their wisdom any wise men.

For, Your Majesty, you have obtained the happiness of your subjects both in this world and the next, as the effect of your sacrifice being performed in righteousness, free from the blameable sin of animal-slaughter. The hard times are all over, and the sufferings of poverty have ceased since men have been established in the precepts of good conduct. Why use many words? Your subjects are happy."

31. "The black antelope's skin which covers your limbs resembles the spot on the bright Moon's surface, nor can the natural loveliness of your demeanour be hindered by the restraint imposed on you by your being a *dikshita*. Your head, adorned with such hair-dress as complies with the rites of the diksha, possesses no less lustre than when it was embellished with the splendour of the royal umbrella. And, last but not least, by your largesse, you have surpassed the renown and abated the pride of the famous performer of a hundred sacrifices."

32. "As a rule, O wise ruler, the sacrifice of those who long for the attainment of some good is a vile act, accompanied as it is by injury done to living beings. Your sacrifice, on the contrary, this monument of your glory, is in complete accordance with your lovely behaviour and your aversion to vices."

33. "O! happy are the subjects who have their protector in you! No father could certainly be a better guardian to his children." Another said:

34. "If the wealthy practise charity, they are commonly impelled to do so by the hopes they put in the cultivation of that virtue; good conduct too may be accounted for by the wish to obtain high regard among men or the desire of reaching heaven after death. But such a practice of both, as is seen in your skill in securing the benefit of others, cannot be found but in those who are accomplished both in learning and virtuous exertions. In such a way, then, those whose hearts are pure do not act up to the enticement of the wicked. Knowing this pure-heartedness is to be striven after." (In the spiritual lessons for princes, also this is to be said: "He who, wishing good to his subjects, himself exerts, thus brings about salvation, glory, and happiness. No other should be a king's business."

And it may be added as follows: "The prince who strives after material prosperity ought to act by the precepts of religion, thinking, 'a religious conduct of his subjects to be the source of prosperity.'"

Further, this is to be said: "Injuring animals never tend to bliss, but charity, self-restraint, continence, and the like have this power; for this reason he who longs for bliss must devote himself to these virtues." And also, when discoursing on the Tathagata: "In this manner, the Lord showed his inclination to care for the interests of the world when he was still in his previous existences."

IV

Another powerful attack against Yagna is contained in his discourses known as the *Kutadanta Sutta*. It is as follows:

The Wrong Sacrifice and the Right

1. Thus have I heard. The Blessed One once, when going on a tour through Magadha with a great multitude of the brethren —about five hundred brethren—came to a Brahmin village

in Magadha called Khanumata. And there at Khanumata, he lodged in the Ambalatthika pleasance.

Now, at that time, the Brahmin Kutadanta was dwelling at Khanumata, a place teeming with life, with much grassland, woodland, water, and corn, on a royal domain presented to him by Seniya Bimbisara, the king of Magadha, as a royal gift, with power over it as if he were the king.

And just then, a great sacrifice was being prepared on behalf of Kutadanta the Brahmin. A hundred bulls, a hundred steers, a hundred heifers, a hundred goats, and a hundred rams had been brought to the post for the sacrifice.

2. Now, the Brahmins and householders of Khanumata heard the news of the arrival of the Samana Gautama. And they began to leave Khanumata in groups and bonds to go to the Ambalatthika pleasance.

3. And just then, Kutandanta, the Brahmin had gone to the upper terrace of his house for his siesta and seeing the people thus going by, he asked his doorkeeper the reason. The doorkeeper told him.

4. Then Kutandanta thought: "I have heard that the Samana Gautama understands the successful performance of a sacrifice with its threefold method and sixteen accessory instruments. Now, I do not know all this, and yet I want to carry out a sacrifice. It would be good for me to go to the Samana Gautama and ask him about it." '

So, he sent his doorkeeper to the Brahmins and householders of Khanumata to ask them to wait until he could go with them to call upon the Blessed One.

5. But there were at that time several Brahmins staying at Khanumata to take part in the great sacrifice. When they heard this, they went to Kutadanta and persuaded him, on the same grounds as the Brahmins had laid before Sonadanda, not to go. But he answered them in the same terms as Sonadanda had used to those Brahmins. Then they

were satisfied and went with him to call upon the Blessed One.

6. When he was seated, Kutadanta, the Brahmin told the Blessed One what he had heard and requested him to tell him about success in performing a sacrifice in its three modes and with its accessory articles of furniture of sixteen kinds.

"Well then, O Brahmin, give ear and listen attentively, and I will speak."

"Very well, Sir," said Kutadanta in reply; and the Blessed One spoke as follows:

7. "Long ago, O Brahmin, there was a king by the name Wide-realm (Maha Vigita), mighty, with great wealth and large property: with stores of silver and gold, of aids to enjoyment, of goods and corn; with his treasure-houses and his garners full. Now, when King Wide-realm was once sitting alone in meditation, he became anxious at the thought: 'I have in abundance all the good things a mortal can enjoy. The whole wide circle of the earth is mine by conquest to possess. 'Twere well if I were to offer a great sacrifice that should ensure me weal and welfare for many days."

And he had the Brahmin, his chaplain, called, and telling him all that he had thought, he said: "Fain would I, O Brahmin, offer a great sacrifice—let the venerable one instruct me how—for my weal and my welfare for many days."

8. Thereupon, the Brahmin, who was chaplain, said to the king: "The king's country, Sir, is harassed and harried. There are decoits abroad who pillage the villages and townships and who makes the roads unsafe. Were the king, so long as that is so, to levy a fresh tax, verily his majesty would be acting wrongly. But perchance, his majesty might think, I will soon put a stop to these scoundrels' game by degradation, banishment, fines, bonds and death!' But their license cannot be satisfactorily put a stop to. The remnant

left unpunished would still go on harassing the realm. Now, there is one method to adopt to put a thorough end to this disorder. Whosoever there be in the king's realm who devote themselves to keeping cattle and farming, to them let his majesty the king give food and seedcorn. Whosoever there be in the king's realm who devote themselves to trade, to them let his majesty the king give capital. Whosoever there be in the king's realm who devote themselves to government service, to them let his majesty the king give wages and food. Then those men, each following his own business, will no longer harass the realm; the king's revenue will go up; the country will be quiet and at peace; and the populace, pleased with one another and happy; dancing with their children in their arms, will dwell with open doors."

Then King Wide-realm, O Brahmin, accepted the word of his chaplain and did as he had said. And those men, each following his business, harassed the realm no more. The king's revenue went up, and the country became quiet and at peace. And the populace, pleased with one another and happy; dancing with their children in their arms, dwelt with open doors.

9. So King Wide-realm had his chaplain called and said: "The disorder is at an end. The country is at peace. I want to offer that great sacrifice—let the venerable one instruct me how—for my weal and my welfare for many days."

Then let his majesty the king send invitations to whomsoever there may be in his realm who are Kshatriyas, vassals of his, either in the country or the towns; or who are ministers and officials of his, either in the country or the towns; or who are Brahmins of position, either in the country or the towns; or who are householders of substance, either in the country or the towns, saying: "I intend to offer a great sacrifice. Let the venerable ones give their sanction to what will be to me for weal and welfare for many days."

Then King Wide-realm, O Brahmin, accepted the word of his chaplain and did as he had said. And they each—Kshatriyas and ministers and Brahmins and householders—made alike reply: "Let His Majesty the king, celebrate the sacrifice. The time is suitable, O King!" 'Thus did these four, as colleagues by consent, become wherewithal to furnish forth that sacrifice falls to.

10. King Wide-realm was gifted in the following eight ways:

"He was well born on both sides, on the mother's side and on the father's, of pure descent back through seven generations, and no slur was cast upon him, and no reproach, in respect of birth."

"He was handsome, pleasant in appearance, inspiring trust, gifted with great beauty of complexion, fair in colour, fine in presence, stately to behold."

"He was mighty, with great wealth and large property, with stores of silver and gold, of aids to enjoyment, of goods and corn, with his treasure-houses and his garners full."

"He was powerful, in command of an army, loyal and disciplined in four divisions (of elephants, cavalry, chariots, and bowmen), burning up, methinks, his enemies by his very glory."

"He was a believer and generous, a noble giver, keeping open house, a well spring whence Samanas and Brahmins, the poor and the wayfarers, beggars, and petitioners might draw, a doer of good deeds."

"He was learned in all kinds of knowledge."

"He knew the meaning of what had been said and could explain, "This saying has such and such a meaning, and that is such and such."

"He was intelligent, expert, and wise, and able to think out things present, past, or future."

"And these eight gifts of his, too, became wherewithal to furnish forth that sacrifice."

11. "The Brahmin, his chaplain, was gifted in the following four ways:

"He was well born on both sides, on the mother's and on the father's, of pure descent back through seven generations, with no slur cast upon him, and no reproach in respect of birth."

"He was a student-repeater who knew the mystic verses by heart, master of the three Vedas, with the indices, the ritual, the phonology, and the exegesis (as a fourth), and the legends as a fifth, learned in the idioms and the grammar, versed in Lok Katha (Folklore) and in the thirty marks on the body of a great man."

"He was virtuous, established in virtue, gifted with virtue that had grown great."

"He was intelligent, expert, and wise; foremost, or at most the second, among those who hold out the ladle."

"Thus these four gifts of his, too, became wherewithal to furnish forth that sacrifice."

12. And further, O Brahmin, the chaplain, before the sacrifice had begun, explained to King Wide-realm the three modes:

"Should His Majesty, the King, before starting on the great sacrifice, feel any such regret as: 'Great, alas, will be the portion of my wealth used up herein,' let not the king harbour such regret. Should His Majesty, the King, whilst offering the great sacrifice, feel any such regret as: 'Great, alas, will be the portion of my wealth used up herein' let not the king harbour such regret. Should His Majesty, the King, when the great sacrifice has been offered, feel any such regret as: 'Great, alas, will be the portion of my wealth used up herein," let not the king harbour such regret."

Thus did the chaplain, O Brahmin, before the sacrifice had begun, explain to King Wide-realm the three modes.

13. And further, O Brahmin, the chaplain, before the sacrifice had begun, to prevent any compunction that might

afterwards arise in ten ways as regards those who had taken part therein, said: "Now there will come to your sacrifice, Sire, men who destroy the life of living things, and men who refrain therefrom; men who take what has not been given, and men who refrain therefrom; men who speak lies, and men who do not; men who slander, and men who do not; men who speak rudely, and men who do not; men who chatter vain things, and men who refrain therefrom; men who covet, and men who covet not; men who harbour ill will, and men who harbour it not; men whose views are wrong; and men whose views are right. Of these, let those, who do evil with their evil. For those who do well, let your majesty offer, for them, Sire, arrange the rites, for them let the king gratify in them shall our heart within find peace."

14. And further, O Brahmin, the chaplain, whilst the king was carrying out the sacrifice, instructed and aroused and incited and gladdened his heart in sixteen ways: "Should there be people who say of the king, as he is offering the sacrifice: 'King Wide-realm is celebrating sacrifice without having invited the four classes of his subjects, without himself having the eight personal gifts, without the assistance of a Brahmin who has the four personal gifts.' Then would they speak not acording to the fact. For the consent of the four classes has been obtained, the king had the eight, and his Brahmin had the four personal gifts. With regard to each and every one of these sixteen conditions, the king may rest assured that it has been fulfilled. He can sacrifice, and be glad, and possess his heart in peace.

15. And further, O Brahmin, at that sacrifice, neither were any oxen slain neither goats, nor fowls, nor fatted pigs, nor were any living creatures put to death. No trees were cut down to be used as posts, and no Dabha grasses were mown to strew around the sacrificial spot. And the slaves and messengers and workmen there employed were driven neither by rods nor fear, nor carried on their work weeping with tears upon

their faces. Whoso chose to help, he worked; whoso chose not to help, worked not. What each chose to do, he did; what they chose not to do, that was left undone, With ghee and oil, and butter and milk, and honey and sugar, only was that sacrifice accomplished.

16. And further, O Brahmin, the Kshatriya vassals, and the ministers and officials, and the Brahmins of position, and the householders of substance, whether of the country or the towns, went to King Wide-realm, taking with them much wealth, and said: "This abundant wealth, Sire, have we brought hither for the king's use. Let His Majesty accept it at our hands!"

"Sufficient wealth have I, my friends, laid up, the produce of taxation that is just. You keep yours and take away more with you!"

When they had thus been refused by the king, they went aside and considered thus with the one another: "It would not befit us now, were we to take this wealth away again to our own homes. King Wide-realm is offering a great sacrifice. Let us too make an after-sacrifice!"

17. So the Kshatriyas established a continual largesse to the east of the king's sacrificial pit, the officials to the south thereof, the Brahmins to the west thereof, and the householders to the north thereof. And the things are given, and the manner of their gift was in all respects like unto the great sacrifice of King Wide-realm himself.

"Thus, O Brahmin, there was a fourfold cooperation, and King Wide-realm was gifted with eight personal gifts, and his officiating Brahmin with four. And there were three modes of the giving of that sacrifice. This, O Brahmin, is what is called the due celebration of a sacrifice in its threefold mode and with its furniture of sixteen kinds."

18. And when he had thus spoken, those Brahmins lifted their voices in tumult, and said: "How glorious the sacrifice, how

pure its accomplishment!" But Kutadanta, the Brahmin, sat there in silence.

Then those Brahmins said to Kutadanta: "Why do you not approve the good words of the Samana Gautama as well-said?"

"I do not fail to approve, for he who approves not as well-said that which has been well spoken by the Samana Gautama, surely his head would split in twain. But I was considering that the Samana Gautama does not say: 'Thus have I heard,' nor 'Thus behoves it to be,' but says only, 'Thus it was then,' or 'It was like that then." So I thought; 'For a certainty, the Samana Gautama himself must have been King Wide-realm or the Brahmin who officiated for him at that sacrifice. Does the Venerable Gautama admit that he who celebrates such a sacrifice, or causes it to be celebrated, is reborn at the dissolution of the body, after death, into some state of happiness in heaven?'"

"Yes, O Brahmin, that I admit. And at that time, I was the Brahmin who, as chaplain, had that sacrifice performed."

19. "Is there, O Gautama, any other sacrifice less difficult and less troublesome, with more fruit and more advantage still than this?" Yes, O Brahmin, there is. "And what, O Gautama, may that be?"

"The perpetual gifts kept up in a family where they are given specifically to virtuous recluses."

20. "But what is the reason, O Gautama, and what the cause, why such perpetual giving specifically to virtuous recluses, kept up in a family, is less difficult and troublesome, of greater fruit and greater advantage than that other sacrifice with its three modes and its accessories of sixteen kinds?"

"To the latter sort of sacrifice, O Brahmin, neither will the Arhats go, nor such as have entered on the Arhat way. And why not? Because in it beating with sticks takes place, and seizing by the throat. But they will go to the former, where such things are not. And therefore are such perpetual gifts above the other sort of sacrifice."

21. "And is there, O Gautama, any other sacrifice less difficult, and less troublesome, of greater fruit and greater advantage than either of these?" "Yes, O Brahmin, there is." "And what, O Gautama, may that be?"

    "The putting up of a dwelling place (Vihara) on behalf of the Order in all the four directions."

22. "And is there, O Gautama, any other sacrifice less difficult and less troublesome, of greater fruit and greater advantage than each and all of these three?" "Yes, O Brahmin, there is." "And what, O Gautama, may that be?"

    "He who with a trusting heart takes a Buddha as his guide, and the Truth, and the Order—that is a sacrifice better than open largeses, better than perpetual alms, better than the gift of a dwelling place."

23. "And is there, O Gautama, any other sacrifice less difficult and less troublesome, of greater fruit and greater advantage than all these four?"

    "When a man with a trusting heart takes upon himself the precepts—abstinence from destroying life; abstinence from taking what has not been given; abstinence from evil conduct in respect of lusts; abstinence from lying words; abstinence from strong, intoxicating, maddening drinks, the root of carelessness—that is a sacrifice better than open largesse, better than perpetual alms, better than the gift of dwelling places, better than accepting guidance."

24. "And is there, O Gautama, any other sacrifice less difficult and less troublesome, of greater fruit and greater advantage than all these five?" "Yes, O Brahmin, there is." "And what, O Gautama, may that be?"

(The answer is the long passage from the *Samaññaphala Sutta* 40, p. 62 (of the text,), down to 75 (p. 74) on the First Jhana, as follows:

1. The introductory paragraphs on the appearance of a Buddha, his preaching, the conversion of a hearer, and his renunciation of the world.
2. The Silas (minor morality).
3. The paragraph on Confidence.
4. The paragraph on 'Guarded is the Door of His Senses.'
5. The paragraph on 'Mindful and Self Possessed.'
6. The paragraph on Contentment.
7. The paragraph on Solitude.
8. The paragraph on the Five Hindrances.
9. The description of the First Jhana.)

"This, O Brahmin, is a sacrifice less difficult and less troublesome, of greater fruit and greater advantage than the previous sacrifices"

(The same is then said of the Second, Third, and Fourth Jhanas, in succession as in the *Samaññaphala Sutta* 77-82 and of the Insight arising from knowledge *(ibid.* 83, 84), and further omitting direct mention either way of 85-96 inclusive of the knowledge of the destruction of the Asavas, the deadly intoxications or floods *(ibid.* 97-98).

"And there is no sacrifice a man can celebrate, O Brahmin, higher and sweeter than this."

25. And when he had thus spoken, Kutadanta, the Brahmin, said to the Blessed One:

"Most excellent, O Gautama, are the words of thy mouth, most excellent! Just as if a man were to set up what has been thrown down, or were to reveal that which has been hidden away, or were to point out the right road to him who has gone astray, or were to bring a light into the darkness so that those who had eyes could see external forms—just even so has the Truth been made known to me in many a figure by the Venerable Gautama. I, even I, betake myself to the Venerable Gautama as my guide to the Doctrine and the Order. May the Venerable One accept me as a disciple, as one who, from this day forth, as long as life endures, has taken him as his guide. And I, O Gautama, will have the seven hundred bulls, the seven hundred steers, and the seven hundred heifers, the seven hundred goats, and the seven hundred rams set free. To them I grant their life. Let them eat green grass and drink fresh water, and may cool breezes waft around them."

26. Then the Blessed One discoursed to Kutadanta, the Brahmin, in due order; that is to say, he spoke to him of generosity, right conduct, heaven, the danger, the vanity, and the defilement of lusts, and the advantages of renunciation. And when the Blessed One became aware that Kutadanta, the Brahmin, had become prepared, softened, unprejudiced, upraised, and believing in heart, then did he proclaim the doctrine the Buddhas alone have won; that is to say, the doctrine of sorrow, its origin, its cessation and the Path. And just as a clean cloth, with all stains washed away, will readily take the dye, just even so did Kutadanta, the Brahmin, even while seated there, obtain the pure and spotless Eye for the Truth. And he knew that whatsoever has a beginning, in that is inherent also the necessity of dissolution.

27. And then the Brahmin Kutadanta, as one who had seen the Truth, had mastered it, understood it, and dived deep down into it; who had passed beyond doubt, put away perplexity, and gained full confidence; who had become dependent on no other for his knowledge of the teaching of the Master, addressed the Blessed One and said:

28. "May the Venerable Gautama grant me the favour of taking his meal with me tomorrow along with the members of the Order."

And the Blessed One signified, by silence, his consent. Then the Brahmin Kutadanta, seeing that the Blessed One had accepted, rose from his seat, and, keeping his right towards him as he passed, he departed thence. And at daybreak, he had sweet food, both hard and soft, prepared at the pit for his sacrifice and had the time announced to the Blessed One: "It is time, O Gautama and the meal is ready." And the Blessed One having dressed early in the morning, put on his outer robe and, taking his bowl with him, went with the brethren to Kutadanta's sacrificial pit and sat down on the seat prepared for him. And Kutadanta, the Brahmin, satisfied the brethren, with the Buddha at their head, with his own hand, with sweet food, both hard and soft, until they refused any more. And when the Blessed One had finished his meal and cleansed his bowl and hands, Kutadanta, the Brahmin, took a low seat and seated himself beside him. And when he was thus seated, the Blessed One instructed, aroused, incited and gladdened Kutadanta, the Brahmin, with religious discourse; then, arose from his seat and departed thence.

V

Thirdly, the Buddha denounced the caste system. The caste system in its present form was not then in existence. The bar against inter-dining and inter-marriage had not yet become operative. Things were flexible and not rigid as they are now. However, the principle of inequality, which is the basis of the caste system, had become well-established, and it was against this principle that Buddha carried on a determined and bitter fight. How strongly he was opposed to the pretensions of the Brahmins for superiority over other classes and how convincing the grounds of his opposition are to be found in many of his dialogues. The most important one of these is known as the *Ambattha Sutta*.

Ambattha Sutta

A young Brahmin's rudeness and an old one's faith.

1. Thus have I heard: The Blessed One, once on a tour through the Kosala country with a great company of the brethren, about five hundred in all, arrived at a Brahmin village in Kosala named Ikkhanankala. And while there, he stayed in the Ikkhanankala Wood.

   At that time, the Brahmin Pokkharsadi was dwelling at Ukkattha, a spot teeming with life, with much grassland and woodland and corn, on a royal domain granted him by King Pasenadi of Kosala as royal gift, with power over it as if he were the king."

2. Now, the Brahmin Pokkharasadi heard the news: "They say that the Samana Gautama, of the Sakya clan, who went out from a Sakya family to adopt the religious life, has now arrived with a great company of the brethren of his Order, at Ikkhanankala, and is staying there in the Ikkhanankala Wood. Now, regarding that Venerable Gautama, such is the high reputation that has been noised abroad. The Blessed One is an Arahat, a fully awakened one, abounding in wisdom and goodness, happy, with knowledge of the worlds, unsurpassed as a guide to mortals willing to be led, a teacher for gods and men, a Blessed One, a Buddha. He, by himself, thoroughly knows and sees, as it were, face to face this universe, including the worlds above of the gods, the Brahmins, and the Maras, and the world below with its recluses and Brahmins, its princes and peoples, and having known it, he makes his knowledge known to others. The truth, lovely in its origin, lovely in its progress, lovely in its consummation, doth he proclaim, both in the spirit and the letter, the higher life doth he make known, in all its fullness and purity. And it's good to pay visits to Arahats like that.

3. At the time, a young Brahmin, an Ambattha, was a pupil under Pokkharasadi, the Brahmin. And he was a repeater

(of the sacred words) knowing, the mystic verses by heart, one who had mastered the Three Vedas, with the indices, the ritual, the phonology, and the explanation as a fourth, and the legends as a fifth, learned in the idioms and the grammar, versed in Lokayata sophistry and the theory of the signs on the body of a great man— so recognised authority in the system of the threefold Vedic knowledge as expounded by his master, that he could say of him: "What I know that you know, and what you know that I know."

4. And Pokkharasadi told Ambattha the news and said: "Come now, dear Ambattha, go to the Samana Gautama, and find out whether the reputation so noised abroad regarding him is in accord with the facts or not, whether the Samana Gautama is such as they say or not".

5. "But how. Sir, shall I know whether that is so or not?" "There have been handed down, Ambattha, in our mystic verses, thirty-two bodily signs of a great man—signs which, if a man has, he will become one of two things and no other. If he dwells at home, he will become a sovereign of the world, a righteous king, bearing rule even to the shores of the four great oceans, a conqueror, the protector of his people, possessor of the seven royal treasures. And these are the seven treasures that he has: the Wheel, the Elephant, the Horse, the Gem, the Woman, the Treasurer, and the Adviser as a seventh. And he has more than a thousand sons, heroes, mighty in frame, beating down the armies of the foe. And he dwells in complete ascendancy over the wide earth from sea to sea, ruling it in righteousness without the need of baton or sword. But if he goes forth from the household life into the houseless state, then he will become a Buddha who removes the veil from the eyes of the world. Now I, Ambattha, am a giver of the mystic verses; you have received them from me."

6. "Very good, Sir, said Ambattha in reply, and rising from his seat and paying reverence to Pokkharasadi, he mounted a

chariot drawn by mares and proceeded, with a retinue of young Brahmins, to the Ikkhanankala Wood. And when he had gone in the chariot as far as the road was practicable for vehicles, he got down and went, into the park on foot.

7. Now, at that time, a number of the brethren were walking up and down in the open air. And Ambattha went up to them and said: "Where may the Venerable Gautama be lodging now? We have come hither to call upon him."

8. Then the brethren thought: "This young Brahmin Ambattha is of distinguished family and a pupil of the distinguished Brahmin Pokkharasadi. The Blessed One will not find it difficult to hold conversation with such." And they said to Ambattha: "There Gautama is lodging, where the door is shut, go quietly up, enter the porch gently, give a cough, and knock on the crossbar. The Blessed One will open the door for you.'

9. Then Ambattha did so. And the Blessed One opened the door, and Ambattha entered in. The other young Brahmins also went in, and they exchanged with the Blessed One the greetings and compliments of politeness and courtesy and took their seats. But Ambattha, walking about, said something or other of a civil kind in an off-hand way, fidgetting about the while or standing up to the Blessed One sitting there.

10. And the Blessed One said to him: "Is that the way, Ambattha, that you would hold converse with aged teachers, and teachers of your teachers well stricken in years, as you now do, moving about the while or standing, with me thus seated?"

11. "Certainly not, Gautama. It is proper to speak with a Brahmin as one goes along only when the Brahmin himself is walking, and standing to a Brahmin who stands, and seated to a Brahmin who has taken his seat, or reclining to a Brahmin who reclines. But with shavelings, sham friars,

menial black fellows, the offscouring of our kinsman's heels—with them, I would talk as I now do to you."

"But you must have been wanting something, Ambattha when you come here. Turn your thoughts rather to the object you had in view when you came. This young Brahmin Ambattha is ill-bred, though he prides himself on his culture; what can this come from except from want of training?"

12. Then Ambattha was displeased and angry with the Blessed One for being called rude. At the thought that the Blessed One was vexed with him, he said, scoffing, jeering, and sneering at the Blessed One: "Rough is this Sakya breed of yours, Gautama, and rude, touchy is this Sakya breed of yours, and violent. Menials, mere menials, they neither venerate, nor value, nor esteem, nor give gifts to, nor pay honour to Brahmins. That Gautama, is neither fitting, nor is it seemly." Thus did the young Brahmin Ambattha, for the first time, charge the Sakyas with being menials.

13. "But in what then, Ambattha, have the Sakyas given you offence?"

"Once, Gautama, I had to go to Kapilvastu on some business or other of Pokkharasadi's and went into the Sakyas' Congress Hall. Now, at that time, there were several Sakyas, old and young, seated in the hall on grand seats, making merry and joking together, nudging one another with their fingers; and for a truth, methinks, it was I that was the subject of their jokes; and not one of them even offered me a seat. That Gautama, is neither fitting, nor is it seemly, that the Sakyas, menials as they are, mere menials, should neither venerate, nor value, nor esteem, nor give gifts to, nor pay honour to Brahmams." Thus did the young Brahmin Ambattha, for the second time, charge the Sakyas with being menials.

14. "Why a quail, Ambattha, little hen-bird though she be, can say what she likes in her own nest. And there, the Sakyas are at their own home in Kapilvastu. It is not fitting for you to take offence at so trifling a thing."

15. "There are these four grades, Gautama,—the nobles, the Brahmins, the trades folk, and the workpeople. And of these four, three—the nobles, the trades folk, and workpeople—are, verily, but attendants on the Brahmins. So, Gautama, that is neither fitting nor is it seemly that the Sakyas, menials as they are, mere menials should neither venerate, nor value, nor esteem, nor give gifts to, nor pay honour to the Brahmins.

"Thus did the young Brahmin Ambattha, for the third time, charged the sakyes with being menials.

16. Then the Blessed One thought thus: "This Ambattha is very set on humbling the Sakyas with his charge of servile origin. What if I were to ask him as to his own lineage." And he said to him:

"And what family do you then, Ambattha, belong to?" "Yes, but if one were to follow up your ancient name and lineage, Ambattha, on the father's and the mother's side, it would appear that the Sakyas were once your masters and that you are the offspring of one of their slave girls. But the Sakyas trace their line back to Okkaka, the king."

"Long ago, Ambattha, King Okkaka, wanting to divert the succession in favour of the son of his favourite queen, banished his elder children—Okkamukha, Karanda, Hatthinika, and Sinipura—from the land. And being thus banished, they took up their dwelling on the slopes of the Himalaya, on the borders of a lake where a mighty oak tree grew. And through fear of injuring the purity of their line, they intermarried with their sisters."

Now, Okkaka, the king, asked the ministers at his court: "Where, Sirs, are the children now?"

"There is a spot, sirs, on the slopes of the Himalayas, on the borders of a lake, where there grows a mighty oak (*sako*). There do they dwell. And lest they should injure the purity of their line, they have married their own (*sakahi*) sisters."

"Then did Okkaka, the king, burst forth in admiration: "Hearts of oak (*sakya*) are those young fellows! Right, well, they hold their own (*parama sakya*)!"

"That is the reason, Ambattha, why they are known as Sakyas. Now, Okkaka had a slave girl called Disa. She gave birth to a black baby. And no sooner was it born than the little black thing said, "Wash me, mother. Bathe me, mother. Set me free, mother, of this dirt. So shall I be of use to you."

Now, just as now, Ambattha, people call devils "devils", so then they called devils "black fellows" (*kanhe*). And they said, "This fellow spoke as soon as he was born." Tis a black thing (*Kanha*) that is born a devil has been born!" And that is the origin, Ambattha, of the Kanhayanas. He was the ancestor of the Kanhayanas. And thus is it, Ambattha, that if one were to follow up your ancient name and lineage on the father's and the mother's side, it would appear that the Sakyas were once your masters and that you are the offspring of one of their slave girls."

17. When he had thus spoken, the young Brahmins said to the Blessed One: "Let not the Venerable Gautama, humble Ambattha too sternly with this reproach of being descended from a slave girl. He is well-born, Gautama, and of a good family; he is versed in the sacred hymns, an able reciter, and a learned man. And he can give answer the Venerable Gautama in these matters."

18. Then the Blessed One said to them: "Quite so. If you thought otherwise, then it would be for you to carry on our discussion further. But as you think so, let Ambattha himself speak."

19. "We do not think so, and we will hold our peace. Ambattha can answer the Venerable Gautama in these matters."

20. Then the Blessed One said to Ambattha, the Brahmin: 'Then this further question arises, Ambattha, a very reasonable one which, even though unwillingly, you should answer. If

you do not give a clear reply, go off upon another issue, remain silent, or go away, then your head will split in pieces on the spot. What have you heard, when Brahmins old and well-stricken in years, teachers of yours or their teachers, were talking together, as to whence the Kanhayanas draw their origin, and who the ancestor was to whom they trace themselves back?"

And when he had thus spoken, Ambattha remained silent. And the Blessed One asked the same question again. And still, Ambattha remained silent. Then the Blessed One said to him: "You had better answer now, Ambattha. It is no time for you to hold your peace. For whosoever, Ambattha, does not, even up to the third time of asking, answer a reasonable question put by a Tathagata (by one who has won the truth), his head splits into pieces on the spot."

21. Now, at that time, the spirit who bears the thunderbolt stood over above Ambattha in the sky with a mighty mass of iron, all fiery, dazzling, and aglow, with the intention, if he did not answer, there and then to split his head in pieces. And the Blessed One perceived the spirit bearing the thunderbolt, and so did Ambattha, the Brahmin. And Ambattha, on becoming aware of it, terrified, startled, and agitated, seeking safety and protection and help from the Blessed One, crouched besides him in awe and said: 'What was it the Blessed One said? Say it once again !"

"What do you think, Ambattha? What have you heard, when Brahmins old and well-stricken in years, teachers of yours or their teachers, were talking together, as to whence the Kanhayanas draw their origin, and who the ancestor was to whom they trace themselves back?"

"Just so, Gautama, did I hear, even as the Venerable Gautama hath said? That is the origin of the Kanhayana, and that the ancestor to whom they trace themselves back."

22. And when he had thus spoken, the young Brahmins fell into tumult, uproar, and turmoil, and said: "Low-born, they say, is Ambattha, the Brahmin; his family, they say, is not of good standing; they say he is descended from a slave girl, and the Sakyas were his masters. We did not suppose that the Samana Gautama, whose words are righteousness itself, was not a man to be trusted!"

23. And the Blessed One thought: "They go too far, these Brahmins, in their depreciation of Ambattha as the offspring of a slave girl. Let me set him free from their reproach. And he said to them: Be not too severe in disparaging Ambattha, the Brahmin on the ground of his descent. That Kanha became a mighty seer. He went into the Dekkan, where he learned mystic verses and, returning to Okkaka, the king, he demanded his daughter Madda-rupi in marriage. To him, the king, in answer, said: "Who forsooth, is this fellow who, son of my slave girl as he is, asks for my daughter in marriage." Angry and displeased, he fitted an arrow to his bow. But neither could he let the arrow fly nor could he take it off the string again.

Then the ministers and courtiers went to Kanha, the seer, and said: "Let the king go safe, Sir, let the king go safe."

"The king shall suffer no harm. But should he shoot the arrow downwards, then would the earth dry up as far as his realm extends." "Let the king, Sir, go safe, and the country too."

"The king shall suffer no harm, nor his land. But should he shoot the arrow upwards, the god would not rain for seven years as far as his realm extends."

"Let the king, Sir, go safe, and the country too."

"The king shall suffer no harm, nor his land. But should he shoot the arrow upwards, the god would not rain for seven years as far as his realm extends."

"Let the king, Sir, go safe, and the country too, and let the god rain."

"The king shall suffer no harm, nor the land either, and the god shall rain. But let the king aim the arrow at his eldest son. The prince shall suffer no harm, not a hair of him shall be touched."

"Then, O Brahmins, the ministers told this to Okkaka and said: "Let the king aim at his eldest son. He will suffer neither harm nor terror." And the king did so, and no harm was done. But the king, terrified at the lesson given him, gave the man his daughter Madda-rupi as a wife. You should not, O Brahmins, be too severe in disparaging Ambattha in the matter of his slave-girl ancestry. That Kanha was a mighty seer."

24. Then the Blessed One said to Ambattha: "What think you, Ambattha? Suppose a young Kshatriya should have a connection with a Brahmin maiden, and from their intercourse, a son should be born. Now would the son thus born to the Brahmin maiden through the Kshatriya youth receive a seat and water (as token of respect) from the Brahmins?

"Yes, he would, Gautama."

"But would the Brahmins allow him to partake of the feast offered to the dead, the food boiled in milk, or offerings to the gods or of food sent as a present?"

"Yes. they would Gautama."

"But would the Brahmins teach him their verses or not?"

"They would Gautama."

"But would he be shut off or not from their women?"

"He would not be shut off.'

"But would the Kshatriyas allow him to receive the consecration ceremony of a Kshatriya?"

"Certainly not, Gautama."

"Because he is not of pure descent on the mother's side."

25. "Then what think you, Ambattha? Suppose a Brahmin youth should have a connection with a Kshatriya maiden, and from their intercourse a son should be born. Now would the son come to the Kshatriya maiden through the Brahmin youth receive a seat and water (as token of respect) from the Brahmins?"

"Yes, he would, Gautama."

"But would the Brahmins allow him to partake of the feast offered to the dead, food boiled in milk, an offering to the gods, or food sent as a present?"

"Yes, they would, Gautama."

"But would the Brahmins teach him their verses or not?"

"They would, Gautama."

"But would the Kshatriyas allow him to receive the consecration ceremony of a Kshatriya."

"Certainly not, Gautama." "Why not that?"

"Because he is not of pure descent on the father's side."

26. "Then, Ambattha, whether one compares women with women or men with men, the Kshatriyas are higher and the Brahmins inferior."

"And what think you, Ambattha? Suppose the Brahmins, for some offence or other, were to outlaw a Brahmin by shaving him and pouring ashes over his head Gautama were to banish him from the land, from the township. Would he be offered a seat or water among the Brahmins?" "Certainly not, Gautama."

"Or would the Brahmins allow him to partake of the food offered to the dead, the food boiled in milk, the offerings to the gods, or food sent as a present?: "Certainly not, Gautama."

"Or would the Brahmins teach him their verses or not?" "Certainly not, Gautama."

"And would he be shut off, or not, from their women?"

"He would be shut off."

27. "But what think you, Ambattha? If the Kshatriyas had in the same way outlawed a Kshatriya and banished him from the land or the township, would he, among the Brahmins, be offered water and a seat?"

"Yes, he would, Gautama."

"And would he be allowed to partake of the food offered to the dead, the food boiled in milk, the offerings to the gods, or food sent as a present?"

"He would, Gautama."

"And would the Brahmins teach him their verses?"

"They would, Gautama?"

"And would he be shut off, or not from their women?"

"He would not, Gautama."

"But thereby, Ambattha, the Kshatriya, would have fallen into the deepest degradation, shaven as to his head, cut dead with the ash-basket, banished from land and townships. So that, even when a Kshatriya has fallen into the deepest degradation, still it holds good that the Kshatriyas are higher, and the Brahmins inferior."

28. Moreover, it was one of the Brahma gods, Sanam-kumara, who uttered this stanza:

"The Kshatriya is the best of those among this folk who put their trust in lineage.

But he who is perfect in wisdom and righteousness, he is the best among gods and men."

Now this stanza, Ambattha, was well sung and not ill sung by the Brahma Sanam-kumara, well said and not ill said, full of meaning and not void thereof. And I, too, approve it. "I also" Ambattha says:

"The Kshatriya is the best of those among this folk who put their trust in lineage.

But he who is perfect in wisdom and righteousness, he is the best among gods and men."

Here ends the first portion of the recitation.

1. "But what, Gautama, is the righteousness and what the wisdom spoken of in that verse?"

   "In the supreme perfection in wisdom and righteousness, Ambattha, there is no reference to the question either of birth or lineage or the pride that says: 'You are held as worthy as I', or 'You are not held as worthy as I.' It is where the talk is of marrying or giving in marriage, that reference is made to such things as that. For whosoever, Ambattha, are in bondage to the notions of birth or lineage, or to the pride of social position, or connection by marriage. They are far from the best wisdom and righteousness. It is only by having rid of all such bondage that one can realise oneself that supreme perfection in wisdom and conduct for oneself.

2. "But what, Gautama, is that conduct, and what that wisdom?" [Here follow, under 'Morality' (Sila)]

   The introductory paragraphs (40-42 of the 'Samaññaphala' pp. 62-63 of the text) on the appearance of a Buddha, his preaching, the conversion of a hearer, and his renunciation of the world. Then come:

   1. The Silas above, pp. 4-12 (8-27) of the text. Only the refrain differs. It runs here, at the end of each clause, through the whole of this repeated passage: 'This is reckoned in him as morality.' Then, under 'Conduct' (*Karuna*).

   2. The paragraph on 'Confidence' above, p. 69 of the text 63. The refrain from here onwards: 'This is reckoned to him as conduct.'

3. The paragraph on 'Guarded is the Door of the Senses' above, p. 70 of the text 64.

4. The paragraph on 'Mindful and Self-Possessed' above, p. 70 of the text 65.

5. The paragraph on 'Content' above, p. 71 of the text 66.

6. The paragraph on 'Solitude' above, p. 71 of the text 67.

7. The paragraphs on the 'Five Hindrances' above p. 71-72 of the text 68-74.

8. The paragraphs on the 'Four Rapt Contemplations' above, 73-76, p. 75-82.

   The refrain at the end of each of them ('higher and better than the last') is, of course, to be read not as a higher fruit of the life of a recluse but as higher conduct.

Under Wisdom (VIGGA)

9. The paragraphs on 'Insight Arising from Knowledge' (*Nana-dassanam*), above, p. 76 of the text 83, 84. The refrain from here onwards is: 'This is reckoned in him as wisdom, and it is higher and sweeter than the last.'

10. The paragraphs on the 'Mental Image', above, p. 77 of the text 85, 86.

11. The paragraphs on 'the Mystic Gifts' (*lddhi*), above, p. 77 of the text 87, 88.

12. The paragraphs on the 'Heavenly Ear' (*Dibbasota*), above p. 79 of the text 89, 90.

13. The paragraphs on 'Knowledge of the Hearts of o thers' (*Kato-pariya-nanam*), above, p. 79 of the text 91, 92.

14. The paragraphs on the 'Memory of One's Own Previous Births' (*Pubbe-nivasa-anussati-nama*) above, p. 81 of the text 93, 94.

15. The paragraph on the 'Divine Eye' (*Dibbakakkhu*), above, p. 82 of the text 95, 96.

16. The paragraphs on the 'Destruction of the Deadly Floods' (*Asavanam Khaya-nanam*), above, p. 83 of the text 97, 98.

"Such a man, Ambattha, is said to be perfect in wisdom, perfect in conduct, perfect in wisdom and conduct. And there is no other perfection in wisdom and conduct higher and sweeter than this."

3. "Now, Ambattha, to this supreme perfection in wisdom and goodness, there are four leakages. And what are the four?"

"In case, Ambattha, any recluse or Brahmin, without having thoroughly attained unto this supreme perfection in wisdom and conduct, with his yoke on his shoulder (to carry firesticks, a water-pot, needles, and the rest of a mendicant friar's outfit), should plunge into the depths of the forest, vowing to himself: 'I will henceforth be one of those who live only on fruits that have fallen of themselves," Then, verily, he turns that out worthy only to be a servant unto him that hath attained to wisdom and rightsouness."

"And again, Ambattha, in case any recluse or Brahmin, without having thoroughly attained unto this supreme perfection in wisdom and conduct, and without having attained to living only on fruits fallen of themselves, taking a hoe and a basket with him, should plunge into the depths of the forest, vowing to himself: 'I will henceforth be one of those who live only on bulbs and roots of fruits.' Then, verily, he turns out worthy only to be a servant unto him who hath attained wisdom and righteousness."

"And again, Ambattha, in case any recluse or Brahmin, without having thoroughly attained unto this supreme perfection in wisdom and conduct, and without having attained to living only on fruits fallen of themselves, and without having attained to living only on bulbs, roots, and fruits, should build himself a fire shrine near the boundaries of some village or town and there dwell serving the fire-god, then verily he turns out worthy only to be a servant unto him that hath attained to wisdom and righteousness."

"And again, Ambattha, in case any recluse or Brahmin, without having thoroughly attained unto this supreme perfection in wisdom and conduct, and without having attained to living only on fruits fallen of themselves, and without having attained to living only on bulbs, roots, and fruits, and without having attained to serving the fire-god, should build himself a founded almshouse at a crossing where four high roads meet, and dwell there, saying to himself: 'Whosoever, whether recluse or Brahmin shall pass here, from either of these four directions, him will I entertain according to my ability and according to my power.' Then, verily, he turns out worthy only to be a servant unto him who hath attained to wisdom and righteousness.:

"These are the four leakage, Ambattha, to supreme perfection in righteousness and conduct."

4. "Now, what think you, Ambattha? Have you, as one of a class of pupils under the same teacher, been instructed in this supreme perfection of wisdom and conduct?"

"Not that, Gautama. How little is it that I can profess to have learnt! How supreme this perfection of wisdom and conduct! Far is it from me to have been trained therein."

"Then what think you, Ambattha? Although you have not thoroughly attained unto this supreme perfection of wisdom and goodness, have you been trained to take the yoke upon your shoulders and plunge into the depths of the forest as one who would fain observe the vow of living only on fruits fallen of themselves?" "Not even that, Gautama".

"Then what think you Ambattha? Although you have not attained unto this supreme perfection of wisdom and goodness, nor have attained to living on fruits fallen of themselves, have you been trained to take a hoe and basket and plunge into the depths of the forest as one who would fain observe the vow of living only on bulbs, roots, and fruits?" "Not even that, Gautama".

"Then what think you, Ambattha? Although you have not attained unto this supreme perfection of wisdom and goodness, and have not attained to living on fruits fallen of themselves, and have not attained to living on bulbs and roots and fruits, have you been taught to build yourself a fireshrine on the borders of some village or town. and dwell there as one who would fain serve the fire-god?' 'Not even that, Gautama.'

"Then what think you, Ambattha? Although you have not attained unto this supreme perfection of wisdom and goodness, and have not attained to living on fruits fallen of themselves, and have not attained to living on bulbs, roots, and fruits, and have not attained to serving the fire-god, have you been taught to build yourself a four-doored almshouse at a spot where four high roads cross, and dwell there as one who would fain observe the vow to entertain whosoever might pass that way, from any of the four directions, according to your ability and power?" "Not even that, Gautama.'

5. "So then you, Ambattha, as a pupil, have fallen short of due training, not only in the supreme wisdom and conduct but even in any one of the four leakages by which the complete attainment thereof is debarred. And your teacher too, the Brahmin Pokkharasadi, has told you this saying: "Who are these shavelings, sham friars, menial black fellows, the offscouring of our kinsman's heels, that they should claim converse with Brahmins versed in the threefold Vedic Lore!' He himself has not even fulfilled any one of these

lesser duties (which leads men to neglect the higher ones). See, Ambattha, how deeply your teacher, the Brahmin Pokkharasadi, has herein done you wrong."

6. "And the Brahmin Pokkharasadi, Ambattha, is in the enjoyment of a grant from Pasenadi, the King of Kosala. But the king does not allow him to come into his presence. When he consults with him, he speaks to him only from behind a curtain. How is it, Ambattha, that the very king from whom he accepts this pure and lawful maintenance, King Pasendadi of Kosala, does not admit him to his presence? See, Ambattha, how deeply your teacher the Brahmin Pokkharasadi, has herein done you wrong."

7. "Now, what think you, Ambattha? Suppose a king, either seated on the neck of his elephant on the back of his horse, or standing on the foot rug of his chariot, should discuss some resolution of state with his chiefs or princes, and suppose as he left the spot and stepped on one side, a workman (Shudra) or the slave of a workman should come up and, standing there, should discuss the matter, saying: 'Thus and thus said Pasendadi the King.' Although he should speak as the king might have spoken or discuss as the king might have done, would he thereby be the king or even as one of his officers?' 'Certainly not, Gautama."

8. "But just so, Ambattha, those ancient poets (Rishis) of the Brahmins, the authors of the verses, the utterers of the verses whose ancient form of words so chanted, uttered, or composed, the Brahmins of today chant over again and rehearse, intoning or reciting exactly, as has been intoned or recited—to wit, Atthaka, Vamaka, Vamadeva, Jamadagni, Angiras, Bharadwaja, Vashistha, Vishwamitra, Kashyapa, and Bhrigu—though you can say: 'I as a pupil, know by heart their verses,' that you should on that account be a Rishi, or have attained to the state of a Rishi—such a condition of things has no existence!"

9. "Now, what think you, Ambattha? What have you heard when Brahmins, old and well stricken in years, teachers or

yours of their teachers, were talking together—did those ancient Rishis whose verses you so chant over and repeat parade about well groomed, perfumed, trimmed as to their hair and beard, adorned with garlands and gems, clad in white garments, in the full possession and enjoyment of the five pleasures of sense, as you and your teacher do now?" "Not that, Gautama."

"Or did they live, as their food, on boiled rice of the best sorts, from which all the black specks had been sought out and removed, and flavoured with sauces and curries of various kind as you and your teacher do now?" "Not that, Gautama."

"Or were they waited upon by women with fringes and furbelows round their loins, as you and your teacher do now?"

"Or did they go about driving chariots, drawn by mares with plaited manes and tails, using long wands and goads the while, as you and your teacher do now?" "Not that, Gautama."

"Or did they have themselves guarded in fortified towns, with moats dug out around them and crossbars let down before the gates, by men girt with long swords, as you, and your teacher do now?" "Not that Gautama."

10. "So then, Ambattha, neither are you a Rishi nor your teacher nor do you live under the conditions under which the Rishis lived. But whatsoever it may be, Ambattha, concerning which you are in doubt or perplexity about me, ask me as to that, and I will make it clear by explanation."

11. Then the Blessed One went forth from his chamber and began to walk up and down, and Ambattha did the same. And as he thus walked up and down, following the Blessed One, he took stock of the thirty-two signs of a great man, whether they appeared on the body of the Blessed One or

not. And he perceived them all save only two. With respect to those two—the concealed member and the extent of tongue—he was in doubt and perplexity, not satisfied, not sure.

12. And the Blessed One knew that he was in doubt. And he so arranged matters by his Wondrous Gift that Ambattha, the Brahmin, saw how that part of the Blessed One that ought to be hidden by clothes was enclosed in a sheath. And the Blessed One so bent round his tongue that he touched and stroked both his ears, touched and stroked both his nostrils, and covered the whole circumference of his forehead with his tongue.

    And Ambattha, the young Brahmin, thought: 'The Samana Gautama is endowed with the thirty-two signs of a great man, with them all, not only with some of them.' And he said to the Blessed One : ' And now, Gautama, we would fain depart. We are busy and have much to do.'

    "Do Ambattha, what seemed to you fit."

    And Ambattha mounted his chariot, drawn by mares, and departed thence.

13. Now, at that time, the Brahmin Pokkharasadi had gone forth from Ukkattha with a great retinue of Brahmins and was seated in his own pleasance, waiting there for Ambattha. And Ambattha came on to the pleasance. And when he had come in his chariot as far as the path was practicable for chariots, he descended from it and came on foot to where Pokkharasadi was, saluted him, and took his seat respectfully on one side. And when he was so seated, Pokkharasadi said to him:

14. "Well, Ambattha! Did you see the Blessed One?" "Yes, Sir, we saw him."

"Well! Is the Venerable Gautama as the reputation about him I told you of declares, and not otherwise: Is he such a one, or is he not?"

"He is so, Sir, as his reputation declares and not otherwise. Such is he, not different. And he is endowed with the thirty-two signs of a great man, with all of them, not only with some." "And did you have any talk, Ambattha, with the Samana Gautama?" "Yes, Sir, I had." "And how did the talk go?'

Then Ambattha told the Brahmin Pokkharasadi all the talk that he had with the Blessed One.

15. When he had thus spoken, Pokkharasadi said to him: "Oh, you wiseacre! Oh! You dullard! Oh! You expert, forsooth, in our threefold Vedic lore! A man, they say, who should carry out his business thus must, on the dissolution of the body, after death, be reborn into some dismal state of misery and woe. What could the very points you pressed in your insolent words lead up to, if not to the very disclosures the Venerable Gautama made? What a wiseacre, a dullard: what an expert, forsooth, in our threefold Vedic lore!" Angry and displeased, he struck out with his foot and rolled Ambattha over. And he wanted, there and then, himself to go and call on the Blessed One.

16. But the Brahmanas there spake thus to Pokkharasadi: "It is much too late, Sir, today to go to call on the Samana Gautama. The Venerable Pokkharasadi can do so tomorrow."

So Pokkharasadi had sweet food, both hard and soft, prepared at his own house and taken on wagons, by the light of blazing torches, out to Ukkattha. And he went on to the Ikkhanankala Wood, driving in his chariot as far as the road was practicable for vehicles and then going on foot to where the Blessed One was. And when he had exchanged with the Blessed One the greetings and compliments of politeness and courtesy, he took his seat on one side, and said to the Blessed One:

17. "Has our pupil Gautama the young Brahmin Ambattha, been here?" "Yes. Brahmin, he has."

"And did you, Gautama, have any talk with him?" "Yes. Brahmin, I had."

"And in what manner was the talk that you had with him?"

18. Then the Blessed One told the Brahmin Pokkharasadi all the talk that had taken place. And when he had thus spoken, Pokkharasadi said to the Blessed One:

"He is young and foolish, Gautama, that young Brahmin Ambattha. Forgive him, Gautama."

"Let him be quite happy, Brahmin, that young Brahmin Ambattha."

19. And the Brahmin Pokkharasadi took stock, on the body of the Blessed One, of the thirty-two marks of a great being. And he saw them all plainly, save only two. As for two of them—the sheath-concealed member and the extensive tongue—he was still undecided. But the Blessed One showed them to Pokkharasadi, even as he had shown them to Ambattha. And Pokkharasadi perceived that the Blessed One was endowed with the thirty-two marks of a great being, with all of them, not only with some. And he said to the Blessed One: "May the Venerable Gautama grant me the favour of taking his tomorrow's meal with me and also the members of the Order with him." And the Blessed One accepted. His request silently.

20. Then the Brahmin Pokkharasadi, seeing that the Blessed One had accepted, had (on the morrow) the time announced to him: "It is time, O Gautama, the meal is ready." And the Blessed One, who had dressed in the early morning, putting on his outer robe and taking his bowl with him, went with the brethren to Pokkharasadi's house and sat down, on the

seat prepared for him. And Pokkharasadi, the Brahmin, satisfied the Blessed One, with his hand, with sweet food, both hard and soft, until he refused any more, and the young Brahmins the members of the Order. And when the Blessed One had finished his meal, and cleansed the bowl and his hands, Pokkharasadi took a low seat, and sat down beside him.

21. Then to him, thus seated, the Blessed One discoursed in due order, that is to say, he spoke to him of generosity, right conduct, heaven, the danger, the vanity, and the defilement of lusts, of the advantages of renunciation. And when the Blessed One saw that Pokkharasadi, the Brahmin, had become prepared, softened, unprejudiced, uplifted, and believing in heart, then he proclaimed the doctrine the Buddhas alone have won; that is to say, the doctrine of sorrow, its origin, its cessation, and the Path. And just as a clean cloth from which all stain has been washed away will readily take the dye, just even so did Pokkharasadi, the Brahmin, obtain, even while sitting there, the pure and spotless Eye for the Truth, and he knew: 'Whatsoever has a beginning in that is inherent also the necessity of dissolution."

22. And then the Brahmin Pokkharasadi as one who had seen the Truth, had mastered it, understood it, dived deep down into it, who had passed beyond doubt and put away perplexity and gained full confidence, who had become dependent on no other man for his knowledge of the teaching of the Master, addressed the Blessed One and said:

"Most excellent, O Gautama (are the words of thy mouth), most excellent! Just as if a man were to set up that which has been thrown down, or were to reveal that which has been hidden away, or were to point out the right road to him who has gone astray, or were to bring a light into the darkness so that those who had eyes could see external forms—just even so, Lord, has the Truth been made known to me, in many a figure, by the Venerable Gautama. And I, O Gautama, with my sons, and my wife, and my people, and my companions, betake myself to the Venerable Gautama as my guide, to the Truth, and the Order. May the Venerable Gautama accept me as a disciple, as one who, from this day forth, as long as life endures, has taken him as his guide. And just as the Venerable Gautama visits the families of others, his disciples at Ukkattha, so let him visit mine. Whosoever there may be there, of Brahmins or their wives, who shall pay reverence to the Venerable Gautama, or stand up in his presence, or offer him a seat or water, or take delight in him, to him that will be for long, a cause of weal and bliss."

"It is well, Brahmin, what you say."

Here ends the Ambattha Sutta.

VI

In the matter of his opposition to caste, Buddha practised what he preached. He did what Aryan society refused to do. In Aryan society, the Shudra or low-caste man could never become a Brahmin. But Buddha not only preached against caste but admitted the Shudra and the low caste to the rank of a Bhikku, who held the same rank in Buddhism as the Brahmin did in Brahmanism.

In the first place, as regards his Order, over which alone he had complete control, he ignores completely all advantages or disadvantages arising from birth, occupation, and social status and sweeps away all barriers and disabilities arising from the arbitrary rules of mere ceremonial or social impurity.

One of the most distinguished members of his Order, the very one of them who was referred to as the chief authority after Gautama himself on the rules of the Order, was Upali, who had formerly been a barber, one of the despised occupations. So Sunita, one of the brethren whose verses are chosen for insertion in the Therigāthā, was a Pukkusa, one of the low tribes. Sati, the profounder of a deadly heresy, was of the sons of the fisher folk, afterwards a low caste, and even then an occupation, on account of its cruelty, particularly abhorred. Nanda was a cowherd. The two Panthakas were born out of wedlock to a girl of good family through intercourse with a slave (so that by the rule laid down in *Manusmriti* they were actually outcasts). Kapa was the daughter of a deers stalker, Punna and Punnika had been slave girls. Sumangalamata was daughter and wife of workers in rushes, and Subha was the daughter of a smith. More instances could undoubtedly be quoted, and others will become known when more texts are published.

It does not show much historical insight to sneer at the numbers as small and to suggest that the supposed enlightenment or liberality was mere pretence. The facts speak for themselves, and the percentage of low-born members of the Order was probably in fair proportion to the percentage of people belonging to the despised *jatis* and *sippas* as compared with the rest of the population. Thus, of the *Theris* mentioned in the Therigāthā, we know the social position of sixty, of whom five are mentioned above—that is, $8^1/_2$ per cent of the whole number were base-born. It is most likely that this is just about the proportion that people in similar social rank bore to the rest of the population.

Just as Buddha levelled up the position of the Shudras and the low-caste men by admitting them to the highest rank, namely that of Bhikkus, he also levelled up the position of women. In Aryan society, women were placed in the same position as the Shudras, and in all Aryan literature, women and Shudras are spoken of together as people belonging to the same status. Both of them were denied the right to take *Sanyas, a*s *Sanyas* was the only way open to salvation.

Women and Shudras were beyond salvation. Buddha broke this Aryan rule in the case of women, as he did in the case of the Shudras. Just as a Shudra could become a Bhikku, so a woman could become a nun. This was taking her to the highest status then conceivable in the eyes of Aryan society.

Another issue on which Buddha fought against the leaders of Aryan society was the issue of the ethics of teachers and teaching. The leaders of Aryan society held the view that learning and education were the privileges of the Brahmins, Kshatriyas and Vaishyas. The Shudras were not entitled to education. They insisted that it would be danger to social order if they taught women or any males not twice-born. Buddha repudiated this Aryan doctrine. As pointed out by Rhys Davis on this question: "That everyone should be allowed to learn; that everyone, having certain abilities, should be allowed to teach; and that, if he does teach, he should teach all to all; keeping nothing back, shutting no one out." In this connection, reference may be made to the dialogue between Buddha and the Brahmin Lohicca, and which is known as the *Lohicca Sutta*.

Lohicca Sutta

(Some points in the Ethics of Teaching)

1. Thus have I heard. The Exalted One, when once passing on a tour through the Kosala districts with a great multitude of the members of the Order, with about five hundred Bhikkus, arrived at Salavatika (Bhikkus village surrounded by a row of Sala trees). Now, at that time, Lohicca, the Brahmin was established at Salavatika, a spot teeming with life, with much grassland, woodland, and corn, on a royal domain granted him by King Pasenadi of Kosala, as a royal gift, with power over it as if he were the king.

2. Now, at that time, Lohicca the Brahmin was thinking of harbouring the following wicked view: "Suppose that a Samana or a Brahmin have reached up to some good state of mind, then he should tell no one else about it. For what can one man do for another? To tell others would be like the man who, having broken through an old bond, should entangle himself in a new one. Like that, I say, is this desire to declare to others; it is a form of lust. For what can one man do for another?"

Now, Lohicca, the Brahmin, heard the news: "They say that the Samana Gautama, of the sons of the Sakyas, who went out from the Sakya clan to adopt the religious life, has now arrived, with a great company of the brethren of his Order, on his tour through the Kosala districts, at Salavatika. Now regarding that Venerable Gautama, such is the high reputation that has been noised abroad: that Exalted One is an Arhat, fully awakened, abounding in wisdom and goodness, happy, with knowledge of the worlds, unsurpassed as a guide to mortals willing to be led, a teacher for gods and men, an exalted one, a Buddha. He, by himself, thoroughly knows, and sees as it were face to face. This universe—including the worlds above of the gods, the Brahmins and the Maras; and the world below with its Samanas and Brahmins, its princes and peoples; and having known it, he makes his knowledge known to others. The Truth, lovely in its origin, lovely in its progress, lovely in consummation, doth he proclaim both in the spirit and the letter. The higher life doth he make known in all its fullness and all its purity. And good is it to pay visits to Arhats like that."

4. Then Lohicca, the Brahmin, said to Bhesika, the barber: "Come now, good Bhesika, go where the Samana Gautama is staying, and on your arrival, ask in my name as to whether his sickness and indisposition have abated, as to his health, vigour, and condition of ease; and speak thus: "May the venerable Gautama, and with him the brethren of the order, accept the tomorrow's meal from Lohicca the Brahmin."

5. "Very well, Sir," said Bhesika the barber, acquiescing in the word of Lohicca the Brahmin, and did so even as he had been enjoined. And the Exalted One consented, by silence, to his request.

6. And when Bhesika, the barber, perceived that the Exalted One had consented, he rose from his seat, and passing the Exalted One with his right hand towards him, went to Lohicca, the Brahmin, and on his arrival spoke to him thus:

"We addressed that Exalted One, Sir, in your name, even as you commanded. And the Exalted One hath consented to come."

7. Then Lohicca the Brahmin, when the night had passed, prepared at his dwelling place, sweet food, both hard and soft, and said to Bhesika, the barber: "Come now, good Bhesika, go where the Samana Gautama is staying, and on your arrival, announce the time to him, saying:' It is time, O Gautama, and the meal is ready.'"

"Very well, Sir," said Bhesika, the barber, in assent to the words of Lohicca, the Brahmin, and did so even as he had been enjoined.

And the Exalted One, who had robed himself early in the morning, went robed, and carrying his bowl with him, with the brethren of the Order, towards Salavatika.

8. Now, as he went, Bhesika, the barber, walked step by step behind the Exalted One. And he said to him:

"The following wicked opinion has occurred to Lohicca the Brahmin: 'Suppose that a Samana or a Brahmin have reached up to some good state of mind, then he should tell no one else about it. For what can one man do for another? To tell others would be like the man who, having broken through an old bond, should entangle himself in a new one. Like that, I say, is this desire to declare to others; it is a form of lust', Twere well, Sir, if the Exalted One would disabuse his mind thereof. For what can one man do for another?"

"That may well be, Bhesika, that may well be."

9. And the Exalted One went on to the dwelling-place of Lohicca, the Brahmin, and sat down on the seat prepared for him. And Lohicca, the Brahmin satisfied the Order, with the Buddha at its head, with his hand, with sweet food, both hard and soft, until they refused any more. And when the Exalted One had finished his meal and, cleansed the bowl

and his hands, Lohicca, the Brahmin, brought a low seat and sat down beside him. And to him, thus seated, the Exalted One spake as follows:

'Is it true what they say, Lohicca, that the following wicked opinion has arisen in your mind; (and he set forth the opinion as above)?' 'That is so Gautama.'

10. "Now what think you, Lohicca? Are you not etablished at Salavatika?" "Yes, that is so, Gautama."

"Then suppose, Lohicca. one were to speak thus: "Lohicca the Brahmin, has domain at Salavatika. Let him alone enjoy all the revenue and all the produce of Salavatika, allowing nothing to anybody else!" Would the utterer of that speech be danger-maker as touching the men who live in dependance upon you or not?" "He would be danger-maker, Gautama.'

"And making that danger, would he be a person who sympathised with their welfare, or not?"

"He would not be considering their welfare, Gautama." "And not considering their welfare, would his heart stand fast in love towards them or in enmity?" "In enmity, Gautama."

"But when one's heart stands fast in enmity, is that unsound doctrine, or sound?" "It is the unsound doctrine, Gautama."

"Now, if a man holds unsound doctrine, Lohicca, I declare that one of two future births will be his lot, either purgatory or rebirth as an animal."

11. "Now what think you, Lohicca? Is not King Pasenadi of Kosala has Kasi and Kosala?" "Yes, that is so, Gautama."

"Then suppose, Lohicca. one were to speak thus: "King Pasenadi of Kosala has Kasi and Kosala. Let him enjoy all the revenue and all the produce of Kasi and Kosala, allowing nothing to anybody else." Would the utterer of that speech be a danger-maker as touching the men who live in dependence on King Pasenadi of Kosala, both you and others, or not?" "He would be danger-maker, Gautama."

"And making that danger, would he be a person who sympathised with their welfare or not?"

"He would not be considering their welfare, Gautama." "And not considering their welfare, would his heart stand fast in love toward them or in enmity?" "In enmity, Gautama."

"But when one's heart stands fast in enmity, is that unsound doctrine, or sound?" "It is the unsound doctrine, Gautama." "Now, if a man holds unsound doctrine, Lohicca, I declare that one of two future births will be his lot, either purgatory or rebirth as an animal."

12. "So then, Lohicca, you admit that he who should say that you, being in occupation of Salavatika, should therefore enjoy all the revenue and produce thereof, bestowing nothing on anyone else; and he who should say that King Pasenadi of Kosala, being in power over Kasi and Kosala, should therefore himself enjoy all the revenue and produce thereof, bestowing nothing on anyone else—would be making danger for those living in dependence upon you, or for those, you and others, living in dependence upon the king. And that those who thus make danger for others must be wanting in sympathy for them. And that the man wanting sympathy has his heart set fast in enmity. And that to have one's heart set fast in enmity is unsound doctrine."

13. "Then just so, Lohicca, he who should say: 'Suppose a Samana or a Brahamin to have reached up to some good state of mind, then should he tell no one else about it. For what can one man do for another? To tell others would be like the man who, having broken through an old bond, should entangle himself in a new one. Like that, I say, is this desire to declare to others; it is a form of lust,'—just so he, who should say thus, would be putting obstacles in the way of those clansmen who, having taken upon themselves the Doctrine and Discipline set forth by Him-who-has-won-the-Truth, have attained great distinction therein—to the fruit of

conversion, for instance, or to the fruit of once returning, or to the fruit of never returning, or even to Arhatship— he would be putting obstacles in the way of those who are bringing to fruition the course of conduct that will lead to rebirth in states of bliss in heaven. But by putting obstacles in their way, he would be out of sympathy for their welfare; being out of sympathy for their welfare, his heart would become established in enmity; and when one's heart is established in enmity, that is unsound doctrine. Now, if a man holds unsound doctrine, Lohicca, I declare that one of two future births will be his lot, either purgatory or rebirth as an animal."

14. "There are three sorts of teachers in the world, Lohicca, who are worthy of blame And whosoever should blame such a one, his rebuke would be justified, in accord with the facts and the truth, not improper. What are the three?"

"In the first place, Lohicca, there is a sort of teacher who has not himself attained that aim of Samanaship for the sake of which he left his home and adopted the homeless life. Without having himself attained it he teaches a doctrine (*Dhamma*) to his hearers, saying: "This is good for you; this will make you happy.' Then those hearers of his neither listen to him, nor give ear to his words, nor become steadfast in heart through their knowledge thereof; they go their own way, apart from the teaching of the master. Such a teacher may be rebuked by setting out these facts and adding: 'You are like one who should make advances to one who keeps repulsing him or should embrace one who turns her face away from him. Like that, do I say, is this lust of yours (to go on posing as a teacher of men, no one heeding, since, they trust you not): For what, then, can one man do for another?'"

"This, Lohicca, is the first sort of teacher in the world worthy of blame. And whosoever should blame such a one, his rebuke would be justified, in accord with the facts and the truth, not improper."

15. "In the second place, Lohicca, there is a sort of teacher who has not attained to that aim of Samanaship for the sake of which he left his home and adopted the homeless life. Without having himself attained it, he teaches a doctrine to his hearers, saying: "This is good for you; this will make you happy.' And to him, his disciples listen; they give ear to his words; they become steadfast in the heart by their understanding of what is said, and they go not do their way, apart from the teaching of the master. Such a teacher may be rebuked by setting out these facts and adding: 'You are like a man who, neglecting his field, should take thought to weed out his neighbour's field." Like that, do I say, is this lust of yours (to go on teaching others when you have not taught yourself): For what, then, can one man do for another?"

"This, Lohicca, is the second sort of teacher in the world worthy of blame. And whosoever should blame such a one, his rebuke would be justified, in accord with the facts and the truth, not improper."

16. And again, Lohicca, in the third place, there is a sort of teacher who has attained that aim of Samanaship for the sake of which he left his home and adopted the homeless life. Having himself attained it, he teaches the doctrine to his hearers, saying: 'This is good for you, this will make you happy.' But those hearers of his neither listen to him, nor give ear to his words, nor become steadfast in heart through understanding thereof; they go their own way, apart from the teaching of the master. Such a teacher may be rebuked, setting out these facts, and adding: 'You are like a man who, having broken through an old bond, should entangle himself in a new one.' Like that, do I say, is this lust of yours (to go on teaching when you have not trained yourself to teach): For what, then, can one man do for another?"

"This, Lohicca, is the third sort of teacher in the world worthy of blame. And whosoever should blame such a one, his rebuke would be justified, in accord with the facts and the truth, not improper. And these, Lohicca, are the three sorts of teachers of which I spoke."

17. 'And when he had thus spoken, Lohicca, the Brahmin spoke to the Exalted One:

"But is there, Gautama, any sort of teacher not worthy of blame in the world?"

"Yes, Lohicca, there is a teacher in the world not worthy of blame." "And what sort of a teacher, Gautama, is so?" The answer is in the words of the exposition set out above in the Samaññaphala, as follows:

1. The appearance of a Tathagata (one who won the Truth), his preaching, the conversion of a hearer, and the hearer's adoption of the homeless state.
2. The minor details of mere morality that he practises.
3. The confidence of heart he gains from this practice.
4. The paragraph on 'Guarded is the Door of His Senses.'
5. The paragraph on 'Mindful and Self-Possessed.'
6. The paragraph on 'Simplicity of Life, Being Content with Little.'
7. The paragraphs one 'Emancipation from Ill-Temper, Laziness, Worry and Perplexity.'
8. The paragraph on the 'Joy and Peace' that, as a result of this emancipation, fills his whole being.
9. The paragraphs on the 'Four Raptures (Jhanas).'
10. The paragraphs on the Insight Arising From Knowledge (the Knowledge of the First Path).
11. The paragraphs on the 'Realisation of the Four Noble Truths, the Destruction of the Intoxications—Lust,

Delusions, Becomings, and Ignorance—and the attainment of Arhatship. The refrain throughout and the closing paragraph is : 'And whosoever the teacher be, Lohicca, under whom the disciple attains to distinction so excellent as that—that, Lohicca, is a teacher not open to blame in the world. And whosoever should blame such a one, his rebuke would be unjustifiable, not in accord either with the facts or with the truth, without good ground.'

18. And when he had thus spoken, Lohicca, the Brahmin, said to the Exalted One:

"Just, Gautama, as if a man had caught hold of a man falling over the precipitous edge of purgatory by the hair of his head and lifted him safely back on the firm land—just so have I, on the point of falling into purgatory, been lifted back on to the land by the Venerable Gautama. Most excellent, O Gautama, are the words of thy mouth, most excellent! Just as if a man were to set up what has been thrown down, or were to reveal what has been hidden away, or were to point out the right road to him who has gone astray, or were to bring light into the darkness so that those who had eyes could see external forms—just even so has the truth been made known to me, in many a figure, by the Venerable Gautama. And I, even I, betake myself to the Venerable Gautama as my guide, to the Doctrine and the Order. May the Venerable Gautama accept me as a disciple, as one who, from this day forth, as long as life endures, has taken him as his guide!"

❑

Part II

Chapter 5

The Decline and Fall of Buddhism

Dr. B. R. Ambedkar wrote "The Decline and Fall of Buddhism" as part of the treatise, 'Revolution and Counter-Revolution'. We have found only five pages in our papers, which were not even corrected. A copy of this essay has been received from Shri S. S. Rege, which shows some corrections in Dr. Ambedkar's handwriting. This essay comprises of eighteen typed pages that are included here.

–Editors

1

The disappearance of Buddhism from India has been a matter of great surprise to everybody who cares to think about the subject, and it is also a matter of regret. But it lives in China, Japan, Burma, Siam, Annam, Indo-China, Ceylon, and parts of Malaya Archipelago. In India alone, it has ceased to exist. Not only does it ceased to live in India, but even the name of Buddha has gone out of memory of most Hindus. How could such a thing have happened? It is an important question for which there has been no satisfactory answer. Not only is there no satisfactory answer, but nobody has attempted to arrive at one. In dealing with this subject, people fail to make a very important distinction. It is a distinction between the fall of Buddhism and the decline of Buddhism. It is necessary to make this distinction because the fall of Buddhism is one thing, the reasons for which are decline very different from those that brought about its decline. The fall is due to quite obvious causes, while the reasons for its decline are not quite so apparent.

There can be no doubt that the fall of Buddhism in India was due to the invasions of the Muslims. Islam emerged as the enemy of the '*But*'. The word '*But',* as everybody knows, is an Arabic word that means an idol. Not many people, however, know the derivation of the word '*But'*. *'But'* is the Arabic corruption of Buddha. Thus, the origin of the word indicates that, in the Muslim mind, idol worship had come to be identified with the religion of the Buddha. To the Muslims, they were one and the same thing. The mission to break the idols thus became the mission to destroy Buddhism. Islam destroyed Buddhism not only in India but wherever it went.

Before Islam came into being, Buddhism was the religion of Bactria, Parthia, Afghanistan, Gandhar, and Chinese Turkestan, as it was of the whole of Asia. In all these countries, Islam destroyed Buddhism. As Vincent Smith points out:

"The furious massacre perpetrated in many places by Muslim invaders was more efficacious than Orthodox Hindu persecutions, and had a great deal to do with the disapperance of Buddhism in several provinces of India."

Not all will be satisfied with this explanation: it does seem inadequate. Islam attacked both, Brahmanism and Buddhism. It will be asked why one should survive while the other perished. The argument is plausible but not destructive the validity of the thesis. To admit that Brahmanism survived does not mean that the fall of Buddhism was not due to the sword of Islam. All that it means is that there were circumstances that made it possible for Brahmanism and impossible for Buddhism to withstand the onslaught of Islam. Fortunately for Brahmanism and unfortunately for Buddhism, that was the fact.

Those who pursue the matter will find that three special circumstances made it possible for Brahmanism and impossible for Buddhism to survive the calamity of Muslim invasions. In the first place, Brahmanism, at the time of the Muslim invasions, had the support of the State. Buddhism had no such support. What is, however, more important is the fact that this state's support to Brahmanism lasted until Islam had become a quiet religion and the flames of its original fury as a mission against idolworship had died out. Secondly, the Buddhist priesthood perished by the sword of Islam and could not be resusciated. On the other hand, Islam could not annihilate the Brahmanic priesthood. In the third place, the Buddhist laity was persecuted by the Brahmanic rulers of India, and to escape this tyranny, the mass of the Buddhist population of India embraced Islam and renounced Buddhism.

Of these circumstances, there is not one which is not supported by history.

Among the provinces of India that came under Muslim domination, Sindh was the first. It was ruled by a Shudra king, but the throne was usurped by a Brahmin who established his own dynasty which naturally supported the Brahmanic religion at the time of the invasion of Sindh by Ibn Qasim in 712 A.D. The ruler of Sindh was Dahir, who belonged to the dynasty of Brahmin rulers.

Hiuen Tsang noted that the Punjab was, in his time, ruled by a Kshatriya Buddhist dynasty. This dynasty ruled Punjab until about 880 A.D. In that year, the throne was usurped by a Brahmin army commander named Lalliya, who founded the Brahmin Shahi dynasty. This dynasty ruled Punjab from 880 A.D. to 1021 A.D. It will thus be seen that at the time when the invasions of the Punjab commenced by Sabuktagin and Muhammad, the native rulers belonged to the Brahmanic religion. Jayapala (960-980 A.D.), Anandpal (980-1000 A.D.), and Trilochanpal (1000-21 A.D.), of whose struggles with Sabuktagin and Mauhammad we read so much, were rulers belonging to the Brahmanic faith.

Central India began to be infested by Muslim invasions, which commenced from the time of Muhammad and continued under the leadership of Shahabuddin Ghori. At that time, Central India consisted of different kingdoms: Mewar (now known as Udaipur) ruled by the Guhilots, Sambhar (now divided into Bundi, Kota, and Sirohi), ruled by the Chauhans, Kanauj ruled by the Pratihars, Dhar ruled by the Parmars, Bundelkhand ruled by Chandellas, Anhilwad ruled by the Chavdas, and Chedi ruled by the Kalachuris. The rulers of all these kingdoms were Rajputs, and the Rajputs, for reasons which are mysterious and which I will discuss later on, had become the staunchest supporters of the Brahmanic religion.

About the time of these invasions, Bengal had fallen into two kingdoms: Eastern and Western. West Bengal was ruled by the kings of the Pal dynasty, and East Bengal was ruled by the kings of the Sena dynasty.

The Palas were Kshatriyas. They were Buddhist, but as Mr. Vadiya says, "probably only in the beginning or in the name." As to the Sena kings, there are different opinions. Dr. Bhandarkar says they were Brahmins who had taken to the military profession of the Kshatriyas. Mr. Vaidya insists that the Sena kings were Aryan Kshatriyas or Rajputs the Lunar race. In any case, there is no doubt that the Senas, like the Rajputs, were supporters of the orthodox faith.

South of the river Narmada, there existed at the time of the Muslim invasions four kingdoms: (1) The Deccan Kingdom of Western Chalukyas, (2) The Southern Kingdom of the Cholas, (3) The Silahara Kingdom in Konkan on the West Coast, and (4) The Ganga Kingdom of Trikalinga on the East Coast. These kingdoms flourished during 1000-1200 A.D., which was the period of the Muslim invasions. There were, under them, certain feudatory kingdons rose to power in the 12th century A.D. and became independent and powerful in the 13th century. They were (1) Devagiri, ruled by the Yadavas, (2) Warangal, ruled by Kakatiyas, (3) Halebidu ruled by the Hoysalas, (4) Madurai ruled by the Pandyas, and (5) Travancore, ruled by the Cheras. All these ruling dynasties were followers of orthodox Brahmanism. The Muslim invasions of India commenced in the year 1001 A.D. The last wave of these invasions reached Southern India in 1296 A.D. when Alauddin Khilji subjugated the Kingdom of Devagiri. The Muslim conquest of India was really not completed by 1296. The wars of subjugation went on between the Muslim conquerors and the local rulers, who, though defeated, were not, subdued. But the point to bear in mind is that during this period of 300 years of Muslim wars of conquests, India was governed all over by princes who professed the orthodox faith of Brahmanism. Brahmanism, beaten and battered by the Muslim invaders, could look to the rulers for support and sustenance and did receive it. Buddhism, beaten and battered by the Muslim invaders, had no such hope. It was an uncared-for orphan and withered in the cold blast of the native rulers, ultimately being consumed in the fire lit by the conquerors.

The Muslim invaders sacked the Buddhist universities of Nalanda, Vikramasila, Jagaddala, and Odantapuri, to name only a few. They razed to the ground Buddhist monasteries with which the country was studded. The monks fled by the thousands to Nepal, Tibet, and other places outside India. A very large number were killed outright by the Muslim commanders. How the Buddhist priesthood perished by the sword of the Muslim invaders has been recorded by the Muslim historians themselves. Summarizing the evidence relating to the slaughter of the Budhist monks perpetrated by the Muslim General in the course of his invasion of Bihar in 1197 A.D., Mr. Vincent Smith says:

"The Muslim General, who had already made his name a terror by repeated plundering expeditions in Bihar, seized the capital by a daring stroke. The almost contemporary historian met one of the survivors of the attacking party in 1243 A.D. and learned from him that the Fort of Bihar was seized by a party of only two hundred horsemen, who boldly rushed the postern gate and gained possession of the place. Great quantities of plunder were obtained, and the slaughter of the 'shaven-headed Brahmins', that is to say, the Buddhist monks, was so thoroughly completed that when the victor sought for someone capable of explaining the contents of the books in the libraries of the monasteries, not a living man could be found who was able to read them. "It was discovered", we are told, "that the whole of that fortress and city was a college, and in the Hindi tongue they call a college Bihar."

Such was the slaughter of the Buddhist priesthood perpetrated by the Islamic invaders. The axe was struck at the very root. For by killing the Buddhist priesthood, Islam killed Buddhism. It was the greatest disaster that befell the religion of Buddha in India. Religion, like any other ideololgy, can be sustained by propaganda. If propoganda fails, religion must disappear. The priestly class, however detestable it may be, is necessary for the sustenance of religion. For it is by its propoganda that religion is kept alive. Without the priestly class, religion must disappear. The sword of Islam fell heavily upon the priestly class. It perished or fled outside India. Nobody remained to keep the flame of Buddhism burning.

It may be said that the same thing must have happened to the Brahmanic priesthood. It is possible, though not to the same extent. But there is this difference between the constitutions of the two religions, and the difference is so great that it contains the entire reason why Brahmanism survived the attack of Islam and why Buddhism did not. This difference relates to the constitution of the clergy.

The Brahmanic priesthood has a most elaborate organization. A clear and succinct account of it has been given by the late Sir Ramkrishna Bhandarkar in the pages of *The Indian Antiquary*.

"Every Brahmanic family," he writes, "is devoted to the study of a particular Veda, and a particular Sakha (recension) of a Veda; and the domestic rites of the family are performed according to the ritual described in the Sutra connected with that Veda. The study consists of memorising the books forming the particular Veda. In Northern India, where the predominant Veda is the White Yajur and the Sākha that of the Mādhyandinas, this study has almost died out, except at Banaras, where Brahmanic families from all parts of India are settled. It prevails to some extent in Gujarat, to a much greater extent in the Maratha country, and in Telangana there is a large number of Brahmins who still devote their lives to this study. Numbers of these go about to all parts of the country in search of dakshina (fee, alms), and all well-to-do natives patronize them according to their means by getting them to recite portions of their Veda, which is mostly the Black Yajur, Apastamba for their Sūtra. Hardly a week passes here in Bombay in which no Telangana Brahmin comes to me to ask for dakshina. On each occasion, I get the men to repeat what they have learned and compare it with the printed texts in my possession.

'With reference to their occupation, Brahmins of each Veda are generally divided into two classes: Grihasthas and Bhikshukas. The former devote themselves to a worldly vocation, while the latter spend their time in the study of their sacred books and the practice of their religious rites.

"Both these classes have to repeat daily the Sandhyā-vandana or twilight–prayers, the forms of which are somewhat different for the different Vedas. But the repetition of the Gāyatri-mantra 'Tat Savitur Varenyam', etc., five, then twenty-eight, or a hundred and eight times, which forms the principal portion of the ceremony, is common to all.

'Besides this, a great many perform everyday what is called Brahmayagna, which on certain occasions is incumbent on all. This for the Rig Veda consists of the first hymn of the first mandala, the opening sentences of the Aitareya Brāhmana, the five parts of the Aitareya Āranyaka, the Yajur-Samhita, the

Sāma-Samhita, the Atharva-Samhita, Aśvalāyana Kalpa-Sutra, Nirukta, Chandas, Nighantu, Jyotiṣa, Sikṣhā, Pāṇini, Yājñavalkya Smriti, Mahabharata, and the Sūtras of Kaṇāda, Jaimini, and Bādarāyaṇa.' The point to be remembered is that in the matter of officiation there is no distinction between a Bhikshuka and a Grihastha. In Brahmanism, both Bhikshuka are priest, and the Grihastha is no less entitled to officiate as a priest than a Bhikshuka is. If a Grihastha does not choose to officiate as a priest, it is because he has not mastered the mantras and the ceremonies or because he follows a more lucrative vocation. Under Brahmanic dispensation, every Brahmin who is not an outcast can be a priest. The Bhikshuka is an actual priest, while a Grihastha is a potential priest. All Brahmins can be recruited to form the army of Brahmanic priesthood. Further, no particular training or initiation ceremony is necessary for a Brahmin to act as a priest. His will to officiate is enough to make him function as a priest. In Brahmanism, the priesthood can never become extinct. Every Brahmin is a potential priest of Brahmanism and can be drafted into service when the need arises. There is nothing to stop the system life and progress. It is not possible in Buddhism. A person must be ordained in accordance with established rites by priests already ordained before he can act as a priest. After the massacre of the Buddhist priests, ordination became impossible, and the priesthood almost ceased to exist. Some attempt was made to fill the depleted ranks of the Buddhist priests. New recruits for the priesthood had to be drawn from all available sources, and they certainly were not the best." According to Haraprasad Shastri.

"The paucity of Bhiksus brought about a great change in the composition of the Buddhist priesthood. It was the married clergy with families, who were called Aryas, that took the place of the Bhiksus proper and began to cater to the religious needs of the Buddhists generally. They commenced attaining the normal status of Bhiksus through the performance of some sacraments. (Intro pp.19.7, quoting Tatakara Guptas' *Adikarmaracana:* 149, pp. 1207-1208). They officiated at the religious ceremonies but at the same time, in addition to their profession of priesthood, earned their livelihood through such avocations as those of a mason, painter, sculptor, goldsmith, and carpenter. These artisan priests, who inlater times were larger in number than the Bhiksus prists became the religious guides of the people. Their avocations left them little time and desire for the acquisition of learning, deep thinking, or devotion to Dhyana and other spiritual exercises. They could not be expected to raise the declining Buddhism to a higher position through their endeavours, nor could they check its course towards its ruin through the introduction of salutary reforms." It is obvious that this new Buddhist priesthood had neither dignity nor learning and was a poor match for their rivals, the Brahmins, whose cunning was not unequal to their learning.

The reason why Brahmanism rose from the ashes and Buddhism did not is to be accounted for by any inherent superiority of Brahmanism over Buddhism. It is found in the peculiar character of their priesthood. Buddhism died because its army of priests died, and it was not possible to recreate it. Though beaten, it was never completely broken. Every Brahmin alive became a priest and took the place of every Brahmin priest who died.

As to the conversion to the faith of Islam by the Buddhist population as a cause of the fall of Buddhism, there can hardly be much doubt.

In his Presidential address to the Early Medieval and Rajput Section of the Indian History Congress held at Allahabad in 1938, Prof. Surendra Nath Sen very rightly observed that there were two problems relating to the Medieval History of India for which no satisfactory answers were forthcoming as yet. He mentiond two: one connected with the origin of the Rajputs and the other with the distribution of the Muslim population in India. Referring to the second, he said:

"But I may be permitted to deal with one question that is not wholly of antiquarian interest today. The distribution of Muslim population in India demands some explanation. It is commonly believed that Islam followed the route of conquest and that the subjugated people were forced to accept the faith of their rulers.

The predominance of the Muslims in the Frontier Province and the Punjab lends some colour to this contention. However, this theory cannot explain an overwhelming Muslim majority in Eastern Bengal. It is quite likely that the North-Western Frontier Province was peopled by Turkish folk during the Kushan days, and their easy conversion to Islam may be explained by racial affinity with the new conquerors but the Muslims of Eastern Bengal are certainly not racially akin to the Turks and the Afghans, and the conversion of the Hindus of that region must have been due to other reasons." What are these other reasons? Prof. Sen then proceeds to lay bare these reasons, which are found in Muslim chronicles. He takes the case of Sindh, for which there is direct testimony and says:

"According to the *Chachnama*, the Buddhists of Sindh suffered all sorts of indignities and humiliations under their Brahmin rulers, and when the Arabs invaded their country, the Buddhists lent their wholehearted support to them. Later on, when Dahir was slain, a Muslim government was firmly established in the country, and the Buddhists found, to their dismay, that as far as their rights and privileges were concerned, the Arabs were prepared to restore the status quo ante bellum. Even under the new order, the Hindus received preferential treatment. The only way out of this difficulty was to accept Islam because the converts were entitled to all the privileges reserved for the ruling classes. So, the Buddhists of Sindh joined the Muslim fold in large numbers." Prof. Sen then adds this significant passage:

"It cannot be an accident that the Punjab, Kashmir, the district around Bihar Sharif, North-East Bengal, where Muslims now predominate, were all strong Buddhist centres in the pre-Muslim days. It would not be fair to suggest that the Buddhists succumbed more easily to political temptations than the Hindus and that the change of religion was due to the prospects of the improvement in their political status."

Unfortunately, the causes that have forced the Buddhist population of India to abandon Buddhism in favour of Islam have not been throughly investigated, and it is, therefore, impossible to say how far the persecution of the Brahmanic kings was responsible for the result. However, some indications suggest this was a principal cause. We have positive evidence of two kings engaged in campaigns of persecuting the Buddhist population.

The first to be mentioned is Mihirkula. He belonged to the Huns, who invaded India around 455 A.D. and established their kingdom in Northern India, with Sakala (modern Sialkot in Punjab) as the capital. Mihirkula ruled around 528 A.D. As Vincent Smith says: "All Indian traditions agree in representing Mihirkula as a bloodthirsty tyrant. 'The Attila of India', stained with more than ordinary degrees of 'implacable cruelty' noted by historians as characteristic of the Hun temperament."

Mihirkula, to use the language of Smith, "Exhibited ferocious hostility against the peaceful Buddhist cult, and remorselessly overthrew the *stupas* and monasteries, which he plundered of their treasures."

The other is Sasanka, the king of Eastern India. He ruled around the first decade of the seventh century and was defeated in a conflict with Harsha. In the words of Vincent Smith.

"Sasanka, who has been mentioned as the treacherous murderer of Harsha's brother and probably was a scion of the Gupta dynasty, was a worshipper of Shiva, hating Buddhism, which he did his best to extirpate. He dug up and burnt the holy Bodhi tree at Buddha Gaya, on which, according to legend, Ashoka had lavished inordinate devotion; broke the stone marked with the footprints of Buddha at Pataliputra; destroyed the convents, scattered the monks, and carried his persecutions to the foot of the Nepalese hills." The seventh century seems to have been a century of religious persecution in India. As Smith points out:

"A terrible persecution of the cognate religion Jainism occurred in Southern India in the seventh century."

Coming nearer to the time of the Muslim invasions, we have the instance of Sindh, where presecution was undoubtedly the cause. That these persecutions continued up to the time of the Muslim invasions may be presumed the fact that in Northern India, the kings were either Brahmins or Rajputs, both of whom were anti Buddhists. That the Jains were persecuted even in the 12th century is amply supported by history. Smith refers to Ajayadeva, a Saiva king of Gujarat who came to the throne in 1174 A.D. to 1176 A.D. and began his reign around a merciless persecution of the Jains, torturing their leader to death. Smith adds, "Several other well-established instances of severe persecution might be cited."

There, is therefore, nothing to vitiate the conclusion that the fall of Buddhism was due to the Buddhists becoming converts to Islam as a way of escaping the tyranny of Brahmanism. The evidence, if it does not fully support the conclusion, at least makes it probable. If it has been a disaster, it is a disaster for which Brahmanism must thank itself.

❑

Chapter 6
The Literature of Brahmanism

We have come across scattered pages of this essay, numbering from 6 to 14 and 17 to 39. These pages seem to be a continuation of the subject dealt with under the title 'The Decline and Fall of Buddhism.' Some pages are first copies, while the rest are carbon copies. There are 14 more pages dealing with the 'Vedanta Sutras' and 'Bhagavad Gita'. The size and quality of the paper on which three chapters, i.e. (1) The Decline and Fall of Buddhism, (2) The Literature of Brahminism, and (3) Vedanta Sutras and Bhagavad Gita, are typed, appear to be similar, but distinct from the size and quality of other chapters in this part.

– Editors

1

The facts which supply the reasons must be gleaned from the literature of Brahmanism, which grew up after its political trimuph under Pushyamitra.

The literature falls under six categories: (1) *Manusmriti* (2) *Gita*, (3) Shankaracharya's *Vedant,* (4) *Mahabharata*, (5) *Ramayana*, and (6) the *Puranas*. In analysing this literature,

I propose to bring out only such facts as are capable of being suggested by inference regarding the reason or reasons for the decline of Buddhism.

There is nothing unusual or unfair in this, for literature is the mirror in which the life of a people can be said to be reflected.

There is one point I feel I must clear up. It relates to the period when this literature came into existence. Not all will agree that the literature referred to came into being after the revolution of Pushyamitra. On the contrary, most Hindus, whether orthodox or not, learned or not, have an ineradicable belief that their sacred literature is a very old one in point of time. Indeed, it seems to be an article of faith with every Hindu, which necessitates a belief in a very high antiquity of their sacred literature.

As to the age of Manu, I have given references to show that Manusmriti was written by Sumati Bhargava after 185 B.C., i.e. after the revolution of Pushyamitra. I need to say nothing more on the subject.

The date of the Bhagavad Gita is a subject about which there has been a difference of opinion.

Mr. Telang believed that the *Gita* must be older than the third century B.C., though he was not able to say how much.

In the opinion of Prof. Garbe, the *Gita* as we have it is different from what it originally was. He agrees that the conviction that the *Bhagavad Gita* has not reached us in its original form but has undergone essential transformations is now, however, shared by many Indologists outside India. According to Prof. Garbe, one hundred and forty-six verses in the *Bhagavad Gita* are new and do not belong to the original *Gita*. As to the date of its composition, Prof. Garbe says that it "cannot possibly be placed before the second century A.D."

Prof. Kausambi insists that the *Gita* was composed in the reign of King Baladitya. Baladitya belonged to the Gupta Dynasty, which supplanted the Andhra Dynasty in the year. Baladitya came to the throne in the year 467 A.D. His reasons for such a late a date are twofold. Before Shankaracharya—who was born in 788 A.D. and who died in 820 A.D.—wrote his commentary on the *Bhagavad Gita*, it was an unknown composition. It was certainly not mentioned in the *Tatvasangraha* by Shantarakshit, who wrote his treatise only 50 years before the advent of Shankaracharya. His second reason is this: Vasubandhu was the originator of a school of thought known as *Vijnyan Vad.* The *Bramha-Sutra-Bhashya* contains a criticism of the Vijnyan Vad of Vasubandhu. The *Gita* contains a reference to the *Bramha-Sutra-Bhashya*. The *Gita* must, therefore, be after Vasubandhu and the *Bramha-Sutra-Bhashya*. Vasubandhu was the preceptor of the Gupta King Baladitya. That being so, the *Gita* must have been composed during or after the reign of Baladitya.

Nothing more needs to be said about the date of Shankaracharya. The age in which he lived and wrote is now generally accepted. Something about his life needs to be said, but I will reserve that for another place.

The question of determining the date of the composition of the *Mahabharata* is next to impossible. Only an attempt to fix the period of its composition can be made. The *Mahabharata* has undergone three editions, and with each editor, the title and subject matter have changed. In its original form, it was known as '*Jaya*' (Triumph).

This original name occurs even in the third edition, both at the beginning as well *as* at the end. The original edition of the book known as *'Jaya'* was composed by one Vyas. In its second edition, it was known as *Bharata*. The editor of this second edition was one Vaishampayana. Vaishampayana's edition was not the only second edition of the *Bharata*. Vyas had many pupils besides Vaishampayana; Sumantu, Jaimini, Paila, and Shuka were his other four pupils. They had all learned at the feet of Vyas. Each one of them produced his version. Thus, there were four other editions of the *Bharata*. Vaishampayana recast the whole and brought out his own version. The third editor is Sauti. He recast Vaishampayana's version of the *Bharata*. Sauti's version ultimately came to be known as the *Mahabharata*. The book has grown both in size and subject matter as well. The *'Jaya'* of Vyas was amall work of not more than 8,800 *shlokas*. In the hands of Vaishampayana, it grew into 24,000 verses. Sauti expanded it to contain 96,836 *shlokas*. As to the subject matter, the original, as composed by Vyas, was only a story of the war between the Kauravas and the Pandavas. In the hands of Vaishampayana, the subject became twofold. To the original story, there was added the sermon. From a purely historical work, it became a didactic work aiming to teach the right code of social, moral, and religious duties. Sauti, the last editor, made it an all-embracing repository of legendary lore. All the smaller floating legends and historical stories that existed independently of the *Bharata* were brought together by Sauti so that they might not be lost or that they may be found togeher. Sauti had another ambition: that was to make the *Bharata* a storehouse of learning and knowledge. This is the reason why he added sections on all branches of knowledge, such as politics, geography, archery, etc. Taking into account Sauti's habit of repetition, it is no wonder that the *Bharata*, in his hands became the *Mahabharata*.

Now, as to the date of its composition. There is no doubt that the war between the Kauravas and the Pandavas is a very ancient event. But that does not mean that the composition of Vyas is as old as the event or contemporaneous with the event. It is difficult to assign specific dates to the different editions. Taking it as a whole, Prof. Hopkins says:

"The time of the whole *Mahabharata*, generally speaking, may then be from 200-400 A.D. This, however, takes into account neither subsequent additions, such as we know to have been made in later times, nor the various recastings in verbal form, which may safely be assumed to have occurred at the hands of successive copyists."

But there are other circumstances which definitely point to a later date.

The *Mahabharata* contains a reference to the Huns. It was Skandagupta who fought the Huns and defeated them in or about the year 455 A.D. Notwithstanding this, the invasions of the Huns continued until 528 A.D. It is obvious that the *Mahabharata* was being written about this time or therefter.

There are other indications which suggest a much later date. The *Mahabharata* refers to the Mlenchhas or the Muslims. In the 190th *Adhyaya* of the *Vana Parva* of the *Mahabharata*, there is a verse 29 wherein the author says that "the whole world will be Islamic. All Yagnas, rites and ceremonies, and religious celebrations will cease." This is a direct reference to the Muslims. Although the verse speaks of what is to happen in the future, the *Mahabharata*, being a *Purana,* must, as in the case of the *Purana*, be taken to speak of the event that has already happened. This verse, so interpreted, shows that the *Mahabharata* was being written after the date of the Muslim invasions of India. There are other references which point to the same conclusion. In the same *Adhyaya*, verse 59, it is said that "Oppressed by the Vrashalas, the *Brahmins*, struck with fear and finding no one to protect them, will roam all over the world groaning and crying in agony."

The Vrashalas referred to in this verse cannot be the Buddhists. There is no particle of evidence that the Brahmins were ever oppressed. On the contrary, the evidence is that the Brahmins, during the Buddhist regime, were treated with the same liberality as the Buddhist *Bhikshus*. The reference to the Vrashalas, meaning the uncultured, must be to the Islamic invaders.

There occur other verses in the same *Adhyaya* of the *Vana Parva*. In these verses, it is said that "Society will become disarranged. People will worship *Yedukas*. They will boycott the gods. The Shudras will not serve the twice-born. The whole world will be covered with *Yedukas*. The Yug will come to an end."

What is the meaning of the term '*Yedukas*'? By some, it has been taken to mean a Buddhist Chaitya. However, according to Mr. Kausambi this interpretation is incorrect. Nowhere in either Buddhist literature or in Vedic literature is the word *Yeduka* used in the sense of 'Chaitya'. On the contrary, according to Amarkosh, as commented upon by Maheshwar Bhatt, the word *Yeduka* means a wall which contains a wooden structure to give it strength. Understood Kausambi contends that the word *Yeduka* must refer to 'Idgah' of the Muslims before which they say their prayers. If this is a correct interpretation, then it is evident that parts of the *Mahabharata* were written after the invasion of Muhammad Ghori. The first Muslim invasion took place in 712 A.D. under lbn Qasim. He captured some towns in Northern India but did not cause much destruction. He was followed by Muhammad of Gazni, who caused great destruction of temples and viharas and massacred priests of both religions. However, he did not engage in building mosques or Idgahs. That was done by Muhammad Ghori. From this, it can be said that the writing of the *Mahabharata* was not complete until 1200 A.D.

It seems that, like the *Mahabharata*, the *Ramayana* has also undergone three editions. There are two types of references to the *Ramayana* in the *Mahabharata*. In one case, the reference is to '*Ramayana*' without any mention of the author. In the other, the reference is to the *Ramayana* of Valmiki. But the present *Ramayana* is not the Ramayana of Valmiki. In the opinion of Mr. C. V. Vaidya:

"That the present *Ramayana*, even as it is approved and adopted by the searching and all-respected commentator Kataka, is not the *Ramayana* originally written by Valmiki, not even the most orthodox thinker will be disposed to doubt. Whoever even cursorily reads the poem cannot but be struck by the inconsistencies, the severances of connections, and juxtapositions of new and old ideas which abound so greatly in the present Ramayana, whether we take the Bengal or the Bombay text of it. One cannot help but conclude that the

Ramayana of Valmiki was substantially reconstructed at some subsequent date."

As in the case of the *Mahabharata,* there has been an accretion to the subject matter of the *Ramayana.* Originally, it was just a story of the war between Rama and Ravana over the abduction of Rama's wife Sita, by Ravana. In the second edition, it became a story with a sermon. From a purely historical work, it also became a didactic work, aiming to teach the right code of social, moral, and religious duties. When it assumed the form of a third edition, it was, again, like the *Mahabharata,* made a repository of legends, knowledge, learning, philosophy, and other arts and sciences.

With regard to the date of the composition of the *Ramayana,* one proposition is well established, namely, that the episode of Rama is older than the episode of the Pandavas. But the composition of the *Ramayana* has gone on pari passu along with the composition of the *Mahabharata.* Portions of *Ramayana* may be earlier than the *Mahabharata.* However, there can be no doubt that a great part of the *Ramayana* was composed after a great part of the *Mahabharata* had already been composed.

(INCOMPLETE)

II

The literature from which I propose to draw consists of (1) The *Bhagavad Gita,* (2) The *Vedanta Sutras,* (3) The *Mahabharata,* (4) The *Ramayana*, and (5) The *Puranas.* In analysing this literature, I propose to bring out only such facts as are capable of being suggested by inference as a reason or reasons for the decline of Buddhism.

Before proceeding to examine the subject matter of this literature, I must deal with the question of the period when this literature came into existence. Not all will agree that the literature referred to came into being after the revolution of Pushyamitra. On the contrary, most Hindus, whether orthodox or not, learned or not, have an ineradicable belief that their sacred literature is a very old one in point of time. Indeed, it seems to be an article of faith with every Hindu, which necessitates a belief in a very high antiquity of their sacred literature.

(1) Bhagavad Gita

Beginning with the *Bhagavad Gita*, the date of its composition has been a matter of controversy. Mr. Telang believed that we should "take the second century B.C. as a terminus before which the *Gita* must have been composed." The late Mr. Tilak was convinced that the date of the present *Gita* must be taken as not later than 500 years before the Saka era, which means that the present *Gita* was composed somewhere about. According to Prof. Garbe· the date of the composition of the *Bhagavad Gita* must be placed somewhere between 200 and 400 A.D. There is another view propounded by Mr. Kausambi, and it is based on quite indisputable data.

Prof. Kausambi insists that the *Gita* was composed in the reign of Gupta King Baladitya. Baladitya belonged to the Gupta Dynasty, which supplanted the Andhra Dynasty in the year Baladitya came to the throne i.e. in the year 467 A.D. His reasons for such a late date for the composition of the *Gita* are twofold. Before Sankaracharya—who was born in 788 A.D. and died in 820 A.D.—wrote his commentary on the *Bhagavad Gita*. It was an unknown composition. It was certainly not mentioned in the *Tatvasangraha* by Shantarakshit, who wrote his treatise only 50 years before the advent of Shankaracharya. His second reason is this: Vasubandhu was the originator of a school of thought known as '*Vijnan Vad*'. The *Brahma-Sutra-Bhashya* contains a criticism of the *Vijnan Vad* of Vasubandhu. The *Gita* contains a reference to the *Brahma-Sutra-Bhashya*. The *Gita* must, therefore, be after Vasubandhu and the *Brahma-Sutra-Bhashya*. Vasubandhu was the preceptor of the Gupta King Baladitya. That being so, the *Bhagavad Gita* must have been composed—or at any rate, portions of *Gita* must have been added to the original edition—during or after the reign of Baladitya, i.e. around 467 A.D.

While there is a difference of opinion regarding the date of the composition of the *Bhagavad Gita*, there is no difference of opinion that the *Bhagavad Gita* has gone through many editions. All share the conviction that the *Bhagavad Gita* has not reached us in its original form but has undergone essential transformations at the hands of different editors, who have added to it from time to time. It is equally clear that the editors through whose hands it has gone were not of equal calibre. As Prof. Garbe points out:

"The *Gita* is certainly 'no artistic work which the all-comprehending vision of a genious has created.' The play of inspiration is indeed often perceptible; not seldom, however, there are merely high-sounding, empty words with which an idea that has been already quite often explained is repeated. Occasionally, the literary expression is exceedingly faulty. Verses are bodily taken over from the Upanishad literature, and this is certainly what a poet filled with inspiration would never have done. The workings of *Sattva*, *Rajas,* and *Tamas* are systematized with a truly Indian pedantry, and much indeed besides this could be brought forward to prove that the Gita is not the product of a genuinely poetic creative impulse."

Hopkins speaks of the *Bhagavad Gita* as characteristic in its sublimity, in its puerilities, in its logic, and in its lack of it. Despite its occasional power and mystic exaltation, the Divine Song, in its present state as a poetic production, is unsatisfactory. The same thing is said over and over again, and the contradictions in phraseology and meaning are as numerous as the repetitions so that one is not surprised to find it described as "the wonderful song, which causes the hair to stand on end."

It is not to be rejected as the view of foreigners. It is fully supported by Prof. Rajwade, who goes on to show that some of those who had a hand in the composition of the *Bhagavad Gita* were ignorant of the rules of grammar.

While all agree that there have been different editions of the *Gita* under various editors, they do not agree regarding what parts of the *Gita* are original and what parts of the *Gita* are additions subsequently made. In the opinion of the late Rajaram Shastri Bhagavad, the original *Gita* consisted only of 60 shlokas. Humboldt was inclined to the view that originally, the *Gita* consisted of only the first eleven *adhyayas* (chapters) and that adhyayas 12 to 18 were subsequent additions to the original. Hopkins' view is that the first fourteen *adhyayas* constitute the heart of the poem. Prof. Rajwade thinks that *adhyayas* 10 and 11 are spurious. Prof. Garbe says that 146 verses in the *Bhagavad Gita* are new and do not belong to the original *Gita* which means that more than one-fifth of the *Gita* is new.

Regarding the author of the *Gita* there is none mentioned. The *Gita* is a conversation between Arjuna and Krishna, which takes place on the battlefield, in which Krishna propounds his philosophy to Arjuna. The conversation is reported by Sanjaya to Dhritarashtra, the father of the Kauravas. The *Gita* should have been a part of the *Mahabharata* for the incident, which formed the occasion, for it is natural to it, but it does not find a place there. It is a separate independent work. Yet there is no author to whom it is attributed. All that we know is that Vyas asks Sanjaya to report to Dhritarashtra the conversation that took place between Arjuna and Krishna. One may, therefore, say that Vyas is the author of the *Gita*.

(2) Vedanta Sutras

As has already been said, the Vedic literature consists of the Vedas, the Brahmanas, the Aranyakas, and the Upanishads. From the point of their subject matter, this literature falls into two classes: (1) literature which deals with religious observances and rites and ceremonies, technically called *Karma Kanda* and (2) literature which deals with the knowledge about God to use the Vedic equivalent; the Brahmanas, technically called '*Jnana Kanda*'. The Vedas and the Brahmanas fall under the first category of literature, while the Aranyakas and the Upanishads fall under the second.

This Vedic literature had grown to enormous proportion, and what is important is that it had grown in a wild manner. Some system, some coordination, was necessary to bring order out of this chaos. As a result of the necessity for this coordination, there grew a branch of inquiry called "Mimamsa," i.e. an inquiry into the connected meaning of sacred texts, i.e. the Vedic literature. Those who thought it necessary to undertake such a task of systematization and coordination divided themselves into two schools: those who systematized the *'Karmakand'* portion and these who systematized the *'Gnanakand'* portion of the Vedic literature. The result was that two branches of the Mimamsa Shastra grew, one called *Purva Mimamsa* and the other *Ultara Mimamsa.* As the names suggest, the *Purva Mimamsa* deals with the early portion of the Vedic literature, namely the *Vedas* and the *Brahmanas.* That is why it is called *Purva* (early) *Mimamsa.* The *Uttara Mimamsa* deals with the later portions of the Vedic literature, namely the Aranyakas and Upanishads. That is why it is called *Uttara (later) Mimamsa.*

The literature connected with the two branches of the Mimamsa Shastra is immense. Of this, two collections of Sutras stand out as the principal and leading works in this field of Mimamsa. The authorship of one is attributed to Jaimini and that of the other is ascribed to Badarayana. Jaimini's Sutras deal with 'Karma Kanda' and Badarayan's deal with 'Jnana Kanda'.There is no doubt that there were prior to Jaimini and Badarayana's, other authors who had written treatises on these subjects. Nonetheless the sutras of Jaimini and Badarayana are taken as the standard works of the two branches of the Mimamsa Shastra.

Although the Sutras of both relate to that branch of inquiry called Mimamsa, Jaimini's Sutras are called *Mimamsa Sutras* while those of Badarayana are called *Vedanta Sutras.* The term 'Vedanta' is taken to mean "the end of the Veda," or the doctrines outlined in the closing chapter of the Vedas, which comprise the Upanishads. As the Upanishads constitute "the final aim of the Vedas," the Sutras of Badarayana, which systematize and coordinate them, have come to be called *Vedanta Sutras.* This is the origin of the *Vedanta Sutras.*

Who is this Badarayana? Why did he compose these Sutras, and when did he compose them? Beyond the name nothing is known about Badarayana. It is not even certain that it is the real name of the author. There is a considerable uncertainty regarding the authorship of these Sutras even among his chief commentators.

Some say that the author is Badarayana. Others say that the author of the Sutra is Vyas. The rest say that Badarayana and Vyas are one and the same person. Such is the bewildering conflict of opinion regarding the author of the Sutras.

Why did he compose these Sutras? That the Brahmins should undertake to systematize the Karma Kanda portion of the Vedic literature, one can quite understand. The Bramhins were deeply concerned with the Karma Kanda. Their very existence, their livelihood depended upon the systematization of the Karmakand portion of the Vedic literature.

The Brahmins, on the other hand, had no interest in the 'Jnana Kand' portion of the Vedic literature. Why should they have attempted to systematize it? The question has not even been raised. But it is an important question, and the answer to that must also be very important. Why the question is important and what the answer is that I shall discuss later on.

There are two other questions regarding to the Vedanta Sutras. The first is this: Is this work theological in character, or is it purely philosophical in its nature? Or is it an attempt to tie down pure philosophy to the apron strings of established theology and thereby make it innocuous and harmless? The other question relates to the commentaries on the Vedanta Sutras.

There have been, altogether, five commentaries on the Vedanta Sutras by five eminent men, all of whom are called Acharyas (doctors of learning) due to their intellectual eminence.

They are: (1) Shankaracharya (788 A.D. to 820 A.D.), (2) Ramanujacharya (1017 A.D. to 1137 A.D.), (3) Nimbarkacharya (died around 1162 A.D.), (4) Madhavacharya (1197-1276 A.D.), and (5) Vallabhacharya (born in 1417 A.D.).

The commentaries of these Acharyas on the Vedanta Sutras have become far more important than the Vedanta Sutras themselves.

The point of some significance is that in the text of the same collection of the *Vedanta Sutras*, those five Acharyas have attempted to find five different systems of thought.

According to Shankara, the *Vedanta Sutras* teach absolute monism, according to Ramanuja, qualified monism; according to Nimbarka, mono dualism; according to Madhava, dualism; and according to Vallabha, pure monism. I will not discuss what these terms mean here. All I want to say is: why should five different schools have arisen as a result of five different interpretations of the same collection of Sutras: Is it a mere matter of grammar? Or is there some other purpose behind these various interpretations? There is also another question that arises out of the plurality of commentaries. While there are five different commentaries, each propounding five different ways of looking at God and the individual soul, really speaking, there are only two: the view taken by Shankaracharya and the view taken by the other four. Although the four differ amongst themselves, they are all united in their opposition to Shankaracharya on two points: (1) the complete oneness between God and the individual soul, and (2) the world is an illusion. Here comes the third question: why did Shankaracharya propound such a unique view of the *Vedanta Sutras* of Badarayana? Is it the result of a critical study of the Sutras? Or is it a wishful interpretation designed to support a preconceived purpose?

I am only raising this question; I do not propose to deal with them here. Here, I am concerned with the age of this literature: is it pre-Buddhist or post-Buddhist?

As to the date of the composition of the *Vedanta Sutras*, the initial difficulty is that, like the *Bhagavad Gita*, it has also gone through several recensions. According to some, there have been three recensions of the *Vedanta Sutras*. That being so, nothing definite can be said regarding the date of its composition. The views expressed are only approximations. There can be no doubt that the *Vedanta Sutras* were composed after the rise of Buddhism, for the Sutras do allude to Buddhism. They must not be after Manu, for Manu refers to them in his Smriti. Prof. Keith holds that they must have been written around 200 A.D., and Prof. Jacobi believes that the Sutras must have been composed between 200 A.D. and 450 A.D.

(3) Mahabharata

The question of determining the date of the composition of the *Mahabharata* is next to impossible. It is only possible to attempt to estimate the period of its composition. The *Mahabharata* has undergone three editions, and in every edition, the title and subject matter of the book have changed. In its original form, it was known as *Jaya* (Triumph). This original name occurs even in the third edition, both at the beginning and in the end. The original edition of the book, known as *Jaya* was composed by one Vyasa. In its second edition, it was known as *Bharata*. The editor of this second edition was Vaishampayana. Vaishampayana's edition was not the only second edition of the *Bharata*. Vyasa had many pupils besides Vaishampayana; Sumantu, Jaimini, Paila and Shuka were his other four pupils. They all had learned under Vyass. Each one of them produced his own edition. Thus, there were four additional editions of the *Bharata*. Vaishampayana recast the whole and brought out his own version. The third editor is Sauti. He recast Vaishampayana's version of the *Bharata*. Sauti's version ultimately came to have the name *Mahabharata*.

The book has grown both in size and subject matter as well. The *Jaya* of Vyasa was a compact work of not more than 8,800 *shlokas*. In the hands of Vaishampayana, it grew into 24,000 verses. Sauti expanded it to contain 96,836 *shlokas*. As for subject matter, the original, composed by Vyasa, was only a story of the war between the Kauravas and the Pandavas. In the hands of Vaishampayana, the subject became two-fold. In the original story, the sermon was added. From a purely historical work, it became a didactic work aimed to teaching a proper code of social, moral, and religious duties. Sauti, the last editor, made it an all-embracing repository of legendary lore. All the compact floating legends and historical stories that existed independently of the *Bharata* were brought together by Sauti so they might not be lost or found together. Sauti had another ambition, which was to make the *Bharata* a storehouse of learning and knowledge. Thus, he added sections on all branches of knowledge, such as politics, geography, archery, etc. Taking into account Sauti's habit of repetition, it is no wonder that the *Bharata* in his hands became the *Mahabharata*.

Now, as to the date of its composition, there is no doubt that the war between the Kauravas and the Pandavas is a very ancient event. But that does not mean that the composition of Vyasa is as old as the event or contemporaneous with it. It is difficult to assign specific dates to the different editions. Taking it as a whole, Prof. Hopkins says:

"The time of the whole, *Mahabharata,* generally speaking, may then be from 200-400 A.D. This, however, takes into account neither subsequent additions, such as we know to have been made in later times, nor the various recastings in verbal form, which may safely be assumed to have occurred at the hands of successive copyists."

But other circumstances point to a later date.

The *Mahabharata* contains a reference to the Huns. It was Skandagupta who fought the Huns and defeated them in or about the year 455. Notwithstanding this, the invasions of the Huns continued until 528 A.D. It is obvious that the *Mahabharata* was being written around this time or thereafter.

There are other indications pointed out by Mr. Kausambi that suggest a much later date. The *Mahabharata* refers to the Mlecchas or the Muslims. In the 190th Adhyaya of the *Vana Parva* of the *Mahabharata*, there is a verse (29) wherein the author says that "the whole world will be Islamic. All Aryan rites and ceremonies and religious celebrations will cease." It is a direct reference to the Muslims, and although the verse speaks of what will happen in the future, the *Mahabharata*, being a Purana must, like other Purana, be taken to speak of the event that have happened. This verse, so interpreted, shows that the *Mahabharata* was being written after the date of the Muslim invasions of India. Other references point to the same conclusion. In the same Adhyaya, verse 59 states that "oppressed by the Vrishalas, the Brahmins, struck with fear, and finding no one to protect them, will roam all over the world groaning and crying in agony."

The Vrishalas referred to in this verse cannot be the Buddhists. There is no particle of evidence that the Brahmins were ever oppressed. On the contrary, the evidence shows that the Brahmins during the Buddhist regimes were treated with the same liberality as the Buddhist bhikshus. The reference to the Vrishalas, which means the uncultured, must be to the Islamic invaders. If that is so, then part of the *Mahabharata* was certainly composed after the Muslim invasions of India began.

Other verses in the same Adhyaya of the *Vana Parva* point to the same conclusion. They are 65, 66, and 67. In these verses, it is said that "society will become disarranged. People will worship *Yedukas*. They will boycott gods. The Shudras will not serve the twiceborn. The whole world will be covered with *Yedukas*. The Yug will come to an end."

Great significance attaches to the term 'Yedukas.' By some, it has been, taken to mean a Buddhist Chaitya, on the ground that 'Yeduka' means bone, particularly the bones of Buddha, and subsequently, Chaitya because a Chaitya contains the bones of the Buddha. However, according to Mr. Kausambi, this is a wrong belief. Nowhere in either Buddhist literature or Vedic literature is the word 'Yeduka' used in the sense of 'Chaitya.' On the contrary, according to Amarkosha, as commented upon by Maheshwar Bhatt, the word 'Yeduka' means a wall that contains a wooden structure to give it strength. So understood, Kausambi contends that the word Yeduka must mean 'Idgah' of the Muslims, before which they say their prayers. If this is a correct interpretation then it is obvious that part of the Mahabharata was written after the Muslim invasions, particularly after those of Muhammad Ghori. The first Muslim invasion took place in 721 A.D. under Ibn Qasim. He captured some of the towns in Northern India but did not cause much destruction of temples and Viharas and massacred priests of both religions. However, he did not engage himself in building mosques or Idgahs. That was done by Muhammad Ghori. Thus it can be said that the writing of the *Mahabharata* was ongoing until 1200 A.D.

Ramayana

It is a fact, that, like the *Mahabharata*, the *Ramayana* has also undergone three editions. There are two types of references to the *Ramayana* in the *Mahabharata*. In one case, the reference is to the *Ramayana* without any mention of the author. The other reference is to the *Ramayana* of Valmiki. However, the present *Ramayana* is not the *Ramayana* of Valmiki. In the opinion of Mr. C. V. Vaidya:

"That the present *Ramayana*, even as it is approved and adopted by the searching and all-respected commentator Kataka, is not the *Ramayana* originally written by Valmiki, not even the most orthodox thinker will be disposed to doubt. Whoever even cursorily reads the poem cannot help but be struck by the inconsistencies, the severances of connections, juxtapositions of new and old ideas which abound so greatly in the present *Ramayana*, whether we take the Bengal or the Bombay text of it. One cannot help but come to the conclusion that the *Ramayana* of Valmiki was substantially reconstructed at some subsequent date."

As in the case of the *Mahabharata*, there has been an accretion to the subject matter of the *Ramayana*. Originally, it was just a story of the war between Rama and Ravana over the abduction of Rama's wife, Sita, by Ravana. In the second edition, it became a story with a sermon. From a purely historical work, it also became a didactic work aiming to teach code of social, moral, and religious duties. When it assumed the form of a third edition, it was again, like the *Mahabharata*, made a repository of legends, knowledge, learning, philosophy, and other arts and sciences.

With regard to the date of the composition of the *Ramayana*, one proposition is well established namely, that the episode of Rama is older than the episode of the Pandavas. However, the composition of the *Ramayana* has gone on peripassu along with the composition of the Mahabharata. Portions of the *Ramayana* may be earlier than the *Mahabharata*, but there can be no doubt that a great part of the *Ramayana* was composed after a significant portion of the *Mahabharata* had already been composed.

Puranas

The Puranas today number 18. This however is not the original number. According to traditions, which there is no reason to doubt, there was only one Purana to start with. Tradition alleges that this Purana was older than the Vedas. The Atharva Veda refers to this Purana and the Bramhanda Puran says that it is more ancient than the Vedas. It was a lore that the king was expected to know for the Satapada. The Brahmana says the Adhvaryu was required to recite the Purana to the king on the 10th day of the Yagna.

The origin of the 18 Puranas is attributed to Vyasa, who is said to have recast the original single Purana and, by additions and substractions, made 18 out of one. The creation of the 18 Puranas is thus the second stage in the evolution of the Puranas. The edition of each of these 18 Puranas, as published or uttered by Vyasa is called the Adi Purana, i.e. the original edition brought out by Vyasa. After Vyasa composed these 18 Puranas, he taught them to his disciple Romaharshana. Romaharshana prepared his edition of the Puranas and taught it to his six disciples. Romaharshana's edition of the Puranas thus became the third edition of the Puranas. Of the six disciples of Romaharshana, three—Kasyapa, Savarni, and Vaisampayana—made three separate editions, which may be called the fourth edition of the Puranas, known by their names. According to the Bhavishya Purana, the Puranas came to be revised sometime during the reign of King Vikramaditya.

As for the subject matter of the Puranas, the Purana, from ancient times has been a recognised department of knowledge. For instance, it was distinguished from Itihas or history. By Itihas, what was understood were past occurences connected with a ruling king. By Akhyana, the recital of an event the occurence of which one had witnessed was mint. By *Upakhyana,* the recital of something one has heard was meant. *Gatha* referred to songs about dead ancestors, nature, and the universe.

Kalpashuddhi refers to ancient ways of acting regarding Shraddha and Kalpa. The Purana was distinguished from all these branches of knowledge. The Purana was concerned with five subjects: (1) Sarga, (2) Pratisarga, (3) Vamsha, (4) Manvantar, and (5) Vamshacharitra. Sarga means the creation of the universe, and Pratisarga means the dissolution of the universe. Vamsha means genealogy, and Manvantar refers to the ages of the different Manus, particularly the fourteen successive Manus who were the progenitors or sovereigns of the Earth. Vamshacharitra means the account of royal dynasties.

There has been a considerable addition made to the scope and subject matter of the Puranas. The Puranas we have today are no longer confined to that subjects. In addition to these subjects, they include their original subjects that fall entirely outside their prescribed scope. Indeed, there has been such a fundamental notion change of what constitutes regarding the scope of the Puranas that some of them no longer contain any treatment of the regular subjects but deal wholly with new or extraneous topics. The additional topics include the following main areas:

(I) Smriti Dharma—which include discussion of:

(1) Varnashrama-dharma, (2) Achara, (3) Ahnika, (4) Bhashyabhasya, (5) Vivaha, (6) Asaucha, (7) Shradha, (8) Dravya-Suddhi, (9) Pataka, (10) Prayaschitta, (11) Naraka, (12) Karma Vipaka, and (13) Yuga Dharma.

(II) Vrata Dharma—Observance of holy vows and holy days

(III) Kshetra Dharma—Pilgrimages to holy places and

(IV) Dana Dharma—Gifts to holy persons.

In addition to these, there are two other topics with which the Puranas are deeply concerned.

The first of these two topics relates to sectarian worship. The Puranas are votaries of particular deities and advocate the cause of a particular deity and the sect devoted to the worship. Five Puranas advocate the worship of Vishnu, eight the worship of Shiva, one the worship of Brahma, one the worship of Surya, two the worship of Devi, and one the worship of Ganesha.

The second topic that the Puranas have incorporated into their subject matter is the history of the Avatars of the gods. The Puranas make a distinction between the identification of two gods and the incarnation of a god. In the case of identification, the theory is that the god is one, although he has two names. In the case of an incarnation, the god becomes another being, whether human or animal miraculous deeds. In reading this history of incarnations, the most fruitful source is Vishnu. For it is only Vishnu who has taken Avatars from time to time and performed miraculous deeds. We find in the Puranas this new topic discussed in elaborate detail.

It is no wonder that, by the addition of these new subjects, the Puranas have been transformed beyond recognition.

There is one other matter regarding the authorship of the Puranas that is noteworthy. It relates to the change in the authorship of the Puranas. Among the ancient Hindus, there were two separate sections within the literary class. One section consisted of the Brahmins, and another section, called the Sutas, were non-Bramhins. Each was in charge of a separate department of literature. The Sutas had a monopoly over the Puranas, and the Brahmins had nothing to do with the composition or the reciting of the Puranas. The responsibility was exclusively reserved for the Sutas, and the Brahmins were not in it. Although the Sutas had specialized in the making and reciting of the Puranas, and despite their hereditary and prescriptive right to compose and recite them, there came a time when the Sutas were ousted from this profession by Brahmins, who took it into their own hands and made a monopoly of it in their favour. Thus, there was a change in the authorship of the Puranas. Instead of the Sutas, it was now the Brahmins who assumed the role of the authors.

It is probably when the Puranas fell into the hands of the Brahmins that they were finally edited and recast to include new subjects. The editing and recasting were carried out in a very daring mannar. In the preress, the Brahmins added new chapters, substituted new chapters for old ones, and even wrote new chapters under old names. As a result, some Puranas retained their earlier content, some lost their early content, some gained new content, and some became entirely new works.

The determination of the date of the composition of the Puranas is a problem that has hardly been tackled. All history written by the Brahmins is history without dates, and the Puranas are no exception. The date of the Puranas has to be determined by circumstantial evidence correlated with events whose dates are well established. The dates of the composition of the different Puranas have not been examined as closely as those of other parts of the Brahminic literature. Indeed, scholars have paid no attention to the Puranas at all—certainly nothing like what they have done in the case of the Vedic literature. Mr. Hazara's work is the only one I know of that attempts determine the date of the composition of the Puranas. I provide below the dates of the Puranas as determined by Mr. Hazara.

	Puranas	**Date of Composition**
1.	Markendeya	Between 200 and 600 A. D.
2.	Vayu	Between 200 and 500 A. D.
3.	Brahmanda	Between 200 and 500 A. D.
4.	Vishnu	Between 100 and 350 A. D.
5.	Matsya	Part about 325 A. D.; part about 1100 A.D.
6.	Bhagavata	Between 500 and 600 A. D
7.	Kurma	Between 550 and 1000 A. D.
8.	Vamana	Between 700 and 1000 A. D.
9.	Linga	Between 600 and 1000 A. D.
10.	Varaha	Between 800 and 1500 A. D.
11.	Padma	Between 600 and 950 A. D.
12.	Brihannaradiya	Between 875 and 1000 A. D.
13.	Agni	Between 800 and 900 A. D.
14.	Garuda	Between 850 and 1000 A. D.
15.	Bramha	Between 900 and 1000 A. D.
16.	Skanda	After 700 A. D.
17.	Brahma Vaivarta	After 700 A. D.
18.	Bhavishya	After 500 A. D.

No more precise date can be fixed for the Puranas, at least for the present. New research in the field may narrow higher and lower limits of their composition, but any difference will only be a matter of degree. It will not result in the subversion of eras.

This short survey is sufficient to remove any doubt regarding the age of this literature, confirming that it is post-Buddhistic. The survey establishes one more point of great significance: this literature arose during the period after the triumph of the Brahmins under the leadership of Pushyamitra. The survey also highlights another point—Vyasa wrote the *Mahabharata,* narrated the *Bhagavad Gita*, and the Puranas. The *Mahabharata* contains 18 Parvas, the *Gita* has 18 Adhyayas, and the Puranas number 18. Is all this a mere coincidence? Or is it the result of a design planned and worked out in concert? We must wait and see.

III

The Vedanta Sutras

The *Vedanta Sutras* of Badarayana, as already pointed out, constitute a department of study along the same line as the *Karma Sutras* of Jaimini. It is natural to ask how the founders of these two schools of thought positioned themselves with each other. When one begins to inquire into the matter, one comes across facts that are quite revealing. In the first place, as Prof. Belvalkar points out, "the *Vedanta Sutras* are very closely modelled upon the *Karma Sutras*". In terms of methodology and terminology, Badarayana almost slavishly follows Jaimini. He accepts Jaiminis rules for interpreting the text of the Shruti. He uses Jaimini's technical terms in the same sense as Jaimini did. He even employs the very illustrations used by Jaimini.

It is a matter for great surprise. What is surprising, however, is the attitude of the two schools towards each other in terms of doctrine. Let me give an illustration.

Badarayana provides the following Sutras as illustrative of Jaimini's position toward Vedanta:

1. Because the Self is supplementary to sacrificial acts, the fruits of the knowledge of the Self are mere praise of the agent, even as in other cases; thus says Jaimini.

   "According to Jaimini, the Vedas merely prescribe acts to attain certain purposes, including Liberation, and nothing more. He argues that the knowledge of the Self does not yield any independent results, as *Vedanta* holds, but is connected with the acts through the agent. No one undertakes a sacrificial act unless he is conscious of the fact that he is different from the body and that after death, he will go to heaven, where he will enjoy the results of his sacrifices. The texts dealing with Self-knowledge merely serve to enlighten the agent and are therefore, subordinate to sacrificial acts. The fruits, however, which the *Vedanta* texts declare about

Self-knowledge are merely praise, just as texts declare such results by way of praise concerning other matters. In short, Jaimini holds that by understanding that his Self will outlive the body, the agent becomes qualified for sacrificial actions, just as other things become fit for sacrifices through purificatory ceremonies.

2. Because we find from the scriptures such conduct of men of realisation.

   "Janaka, emperor of Videha, performed a sacrifice in which gifts were freely distributed" (Brih. 3.1.1); "I am going to perform a sacrifice, Sirs" (Chh. 5.11.5). Now, both Janaka and Asvapati were knowers of the Self. If, by this knowledge of the Self, they had attained Liberation, there would have been no need for them to perform sacrifices. However, the two texts quoted show that they did perform sacrifices. It proves that it is through sacrificial acts alone that one attains Liberation, and not through the knowledge of the Self, as the Vedantians hold.

3. That (viz, that knowledge of the Self stands in a subordinate relation to sacrificial acts) the scriptures directly declare: "That alone which is performed with knowledge, faith, and meditation becomes more powerful" (Chh. 1.1.10). This text clearly shows that knowledge is a part of the sacrificial act.

4. Because the two (knowledge and work) go together with the departing soul to produce the results.

   "It is followed by knowledge, work, and past experience" (Brih. 4.4.2). This text shows that knowledge and work go together with the soul and produce the effect which is destined to be enjoyed. Knowledge, independently, is not able to produce any such effect.

5. Because the scriptures enjoin work for such as know the purport of the Vedas.

"The scriptures enjoin work only for those who know the Vedas, which includes the knowledge of the Self. Hence, knowledge does not independently produce any result."

6. And on account of prescribed rules:

   "Performing works here, let a man wish to live a hundred years" (Is. 2.); "Agnihotra is a sacrifice lasting up to old age and death, for through old age one is freed from it or through death" (Sat. Br. 12.4.1.1). From such prescribed rules, we also find that knowledge stands in a subordinate relation ro work.

   What is the position of Badarayana towards Jaimini and *Karma Kanda* Shastras?

   It is best illustrated by the reply that Badarayana gives to the attack by Jaimini on *Vedanta,* as formulated by Badarayana in the Sutras quoted above. The reply is contained in the following Sutras:

7. But because the scriptures teach that the Supreme Self is different from the agent, Badarayana's view is correct, as this is from the scriptures.

   "Sutras 2-7 give the view of the Mimamsakas, which is refuted by Sutras 8-17. The *Vedanta* texts do not teach the limited Self, which is the agent, but the Supreme Self, which is different from the agent. Thus, the knowledge of the Self that the *Vedanta* texts declare is different from the knowledge of the Self which an agent possesses. The knowledge of such Self, which is free from all limiting adjuncts, not only does not help but puts an end to all actions. That the *Vedanta* texts teach the Supreme Self is clear from such texts as the following: 'He who perceives all and knows all' (Mu. 1.1.9); 'Under the mighty rule of this immutable, O Gargi,' etc. (Brih. 3.8.9).

8. But the declarations of the Shruti equally support both views.

"This Sutra refutes the view expressed in Sutra 3. There it was shown that Janaka and others, even after attaining knowledge, were engaged in work. This Sutra says the scriptural authority equally supports the view that for one who attained knowledge, there is no work. 'Knowing this very Self, the Brahmins renounce the desire for sons, for wealth, and for the worlds, and lead a mendicant life' (Brih. 3.5.1). 'We also see from the scriptures that knowers of the Self like Yajnavalkya gave up work.' 'This much indeed is the means of immortality, my dear.' Saying this, Yajnavalkya left home' (Brih. 4.5.15). The work of Janaka and others was characterized by non-attachment, and as such, it was practically no work, so the Mimamsa argument is weak."

9. The declaration of the scripture referred to in Sutra 4 is not universally applicable.

The declaration of the Shruti that knowledge enhances the fruit of the sacrifice does not apply to all knowledge, as it pertains specifically to the Udgitha, which is the topic of this section. There is a division between knowledge and work, akin to a hundred being divided between two people.

"This Sutra refutes Sutra 5. 'It is followed by knowledge, work, and past experiences' (Brih. 4.4.2). Here, we have to take knowledge and work in a distributive sense, meaning that knowledge follows one and works another. Just as when we say a hundred be given to these two people, we divide it into two halves and give each man fifty. There is no combination of the two. Even without this explanation, Sutra 5 can be refuted. For the text, quoted refers only to knowledge and work, which concern the transmigrating soul and not an emancipated soul. The passage, 'Thus, the man who desires transmigrates' (Brih. 4.4.6), shows that the previous text refers to the transmigrating Self. And of the emancipated soul, Shruti says, 'But the man who never desires does not never transmigrate,' etc. (Brih. 4.4.6)."

10. The scriptures enjoin work only on those who have read the Vedas.

"This Sutra refutes Sutra 6. Those who have read the Vedas and know about the sacrifices are entitled to perform work. No work is prescribed for those who know the Self from the Upanishads. Such knowledge is incompatible with work.

11. Because there is no special mention of Jaimini, it does not apply to him.

"This Sutra refutes Sutra 7. The text quoted there from *Isa Upanishad* is a general statement, and there is no special mention in it that it applies to a Jnani also. In the absence of such a specification, it is not binding on him.

12. Or rather, the permission to do work is for the purpose of praising Knowledge.

"The injunction to do work for the knowers of the Self is for the glorification of this knowledge. The praise involved in it is this: A knower of the Self may work all his life, but on account of this knowledge, he will not be bound by its effects.

13. And some, by their own choice, have refrained from all work.

"In Sutra 3, it was said that Janaka and others were engaged in work even after knowledge. This Sutra states that some have, of their own accord, given up all work. The point is that after knowledge, some may choose to work to set an example to others, while others may give up all work. There is no obligation for the knowers of the Self regarding work.

14. And the scriptures state that the knowledge leads to the destruction of all qualifications for work.

Knowledge destroys all ignorance and its products like agents, acts, and results. "But when to the knower of Brahmin everything has become the Self, then what should one see and through what," etc. (Brih. 4.5.15). The knowledge of the Self is antagonistic to all work and so cannot possibly be subsidiary to work.

15. And knowledge belongs to those who observe continence, i.e., to Sannyasis, because this fourth Ashrama is mentioned in the scriptures.

"The scriptures declare that knowledge is gained in that stage of life in which continence is prescribed, i.e., the fourth stage or Sannyasa Ashrama. To a Sannyasin, there is no work prescribed except discrimination. So, how can knowledge be subservient to work? That there is a stage of life called Sannyasa found in the scriptures in texts like: 'There are three branches of duty: sacrifice, study, and charity are the first. All these attain to the worlds of the virtuous, but only one who is firmly established in Brahmin attains immortality' (Chh. 2.33.1-2); 'Desiring this world (the Self) alone, monks renounce their homes' (Brih. 4.4.22). See also Mu. 1.2.11 and Chh. 5.10.1. Everyone can take to this life without being a householder, etc., which shows the independence of knowledge."

Many such Sutras can be found in Badarayana, indicating the attitude of the two schools of thought towards each other. But one is enough, as it is very typical. If one stops to consider the matter, the position becomes absolutely clear. Jaimini denounces *Vedanta* as a false Shastra, a snare and a delusion—something superficial, unnecessary, and insubstantial. What does Badarayana do in the face of this attack? He defends his own *Vedanta Shastra*. What one would expect from *Badrayana* is denunciation of the *Karma Kanda* of Jaimini as a false religion. Badarayana shows no such courage. On the contrary, he is very apologetic. He concedes that Jaimini's *Karma Kanda* is based on the scriptures and cannot be repudiated. All that he insists is that his *Vedanta* doctrine is also true because it has support of the scriptures. Some explanation is necessary for this attitude of Badarayana.

Bhagavad Gita

The *Bhagavad Gita* forms part of the *Bhishma Parva* of the great epic known as the *Mahabharata*. The epic is mainly concerned with the struggle for sovereignty between cousins, the Kauravas, the sons of Dhritarashtra, and the Pandavas, the sons of Pandu. Pandu was the younger brother of Dhritarashtra, but as Dhritarashtra was blind, the throne went to Pandu. After Pandu's death, a dispute arises between his sons and the sons of Dhritarashtra regarding the right of succession. The struggle for sovereignty culminated in the battle of Kurukshetra (near modern Panipat). In this battle, Krishna sides with the Pandavas and acts as their guide, friend and philosopher,—nay, acts as the charioteer of Arjuna, one of the Pandava brothers, who plays the part of the chief warrior in the battle on the side of the Pandavas.

The two armies of the Kauravas and the Pandavas were arrayed for battle on the field. Arjuna, in his chariot with Krishna, as the driver, comes and takes his place in front of the Pandava army. Strong and valiant, he gazes at the opposing army of the Kauravas and is struck by the horror of the dreadful fratricidal war in which he will have to kill his cousins and slay those whom he reveres and to whom he is greatly attached and indebted. He becomes dejected, lays down his weapons, and refuses to fight. Krishna begins to argue with him and provokes him to fight. This argument takes the form of a question-and-answer conversation between Arjuna and Krishna, at the end of which Arjuna agrees to fight.

At the opening of the *Bhagavad Gita,* we find old Dhritarashtra questioning Sanjaya about the battle. It is because Dhritarashtra, the father of the Kauravas, who, though alive at the time when the battle was fought, was a blind man and could not see or know things for himself. For the knowledge of the happenings, he had to depend upon the reports of others. Anticipating the difficulty of getting someone to tell Dhritarashtra the authentic story, Vyasa, the author of the *Mahabharata*, said to bestow on Sanjaya, the charioteer of Dhritarashtra, the power of knowing all that takes place on the battlefield—even the thoughts in men's minds—so that he may make a faithful report to Dhritarashtra. That is why we find the episode of the *Bhagavad Gita* related to the reply by Sanjaya to questions from Dhritarashtra. However, the *Gita* is a conversation between Arjuna and Krishna and is rightly called *Krishna-Arjuna Samvad.*

In this *Krishna-Arjuna-Samvad*—which is the riginal name of the *Bhagavad Gita*—the main question over which there was disagreement was whether to fight or not to fight. There was no other question. It was the one and the only question that was the subject matter of discussion and argument between the two. Starting from this point of view, it is obvious that the *Gita* could never have been intended by Krishna to be the occasion for moral instruction for the general public or the doctrinal exposition of any religious system or the catechism attached to any creed. Yet this is just what the *Gita* has come to be. Although the occasion was to decide whether to fight or not to fight, the *Gita* is said to contain the religious doctrine Krishna is said to have preached to Arjuna.

The first question that crops up is, who is this Krishna? To this, one gets, quite surprisingly, a variety of answers from the *Gita* itself. At the start, Krishna appears as a mere man with a completely human personality. He is a warrior by profession. He is a great warrior, though he had chosen the humble duty of driving the chariot of Arjuna. From man, he grows into superman, directing and controlling the war and its fortunes. From superman, he grows into a demigod and dictator. When all his arguments fail to move Arjuna to fight, he simply orders him to fight, and the frightened Arjuna gets up and does his biddings. From demigod, he rises to the position of God and is spoken of as Ishwara.

This shows the growth of the personality of Krishna. But what is important is that, in the very same *Gita*, Krishna stands out as a representative of other forms of God. Four such representative characters in which Krishna appears are clear to anyone who happens to read the *Gita*, even casually.

Krishna as Vasudeva:

X.37. Of the Vrishnis, I am Vasudeva; of the Pandavas, Dhananjaya; and also for the Munis, I am Vyasa; of the sages, Ushanas the sage.

Krishna as Bhagwan:

X.12. The Supreme Brahman, the Supreme Abode, the Supreme Purifier, art Thou.

Krishna as an Avatar of Vishnu:

X.21. Of the Adityas, I am Vishnu; of luminaries, the radiant Sun; of the winds, I am Marichi; of the asterisms, the Moon.

XI.24. On seeing Thee touching the sky, shining in many a colour, with mouths wide open, with large fiery eyes, I am terrified at heart, and find no courage nor peace, O Vishnu.

XI.30. Swallowing all the worlds on every side with Thy flaming mouths, Thou art licking Thy lips. Thy fierce rays, filling the whole world with radiance, are burning, O Vishnu.

Krishna as an Avatar of Shankara:

X.23. And of the Rudras, I am Shankara; of the Yakshas and Rakshasas, the Lord of Wealth (Kubera); of the Vasus, I am Pavaka; and of mountains, Meru am I.

Krishna as Brahman:

XV.15. I am centred in the hearts of all; memory and perception, as well as their loss, come from Me. I am verily that which has to be known by all the Vedas. I indeed am the Author of the Vedanta, and the Knower of the Vedas.

XV.16. There are two Purushas in the world—the Perishable and the Imperishable. All beings are the Perishable, and the Kutastha is called Imperishable.

XV.17. But there is another, the Supreme Purusha, called the Highest Self, the immutable Lord, who, pervading the three worlds, sustains them.

XV.18. As I transcend the Perishable and am above even the Imperishable, therefore I am in the world and the Vedas celebrated as the Purushottama (the Highest Purusha).

XV.19. He who, free from delusion, thus knows Me, the Highest Spirit, he knowing all, worships Me with all his heart, O descendant of Bharata.

What is the doctrine that Krishna preaches to Arjuna? The doctrine preached by Krishna to Arjuna is the doctrine of salvation for the human soul. While the question dealt with by Krishna is one relating to Salvation, Krishna teaches three different doctrines of Salvation:

(1) Salvation is possible by *Jnana Marg* as propounded by *Samkhya Yoga*.

II.39. The wisdom of Self-realisation has been declared unto thee. Hearken thou now to the wisdom of Yoga, endued with which, O son of Pritha, thou shalt break through the bonds of *Karma*.

It is the concluding verse of the discourse on *Samkhya Yoga* discussed in Chapter II, verses 11-16 and 18-30.

(2) Salvation is possible by *Karma Marg*.

V. 2. Both renunciation and performance of action lead to freedom: of these, performance of action is superior to the renunciation of action.

(3) Salvation is possible by *Bhakti Marg*.

IX. 13. But the great-souled ones, O son of Pritha, possessed of the Divine Prakriti, knowing Me to be the origin of beings and immutable, worship Me with a single mind.

IX. 14. Glorifying Me always and striving with firm resolve, bowing down to Me in devotion, always steadfast, they worship Me.

IX. 15. Others, too, sacrificing by the Yagna of knowledge (i.e., seeing the Self in all), worship Me, the All-formed, as one, as distinct, as manifold.

IX. 17. I am the Father of this world, the Mother, the Sustainer, the Grandfather; the Purifier, the one thing to be known, the syllable Om, and also the Rik, Saman, and Yajus.

IX. 22. People who, meditating on Me as non-separate, worship Me in all beings, to them thus ever jealously engaged, I para what they lack and preserve what they already have. There are two other features of the *Bhagavad Gita* which arrests one's attention:

(i) There is a sentiment of depreciation of the Vedas and Vedic rituals and sacrifices.

I i) There is a sentiment of depreciation of the Vedas and Vedic rituals and sacrifices.

II. 42-44. O Partha, no set determination is formed in the minds of those that are deeply attached to pleasure and power, and whose discrimination is stolen away by the flowery words of the unwise, who are full of desires and look upon heaven as their highest goal and who, taking pleasure in the panegyric words of the Vedas, declare that there is nothing else. Their flowery words are exuberant with various specific rites as the means to pleasure and power and are the causes of (new) births as the result of their works (performed with desire).

III. 45 The Vedas deal with the three Gunas Be thou free, O Arjuna, from the triad of the Gunas, free from the pairs of opposites, ever balanced, free from the thought of getting and keeping, and established in the Self.

IV. 46. To the Brahmin who has known the Self, all the Vedas are of so much use, as a reservoir is, when there is a flood everywhere.

IX. 21. Having enjoyed the vast Swarga-world, they enter the mortal world, on the exhaustion of their merit; thus, abiding by the injunctions of the three Vedas, desiring desires, they constantly come and go.

(INCOMPLETE)

❑

Chapter 7

The Triumph of Brahmanism: Regicide or the Birth of Counter-Revolution

We have found only three typed pages under this title. Fortunately, a copy of the essay has been preserved by Shri S. S. Rege for inclusion in this hook. Upon examining the pages, we have noticed that the copy given by Mr. Rege also lacks page numbers 3 to 7 and 9 to 17. The total numbers typed pages of this essay has been numbered ninty-two inclusive of the missing pages. The title on the copy of Mr. Rege is the 'Triumph of Brahmanism;' whereas the first page of the script in our papers is entitled as 'Regicide or the Birth of Counter-Revolution'. The classification of the subject into nine chapters is noted in our copy, whereas it is missing from the copy of Mr. Rege. Both the titles and the classification are recorded in the handwriting of Dr. Ambedkar. Hence, they are retained in this print. Incidentally, the page numbered 9 to 17 were found scattered in another file. All those papers have now been introduced in their proper place. Thus, except page numbers. 4 to 7, the script is complete.

– Editors

I. The Brahmanic Revolt against Buddhism. II. Manu, the Apostle of Brahmanism. III. Brahmanism and the Brahmin's Right to Rule and Regicide. IV. Brahmanism and the Privileges of Brahmins. V. Brahmanism and the Creation of Caste. VI. Brahmanism and the Degradation of the Non-Brahmins. VII. Brahmanism and the Suppression of the Shudra. VIII. Brahmanism and the Subjection of Women. IX. Brahmanism and the Legalization of the Social System.

I

Speaking about India, Prof. Bloomfield opens his lectures on the religion of the Vedas by reminding his audience that "India is the land of religions in more than one sense. It has produced out of its own resources several distinctive systems and sects.

In another sense, India is a land of religions. Nowhere else is the texture of life so much impregnated with religious convictions and practices..."

These observations contain profound truth. He would have expressed an even more profound and arresting truth if he had said that India is a land of warring religions. For Indeed, there is no country in which religion has played such a significant role in its history as it has in the history of India. The history of India is nothing but a history of a mortal conflict between Buddhism and Brahmanism. So neglected is this truth that no one will be found to give it his ready acceptance. Indeed, there may be individuals who would repudiate any such suggestion.

Let me, therefore, briefly recount the salient facts of Indian history. For it is important for everyone who seeks to understand the history of India to know that it is nothing but the history of the struggle for supremacy between Brahmanism and Buddhism.

The history of India is said to begin with the Aryans, who invaded India, made it their home, and established their culture. Whatever may be the virtues of the Aryans—their culture, their religion, and their social system—we know very little about their political history. Indeed, notwithstanding the superiority that is claimed by the Aryans against the non-Aryans, the Aryans have left very little of their political achievements for history to speak of. The political history of India begins with the rise of a non-Aryan people called Nagas, who were a powerful group that the Aryans were unable to conquer. The Aryans had to make peace with the Nagas and were compelled to recognise them as their equals. Whatever fame and glory India achieved in ancient times in the political field, the credit for it goes entirely to the non-Aryan Nagas. It is they who made India great and glorious in the annals of the world.

The first landmark in India's political history is the emergence of the Kingdom of Magadha in Bihar in the year 642 B.C. The founder of this kingdom of Magadha is known by the name of Sisunag and belonged to the non-Aryan race of Nagas. From the small beginning made by Sisunag, this Kingdom of Magadha grew in its extent under the capable rulers of the Sisunag Dynasty. Under Bimbisara, the fifth ruler of this dynasty, the kingdom expanded into an empire and came to be known as the Empire of Magadha. The Sisunag Dynasty continued to rule the kingdom till 413 B.C. In that year, the reigning emperor of the Sisunag Dyansty, Mahananda, was killed by an adventurer called Nanda. Nanda usurped the throne of Magadha and founded the Nanda Dynasty.

This Nanda Dynasty ruled over the Empire of Magadha up to 322 B.C. The last Nanda king was deposed by Chandragupta, who founded the Maurya Dynasty. Chandragupta was relatedf to the family of the last ruling emperor of the Sisunag Dynasty, so it may be said that the revolution effected by Chandragupta was really a restoration of the Naga Empire of Magadha.

The Mauryas, by their conquests, enormously extended the boundaries of this Empire of Magadha, which they inherited. So vast became the growth of this empire under Ashoka that it began to be known by another name: It the Maurya Empire or the Empire of Ashoka. *(From here onwards, pages Nos. 4 to 7 of the manuscript are missing.)*

It did not remain as one of the many diverse religions then in vogue; Ashoka made it the religion of the state. This, of course, was the greatest blow to Brahmanism. The Brahmins lost all state patronage and were relegated to a secondary and subsidiary position in the Empire of Ashoka.

Indeed, it may be said to have been suppressed for the simple reason that Ashoka prohibited all animal sacrifices, which constituted the very essence of Brahmanic religion.

The Brahmins had not only lost state patronage, but they also lost their occupation which mainly consisted of performing sacrifices for a fee that often times was very substantial and constituted their chief source of living. The Brahmins, therefore, lived as the suppressed and depressed classes for nearly 140 years, during which the Maurya Empire lasted.

A rebellion against the Buddhist state was the only way of escape left to the suffering Brahmins, and there is a special reason why Pushyamitra should raise the banner of revolt against the rule of the Mauryas. Pushyamitra was a Sunga by *Gotra*.

The Sungas were Samvedi Brahmins, who believed in animal sacrifices and soma sacrifices. The Sungas were, therefore, quite naturally smarting under the prohibition on animal sacrifices throughout the Maurya Empire, as proclaimed in the very *Rock Edict* by Ashoka.

No wonder Pushyamitra, who, as a Samvedi Brahmin, was the first to conceive the passion to end the degradation of the Brahmin by destroying the Buddhist state, which was the cause of it, and to free them to practise their Brahmanic religion.

That the object of the regicide by Pushyamitra was to destroy Buddhism as a state religion and to make the Brahmins the sovereign rulers of India so that with the political power of the state behind it, Brahmanism may triumph over Buddhism is borne out by two other circumstances.

The first circumstance relates to the conduct of Pushyamitra himself. There is evidence that Pushyamitra, after he ascended the throne performed the *Ashvamedha Yagna*, or the horse sacrifice, the Vedic rite, which could only be performed by a paramount sovereign. As Vincent Smith observes:

"The exaggerated regard for the sanctity of animal life, which was one of the most cherished features of Buddhism and the motive of Ashoka's most characteristic legislation, had necessarily involved the prohibition of bloody sacrifices, which are essential to certain forms of Brahmanical worship and were believed by the orthodox to possess the highest saving efficacy. The memorable horse sacrifices of Pushyamitra marked an early stage in the Brahmanical reaction, which was fully developed five centuries later in the time of Samudragupta and his successors."

Then, there is evidence that Pushyamitra, after his accession, launched a violent and virulent campaign of persecution against Buddhists and Buddhism.

How pitiless the persecution of Buddhism by Pushyamitra can be gauged from the proclamation was he issued against the Buddhist monks. By this proclamation, Pushyamitra set a price of 100 gold pieces on the head of every Buddhist monk.

Dr. Haraprasad Shastri, speaking about the persecution of Buddhists under Pushyamitra, says:

"The condition of the Buddhists under the imperial sway of the Sungas, orthodox and bigoted, can be more easily imagined than described. From Chinese authorities, it is known that many Buddhists still do not pronounce the name of Pushyamitra without a curse."

II

If the revolution of Pushyamitra was purely political, there was no need for him to have launched a compaign of persecution against Buddhism, which was not very different from the compaign of persecution launched by the Mahmud of Ghazni against Hinduism. It is one piece of circumstantial evidence that proves the aim of Pushyamitra was to overthrow Buddhism and establish Brahmanism in its place.

Another piece of evidence that shows that the origin and purpose of the revolution by Pushyamitra against the Mauryas was to destroy Buddhism and establish Brahmanism is evidenced by the promulgation of the *Manusmriti* as a code of laws.

The *Manusmriti* is said to be divine in its origin. It is said have been revealed to man by Manu, to whom it was revealed by the *Swayambhu* (i.e., the Creator). This claim, as will be seen from the reference already made to it, is set out in the Code itself. Surprisingly, nobody has cared to examine the grounds of such a claim. The result is that there is a complete failure to realise the significance, place, and position of the *Manusmriti* in the history of India. It is true even of the historians of India, although the *Manusmriti* is a record of the greatest social revolution that Hindu society has undergone. There can, however, be no doubt that the claim made in the *Manusmriti* regarding its authorship is an utter fraud, and the beliefs arising out of this false claim are quite untenable.

The name Manu had great prestige in the ancient history of India, and it is with the object of investing the Code with this ancient prestige that its authorship was attributed to Manu. That this was a fraud to deceive people is beyond question. The Code itself is signed in the family name of Bhrigu, as was the ancient custom. The text Composed by Bhrigu entitled "*The Dharma Code of Manu*" is the real title of the work. The name Bhrigu is subscribed to the end of every chapter of the Code itself. We have, therefore, the family name of the author of the Code. His personal name is not disclosed in the book. All the same, it was known to many. The author of *Naradasmriti*, writing in about the 4th century A.D., knew the name of the author of the *Manusmriti* and gives out the secret. According to Narada, it was one Sumati Bhargava who composed the *Code of Manu*. Sumati Bhargava is not a legendary name, and must have been a historical person, for even Medhatithe, the great commentator on the *Code of Manu*, believed the view that this Manu was 'a certain individual'. Manu, therefore, is the assumed name of Sumati Bhargava, the real author of *Manuamriti*.

When did this Sumati Bhargava compose this Code? It is not possible to give any precise date for its composition. However, quite a precise period during which it was composed can be given. According to scholars whose authority cannot be questioned, Sumati Bhargava must have composed the Code, which he deliberately called *Munusmriti* between 170 B.C. and 150 B.C. Now, if one bears in mind the fact that the Brahmanic revolution by Pushyamitra took place in 185 B.C., there remains no doubt that the Code known as *Manusmriti* was promulgated by Pushyamitra as embodying the principles of Brahmanic Revolution against the Buddhist state of the Mauryas. That the *Manusmriti* forms the institutes of Brahmanism and serves as a proof that Pushyamitra revolution was not a purely personal adventure will be clear to anyone who cares to note the following peculiarities relating to the *Manusmriti*.

The first thing to be noted is that the *Manusmriti* is a new Code of law promulgated for the first time during the reign of Pushyamitra. There was a view once prevalent that there existed a code known as the *Manava-Dharma-Sutra* and that what is known as *Manusmriti* is an adaptation of the old *Manava Dharma Sutra*. This view has been abandoned, as there has been no trace of any such work. Two other works existed before the present *Manusmriti*. One was known as *Manava-Artha-Shastra*, or *Manava-Raja-Shastra* or *Manava-Raja-Dharma-Shastra*. The other work was known as *Manava-Grihya-Sutra*. Scholars have compared the *Manusmriti* with these works. On important points, the provisions of one are not only dissimilar but are in every way contrary to the provisions contained in the other. This is enough to show that *Manusmriti* contains the new law of the new regime.

That the new regime of Pushyamitra was anti-Buddhist is betrayed by the open provisions enacted in the *Manusmriti* against the Buddhists and Buddhism. Note the following provisions in *Manusmriti*:

IX. 225. ...Men who abide in heresy... the king should banish from his kingdom.

IX. 226. These robbers in disguise, living in the king's kingdom, constantly injure the worthy subject by the performance of their misdeeds.

V. 89. Libations of water shall not be offered to the souls of those who neglect the prescribed rites and may be said to have been born in vain, to those born in consequence of an illegal mixture of the castes, to those who are ascetics of heretical sects and to those who have committed suicide.

V. 90. Libations of water shall not be offered to the souls of women who have joined a heretical sect.

IV. 30. Let him (the householder) not honour, even by a greeting, heretics logicians, arguing against the Vedas.

XII. 95. All those traditions and despicable systems of philosophy, which are not based on the Vedas, produce no reward after death, for they are declared to be founded on darkness.

XII. 96. All those doctrines, differing from the Vedas, which spring up and soon perish, are worthless and false, because of modern date.

Who are the heretics to whom Manu refers and wants the new king to banish from his realm and the householder not to honour in life and after death? What is this worthless philosophy of modern date, differing from the Vedas, based on darkness and bound to perish? There can be no doubt that the heretic of Manu is a Buddhist, and the worthless philosophy of modern date differing from the Vedas is Buddhism. Kalluck Bhutt, another commentator on *Manusmriti* expressly states that the references to heretics in these *shlokas* of Manu are to the Buddhists and Buddhism.

The third circumstance is the position assigned to the Brahmins in the *Manusmriti*. Note the following provisions of Manu:

I. 93. As the Brahmin sprang from Brahma's mouth, as he was the first born,and as he possesses the Vedas, he is by right the lord of this whole creation.

I. 96. Of created beings, the most excellent are said to be those which are animated; of the animated, those which subsist by intelligence; of the intelligent, mankind; and of men, the Brahmins.

I. 100. Whatever exists in the world is the property of the Brahmins; on account of the excellence of his origin, the Brahmins is, indeed, entitled to it all.

I. 101. The Brahmin eats but his own food, wears but his own apparel, bestows but his own in alms; other mortals subsist through the benevolence of the Brahmin.

X. 3. On account of his pre-eminance, on account of the superiority of his origin, on account of his observance of particular restrictive rules, and on account of his particular sanctification, the Brahmin is the lord of all castes.

XI. 35. The Brahmin is declared to be the creator of the world, the punisher, the teacher, and a benefactor of all created beings; to him, let no man say anything unpropitious, nor use any harsh words.

Manu warns the king against displeasing the Brahmins in the following terms:

IX. 313. Let him (the king) not, though fallen unto the deepest distress, provoke Brahmins to anger, for they, when angered, could instantly destroy him altogether with his army and vehicles.

Manu further proclaims:

XI. 31. A Brahmin who knows the law need not bring any offence to the notice of the king; by his own power alone, he can punish those men who injure him.

XI. 32. His own power is greater than the power of the king; the Brahmin, therefore, may punish his foes by his own power alone.

This deification of the Brahmins, placing them even above the king, would have been impossible unless the king himself was a Brahmin and in sympathy with the view expressed by Manu. Pushyamitra and his successors could not have tolerated these exaggerated claims of the Brahmins unless they themselves were Brahmins interested in the establishment of Brahmanism. Indeed, it is quite possible that the *Manusmriti* was composed at the command of Pushyamitra himself and forms the book of the philosophy of Brahmanism.

Taking all these facts into consideration, there can remain no doubt the only object of Pushyamitra's revolution was to destroy Buddhism and re-establish Brahmanism.

The preceding summary of the political history of India would have been quite unnecessary for the immediate purpose of this chapter if I were satisfied with the way how the history of India is written. But frankly, I am not satisfied. Too much emphasis is laid on the Muslim conquest of India. Reels and reels have been written to show how wave after wave of Muslim invasions came down like avalanche, enveloped the people, and overthrew their rulers. The whole history of India is made to appear as though the only important thing in it is a catalogue of Muslim invasions. However, even from this narrow point of view, it is clear that the Muslim invasions are not the only invasions worth studying. There have been other invasions equally, if not of greater, importance. If Hindu India was invaded by the Muslim invaders, so was Buddhist India invaded by Brahmanic invaders. The Muslim invasions of Hindu India and the Brahmanic invasions of Buddhist India have many similarities. The Muslim invaders of Hindu India fought among themselves for their dynastic ambitions. The Arabs, Turks, Mongols, and Afghans fought for supremacy among themselves. But they had one thing in common—namely, the mission to destroy idolatory. Similarly, the Brahmanic invadars of Buddhist India fought among themselves for their dynastic ambitions. The Sungas, Kanvas, and the Andhras fought for supremacy among themselves. But they, like the Muslim invaders of Hindu India, had one object in common, which was to destroy Buddhism and the Buddhist Empire of the Mauryas. Surely, if Muslim invasions of Hindu India are worthy of study at the hands of the historians, the invasions of Buddhist India by Brahmanic invaders are equally deserving of study. The ways and methods employed by the Brahmanic invaders of Buddhist India to suppress Buddhism were not less violent or less virulent than the ways and means adopted by Muslim invaders to suppress Hinduism. From the point of view of the permanent effect on the social and spiritual life of the people, the Brahmanic invasions of Buddhist India have been so profound in their effect that, compared to them, the effect of Muslim invasions on Hindu India has been really superficial and ephemeral. The Muslim invaders destroyed only the outward symbols of Hindu religion, such as temples and Maths, etc. They did not extirpate Hinduism, nor did they cause any subversion of the principles or doctrines which governed the spiritual life of the people. The effects of the Brahmanic invasions were a thorough-going change in the principles that Buddhism had preached for a century as true and eternal principles of spiritual life. These principles were accepted and followed by the masses as the way of life. To alter the metaphor, the Muslim invaders only stirred the waters in the bath and that too only for a while. Thereafter, they got tired of stirring and left the waters with the sediments to settle. They never threw the baby—if one can speak of the principles of Hinduism as a baby—out of the bath. Brahmanism, in its conflict with Buddhism, made a clean sweep. It emptied the bath with the Buddhist baby in it, filled the bath with its own water, and placed in it its own baby. Brahmanism did not care to stop and see how filthy its water was compared with the clean and fragrant water which flowed from the noble source of Buddhism. Brahmanism did not care to stop and see how hideous its own baby was compared with the Buddhist baby. Brahmanism acquired, through its invasions, political power to annihilate Buddhism, and it did annihilate Buddhism. Islam did not supplant Hinduism. Islam never did a thorough job of its mission. Brahmanism did. It drove out Buddhism as a religion and occupied its place.

These facts show that Brahmanic invasions of Buddhist India have a far greater significance to the historians of India than the Muslim invasions of Hindu India can be said to have produced. Yet, very little space is devoted by historians to the vicissitudes which befell Buddhist India, built up by the Mauryas, and even where that is done, they have not cared to deal pointedly with questions that quite naturally arise: questions such as, who were the Sungas, Kanvas, and Andhras; why did they destroy the Buddhist India which was built up by the Mauryas. Never has any attempt been made to study the changes that Brahmanism, after it triumphed over Buddhism, brought about in the political and social structure.

The failure to appreciate this aspect of India's history is due to the prevalence of some very wrong notions. It has been commonly supposed that the culture of India has been the same throughout history, that Brahmanism, Buddhism, and Jainism are simply different phases, and that there has never been any fundamental antagonism between them. Secondly, it has been assumed that whatever conflicts have taken place in Indian politics were purely political and dynastic and had no social and spiritual significance. It is because of these wrong notions that Indian history has become a purely mechanical thing, a record of one dynasty succeeding another and one ruler succeeding another ruler. A corrective to such an attitude and to such a method of writing history lies in recognition of two indisputable facts.

In the first place, it must be recognised that there has never been such, a thing as a common Indian culture and that historically, there have been three Indias—Brahmanic India, Buddhist India, and Hindu India—each with its own culture. Secondly, it must be recognised that the history of India before the Muslim invasions is the history of a mortal conflict between Brahmanism and

Buddhism. Anyone who does not recognise these two facts will never be able to write a true history of India, a history which will disclose the meaning and purpose running through it. It is to correct the Indian history written as it is and to disclose the meaning and purposes running through it that I was obliged to recast the history of the Brahmanic invasions of Buddhist India and the political triumph of Brahmanism over Buddhism.

We must, therefore, begin with the recognition of the fact that Pushyamitra's revolution was a political revolution engineered by the Brahmins to overthrow Buddhism.

The curious will naturally ask, "What did this triumphant Brahmanism do?" It is to this question that I will now turn. The deeds or misdeeds of this triumphant Brahmanism may be catalogued under seven heads: (1) It established the right of the Brahmin to rule and commit regicide. (2) It made the Brahmins a class of privileged people. (3) It converted the *Varna* into caste. (4) It brought about a conflict and anti-social feelings between the different castes. (5) It degraded the Shudras and the women. (6) It forged the system of graded inequality. (7) It made legal and rigid the social system, which was conventional and flexible.

To begin with the first:

The revolution brought about by Pushyamitra created an initial difficulty for the Brahmins. People could not be easily reconciled to this revolution. The resentment of the public was well expressed by the poet Bana when, in referring to this revolution, he reviles Pushyamitra as being base-born and calls his act of regicide as *Anarya.* The act of Pushyamitra was properly described by Bana as *Anarya,* i.e., contrary to Aryan law. For three points, the Aryan law at the date of Pushyamitra's revolution was well settled. The then-Aryan law declared (1) That kingship is the right of the Kshatriya only. A Brahmin could never be a king. (2) That no Brahmin shall take to the profession of arms. (3) That rebellion against the king's authority was a sin. Pushyamitra, to foster the rebellion, had committed a crime against each of these three laws. He was Brahmin, and although a Brahmin, he rebelled against the king, took to the profession of arms, and became a king. People were not reconciled to this usurption, which constituted so flagrant a breach of the law that the Brahmins had to regularize the position created by Pushyamitra. The Brahmins did this by taking the bold step of changing the law. This change of law is quite manifest from the *Manusmriti*. I will quote the appropriate *shlokas* from the Code:

XIII. 100. The post of the Commander-in-Chief of the kingdom, the very Headship of Government, the complete empire over everyone, are deserved by the Brahmin.

Here, we have one change in the law. This new law declares that the Brahmin has a right to become *Senapati* (Commander of forces), to conquer a kingdom, and to be the ruler and the Emperor of it.

XI. 31. A Brahmin, who well knows the laws, need not complain to the king of any grievous injury since, even by his own power, he may chastise those who injure him.

XI. 32. His (Brahmin's) own power, which depends on himself alone, is mightier than the royal power, which depends on other men; by his own might, therefore, may a Brahmin coerce his foes.

XI. 261-62. A Brahmin who has killed even the peoples of the three worlds is completely freed from all sins on reciting three times the Rig, Yajur, or Sama Vedas with the Upanishads.

Here is the second change in the law. It authorized the Brahmin to kill not only the king but to engage in a general massacre of men if they sought to do injury to his power and position.

VII. 348. The twice-born man may take arms, when the rightful occupation assigned to each by *Dharma* is obstructed by force; and when, in some evil time, a disaster has befallen the twice-born classes.

IX. 320. Of a Kshatriya (military man or king), who raises his arm violently on all occasions against the Brahmins, Brahmin himself shall be the chastiser; since the soldier originally proceeded from the Brahmin.

This is the third legal change. It recognised the right to rebellion and the right to regicide. The new law is very delicately framed. It gives the right of rebellion to the three higher classes. But it is also given to the Brahmins singly by way of providing for a situation when the Kshatriyas and the Vaishyas may not be prepared to join the Brahmin in bringing about a rebellion. The right of rebellion is well-circumscribed. It can be exercised only when the king is guilty of upsetting the occupations assigned by Manu to the different *Varnas*.

These legal changes were as necessary as they were revolutionary. Their object was to legalize and regularize the position created by Pushyamitra by killing the last Maurya King. By virtue of these legal changes, a Brahmin could lawfully become a king, could lawfully take arms, could lawfully depose or murder a king who was opposed to *Chaturvarna* and could lawfully kill any subject that opposed the authority of the Brahmin. Manu gave the Brahmins a right to commit Bartholomeu if it became necessary to safeguard their interests.

In this way, Brahmanism established the right of Brahmin to rule and set at rest whatever doubt and dispute there was regarding the same. But that could hardly be enough for the Brahmins as a whole. It may be a matter of pride, but not of any advantage. There can be no special virtue in Brahmin rule if the Brahmin was treated as a common man along with the Non-Brahmins, having the same rights and same duties. Brahmin rule, if it is to justify itself, must do so by conferring special privileges and immunities on the Brahmins as a class. Indeed, Pushyamitra's Revolution would have been an ill wind blowing no good if it had not recognised the superior position of the Brahmins and conferred upon them special advantages. Manu was alive to this and accordingly proceeds to create monopolies for Brahmins and grant them certain immunities and privileges, as may be seen from the Code.

First, as to monopolies:

I. 88. To Brahmins, he assigned teaching and studying the Vedas, sacrificing for their own benefit and for others, giving and accepting of alms.

X. 1. Let the three twice-born castes (*Varnas*), discharging their prescribed duties, studying the Vedas, but among them, the Brahmins alone shall teach it, not the other two, that is an established rule.

X. 2. The Brahmin must know the means of subsistence prescribed by law for all, instruct others, and live according to the law.

X. 3. On account of his pre-eminence, on account of the superiority of his origin, on account of his observance of particular restrictive rules, and on account of his particular sanctification, the Brahmin is the Lord of all Castes (*Varnas*).

X. 74. Brahmins who are intent on the means of gaining union with Brahmin and firm in discharging their duties shall live by duly performing the following six acts, which are enumerated in their proper order.

X. 75. Teaching, studying, sacrificing for himself, sacrificing for others, making gifts, and receiving them are the six acts prescribed for a Brahmin.

X. 76. But among the six acts ordained for him, three are his means of subsistence, viz., sacrificing for others, teaching, and accepting gifts from pure men.

X. 77. Passing from the Brahmin to the Kshatriya, three acts incumbent on the former are forbidden, viz., teaching, sacrificing for others, and, thirdly, the acceptance of gifts.

X. 78. The same is likewise forbidden to a Vaishya; that is a settled rule, for Manu, the Lord of Creatures (Prajapati), has not prescribed them for men of those two castes.

X. 79. To carry arms for striking and throwing is prescribed for Kshatriyas as a means of subsistence; to trade, rear cattle, and agriculture for Vaishyas; but their duties are liberality, the study of the Vedas, and the performance of sacrifices.

Here are three things which Manu made the monopoly of the Brahmin: teaching Vedas, performing sacrifices, and receiving gifts.

The following are the immunities that were granted to the Brahmins. They fall into two classes: freedom from taxation and exemption from certain forms of punishment for crimes.

VII. 133. Though dying with want, a king must not levy a tax on *Srotriyas*, and no *Srotriya* residing in his kingdom, must perish from hunger.

VIII. 122. They declare that the wise have prescribed these fines for perjury to prevent a failure of justice and to restrain injustice.

VIII. 123. But a just king shall fine and banish men of the three lower castes (*Varna*), who have given false evidence, but a Brahmin he shall only banish.

XXI. 124. Manu, the son of the Self-existent (*Swamyambhu*), has named ten places on which punishment may be made to fall in the cases of the three lower castes (*Varna*), but a Brahmina shall depart unhurt from the country.

VIII. 379. Tonsure of the head is ordained for a Brahmin instead of capital punishment, but men of other castes shall suffer capital punishment.

VIII. 380. Let him never slay a Brahmin, though he has committed all possible crimes, let him banish such an offender, leaving all his property to him and his body unhurt.

Thus, Manu places the Brahmin above the ordinary penal law for felonies. He is to be allowed to leave the country without a wound on him and with all property, even in proven offences of capital punishment. He is not to suffer forfeiture or fine, nor capital punishment. He suffers only banishment, which, in the words of Hobbes, was only a "Change of air" after having committed the most heinous crimes. Manu also gave him certain privileges. A judge must be a Brahmin.

VIII. 9. But if the king does not personally investigate the suits, then let him appoint a learned Brahmin to try them.

VIII. 10. That man shall enter that most excellent court, accompanied by three assessors, and fully consider all causes brought before the king, either sitting down or standing.

The other privileges were financial:

XXV. 37. When a learned Brahmin has found treasure deposited in former times, he may take even the whole of it, for he is master of everything.

XXVI. 38. When the king finds treasure of old concealed in the ground, let him give one-half to Brahmins and place the other half in his treasury.

IX. 323. But a king who feels his end drawing nigh shall bestow all his wealth, accumulated from fines, on Brahmins, make over his kingdom to his son, and then seek death in battle.

IX. 187. Always to that relative within three degrees who is nearest to the deceased *Sapinda* the estate shall belong; afterwards, a *Sakulya* shall be the heir, then the spiritual teacher or the pupil.

IX. 188. But on the failure of all heirs, Brahmins shall share the estate, (who are) versed in the three Vedas, pure and self-controlled; thus, the law is not violated.

IX. 189. The property of a Brahmin must never be taken by the king that is a settled rule, but the property of men of other castes the king may take on failure of all heirs.

These are some of the advantages, immunities, and privileges which Manu conferred upon the Brahmins. It was a token of a Brahmin having become a king.

Supporters of Brahmanism—so strong is the belief in the excellence of Brahmanism that there are no apologists for it as yet—never fail to point to the disabilities that Manu has imposed upon the Brahmins. Their object in doing so is to show that the ideal placed by Manu before the Brahmin is poverty and service. That Manu has placed certain disabilities upon the Brahmins is a fact. But to conclude from it that Manu's ideal for a Brahmin is poverty, and service is a gross and deliberate concoction for which there is no foundation in Manu.

To understand the real purpose that Manu had while imposing these disabilities, two things must be borne in mind. Firstly, the place Manu has assigned to the Brahmins in the general scheme of society, and secondly, the nature of the disabilities. The place assigned by Manu to the Brahmins is enunciated by him in unequivocal terms. The matter being important, I must quote again the verses already quoted:

I. 93. As the Brahmin sprang from Brahma's mouth, as he was the firstborn, and as he possesses the Vedas, he is by right the Lord of this Whole Creation.

Consider the nature of the disabilities.

IV. 2. A Brahamin must seek a means of subsistence which either causes no, or at least little, pain to others and live by that except in times of distress.

IV. 3. To gain bare subsistence, let him accumulate property by following those irreproachable occupations which are prescribed for his caste, without unduly fatiguing his body.

III. 337. In a case of theft, the guilt of a Shudra shall be eightfold, that of a Vaishya sixteenfold, and that of a Kshatriya two-and-thirty-fold.

III. 338. That of a Brahamin shall be sixty-four-fold, or quite a hundred-fold, or even twice four-and-sixty-fold; each of them knowing the nature of the offence.

III. 383. A Brahamin shall be compelled to pay a fine of one thousand panas if he has intercourse with guarded females of those two castes, for offending with a guarded Shudra female, a fine of one thousand panas shall be inflicted on a Kshatriya or a Vaishya.

VIII. 384. For intercourse with an unguarded Kshatriya a fine of five hundred panas shall fall on a Vaishya, but for the same offence a Kshatriya shall be shaved with the urine of a donkey or pay the same fine.

VIII. 385. A Brahamin who approaches unguarded females of the Kshatriya or Vaishya castes, or a Shudra female, shall be fined five hundred panas; but for intercourse with a female of the lowest castes, he shall be fined one thousand panas.

Examining these disabilities against the background furnished by the place assigned to him by Manu, it is obvious that the object of these disabilities was not to make the Brahmin suffer. On the other hand, it becomes clear that the object of Manu was to save the Brahmin from falling from the high pinnacle on which he had placed him and incurring the disgrace of the non-Brahmins.

That the object of Manu was not to subject the Brahmins to poverty and destitution is clear from other provisions in the *Manusmriti*. In this connection, reference should be made to the rule mentioned in the *Manusmriti* regarding the course of conduct a Brahmin should pursue when he is in distress.

X. 80. Among the several occupations, the most commendable are teaching the Vedas for a Brahmin, protecting the people for a Kshatriya, and trading for a Vaishya.

X. 81. But a Brahmin, unable to subsist by his peculiar occupations just mentioned, may live according to the law applicable to Kshatriyas, for the latter is next to him in rank.

X. 82. If asked, How shall it be if he cannot maintain himself by either of these occupations? The answer is, he may adopt a Vaishya's mode of life, employing himself in agriculture and rearing cattle.

X. 83. But a Brahamin, or a Kshatriya, living by a Vaishya's mode of subsistence, shall carefully avoid the pursuit of agriculture, which causes injury to many beings and depends on others.

X. 84. Some declare that agriculture is something excellent, but that means of subsistence is blamed by the virtuous, for the wooden implement with iron point injures the earth and the beings living in the earth.

X. 85. But he who, through a want of means of subsistence, gives up the strictness concerning his duties, may sell, to increase his wealth, the commodities sold by Vaishyas, making however the following exceptions.

It will be seen that the disabilities imposed upon a Brahmin last as long as he is prospering by the occupations which belong to him as of right. As soon as he is in distress, his disabilities vanish, and he is free to do anything that he likes to do in addition to the occupations reserved to him and without ceasing to be a Brahmin. Further, whether he is in distress or not is a matter left to the Brahmin to be decided at his discretion. There is, therefore, no bar to prevent even a prosperous Brahmin from supplementing his earnings by following any of the professions opened to him in distress by satisfying his conscience.

There are other provisions in the *Manusmriti* intended to materially benefit the Brahmins. They are *Dakshina* and *Dana. Dakshina* is the fee Brahmin is entitled to charge when he is called to perform a religious ceremony. Brahmanism is full of rites and ceremonies. It is not very difficult to imagine how great this source of income must be to every Brahmin. There was no chance of a priest being cheated of his fees. The religious sense attached to *Dakshina* was a sufficient sanction for regular payment. But Manu wanted to give the Brahmins the right to recover his fees.

XI. 38. A Brahmin who, though wealthy, does not give, as a fee for the performance of an *Agnyadheya*, a horse sacred to Prajapati, becomes equal to one who has not kindled the sacred fires.

XI. 39. Let him who has faith and controls his senses perform other meritorious acts, but let him on no account offer sacrifices at which he gives smaller fees than those prescribed.

XI. 40. The organs of sense and action, honour, bliss in heaven, longevity, fame, offspring, and cattle are destroyed by a sacrifice at which too small sacrificial fees are given; hence a man of small means should not offer a *Srauta* sacrifice.

He even goes to the length of excusing a Brahmin by declaring that anything done by him to recover his fees shall not be an offence under the law.

VIII. 349. In their own defence, in a strife for the fees of officiating priests, and to protect women and Brahmins; he who under such circumstances kills in the cause of right, commits no sin.

But it is the provision of dana which makes a fruitful source of income for the Brahmins. Manu exhorts the king to make *dana* to Brahmins.

VII. 79. A king shall offer various *Srauta* sacrifices at which liberal fees are distributed, and in order to acquire merit, he shall give to Brahmins enjoyments and wealth.

VII. 82. Let him honour those Brahmins who have returned from their teacher's house after studying the Vedas; for that money which is given to Brahmins is declared to be an imperishable treasure for kings.

VII. 83. Neither thieves nor foes can take it, nor can it be lost; hence an imperishable store must be deposited by kings with Brahmins.

XI. 4. But a king shall bestow, as is proper, jewels of all sorts, and presents for the sake of sacrifices on Brahmins learned in the Vedas.

This admonition by Manu to the king did not remain a mere hope for the Brahmin. History shows that this exhortation was fully exploited by the Brahmins, as the number of *dana patras* discovered by archialogists indicates. It is astounding how the kings were fooled by the Brahmins to transfer village after village to crafty, lazy, and indolent Brahmins. Indeed, a large part of the wealth of the present-day Brahmins lies in this swindle practised by wily Brahmins upon pious but foolish kings. Manu was not content to let the Brahmin prey upon the king for *dana.* He also allowed the Brahmin to prey upon the public in the mattter of *dana.* This Manu has done in three different ways. In the first place, he exhorts people to make gifts as a part of the duty owed by the pious to themselves, at the same time pointing out that the highest *dana* is to a Brahmin:

VII. 85. A gift to one who is not a Brahmin yields the ordinary reward; a gift to one who calls himself a Brahmana, a double reward; a gift to a well-read Brahmin, a hundred-thousandfold reward; a gift to one who knows the Vedas and the Angas (*Vedaparanga*), a reward without end.

VII. 86. For according to the particular qualities of the recipient and according to the faith of the giver, a small or a great reward will be obtained for a gift in the next world.

In the next place, Manu declares that in certain circumstances *dana* to a Brahmin is compulsory.

XI. 1. Him who wishes to marry for the sake of having offspring, him who wishes to perform a sacrifice, a traveller, him who has given away all his property, him who begs for the sake of his teacher, his father, or his mother, a student of the Vedas, and a sick man.

XI. 2 Out of these nine Brahmins, one should consider as Snatakas, begging to fulfil the sacred law; to such poor men, gifts must be given in proportion to their learning.

XI. 3. To these most excellent among the twice-born, food and presents of money must be given; it is declared that food must be given to others outside the sacrificial enclosure.

XI. 6. One should give, according to one's ability, wealth to Brahmins learned in the Vedas and living alone; thus one obtains after death heavenly bliss.

The third method adopted by Manu to make the rule of *dana* become a source of secure and steady income is beyond question the most ingenious one. Manu linked up *dana* with penance. In the scheme of Manu, an improper act may be a sin, although not an offence, or it may be both a sin and an offence. As a sin, its punishment is a matter of canonical law. As an offence its punishment is a matter of secular law. As a sin, the improper act is called *Pataka* and the punishment for it is called penance. In the scheme of Manu, every *Pataka* must be expunged by the performance of a penance.

XI. 44. A man who omits a prescribed act, performs a blameable act, or cleaves to sensual enjoyments must perform a penance.

XI. 45. All sages prescribe a penance for a sin unintentionally committed; some declare, on the evidence of the revealed texts, that it may be performed even for intentional offences.

XI. 46. A sin unintentionally committed is expiated by the recitation of Vedic texts, but that which men in their folly commit intentionally, by various special penances.

XI. 53. Thus, in consequence of a remnant of the guilt of former crimes, are born idiots, dumb, blind, deaf, and deformed men, who are all despised by the virtuous.

XI. 54. Penances, therefore, must always be performed for purification because those whose sins have not been expiated, are born again with disgraceful marks.

The penances prescribed by Manu are many, and the curious may refer to the *Manusmriti* itself for knowledge of what they are. What is noteworthy is these that penances are calculated to materially benefit the Brahmin. Some penances take the form of a simple *dana* to the Brahmin. Others prescribe the performance of some religious rites. However, as religious rites cannot be performed by anybody except by a Brahmin, and since the performance of religious rites requires the payment of fees, the Brahmin alone can be the beneficiary of the *dana* system.

It is, therefore, absurd to suggest that Manu wanted to place before the Brahmins the ideal of humility, poverty, and service. The Brahmins certainly did not understand Manu that way. Indeed, they believed that they were made a privileged class. Not only they believe in it, but they also sought to extend their privileges in other directions—a matter which will be discussed later on. They were perfectly justified, in their view. Manu called the Brahmins the 'Lords of the Earth', and he framed the law with such care that they shall remain so.

Having made full provision for Brahmin rule and his dominance, Manu next launches out to transform society to suit his purposes.

The transformation of *Varna* into caste is the most stupendous and selfish task in which Brahmanism, after its triumph, became primarily engaged. We have no explicit record of the steps that Brahmanism took to bring about this change. On the contrary, we have a lot of confused thinking on the relation between *Varna* and caste. Some think that *Varna* and caste are the same. Those who think that they are different seem to believe that *Varna* became caste when the prohibition on intermarriage became part of the social order. All this, of course, is erroneous, and the error is because of the fact that Manu, in transforming the *Varna* into caste, has nowhere explained his ends and how his means are related to those ends. Oscar Wilde has said that to be intelligible is to be found out. Manu did not wish to be found out. He is, therefore, silent about his ends and means, leaving people to imagine them. For Hindus, the subject is important beyond measure. An attempt at clarification is absolutely essential so that the confusion due to different people imagining differently the design of Manu may be removed and light thrown on the way how Brahmanism proceeded to give a wrong and pernicious turn to the original idea of *Varna* as the basis of society.

As I said, Manu's ways are silent and subterranean, and we cannot give the detailed and chronological history of this conversion of *Varna* into caste. But fortunately, there are landmarks which are clear enough to indicate how the change was brought about.

Before proceeding to describe how this change was brought about, let me clear the confusion between *Varna* and caste. This can best be done by noting the similarities and differences between the two. *Varna* and caste are identical in their *de jure* connotation. Both connote status and occupation. Status and occupation are the two concepts which are implied both in the notion, *Varna* as well as in the notion of caste. *Varna* and caste, however, differ in one important particular. *Varna* is not hereditary, either in status or occupation. On the other hand caste implies a system in which status and occupation are hereditary and descend from father to son.

When I say that Brahmanism converted *Varna* into caste, what I mean is that it made status and occupation hereditary.

How was this transformation effected? As I said, there are no footprints left of the steps taken by Brahmanism to accomplish this change, but there are landmarks which serve to give us a clear view of how the deed came to be done.

The change was accomplished by stages. In the transformation of *Varna* into a caste, three stages are quite well-marked. The first stage was the stage in which the duration of *Varna*—i.e., of status and occupation of a person—was for a prescribed period of time only. The second stage was a stage in which the status and occupation involved the *Varna* of a person endured during lifetime only. The third stage was a stage in which the status and occupation of the *Varna* became hereditary. To use legal language, the estate conferred by Varna was, at the beginning, an estate for a term only. Thereafter, it became a life estate, and finally, it became an estate of inheritance, which is tantamount to saying that *Varna* became caste. That these are the stages by which *Varna* was converted into caste seems to have ample support from tradition as recorded in the religious literature. There is no reason why this tradition should not be accepted as embodying something that is quite genuine. According to this tradition, the task of determining the *Varna* of a person was effected by a body of officers called Manu and the Sapta Rishis. From the mass of people, Manu selected those who were fit to be Kshatriyas and Vaishyas, and the Sapta Rishis selected those who were fit to be Brahmins. After this selection was made by Manu and the Sapta Rishis for being Brahmins, Kshatriyas, Vaishyas, the rest who were not selected were called Shudras. The *Varna* arrangement so determined lasted for one *Yug,* i.e., a period of four years. Every fourth year, a new body of officers known by the same designation, Manu and Sapta Rishi, was appointed to make a new selection. It happened that at, times, some of those who were left to be fit only for being Shudras were selected for being Brahmins, Kshatriyas, and Vaishyas, while some of those who were elected for being Brahmins, Kshatriyas, and Vaishyas were left as being fit only to be Shudras. Thus, the personnel of the *Varna* changed. It was a sort of periodical shuffling and selection of men according to their mental and physical aptitudes and occupations, which were essential to the life of the community. The time when the reshuffling of the *Varnas* took place was called *Manwantar*, which etymologically means a change of *Varna* made by Manu. The word *Manwantar* also means the period for which the *Varna* of an individual was fixed. The word *Manwantar* is very rich in its contents and expresses the essential elements of the *Varna* system, which were twofold. First, it shows that *Varna* was determined by an independent body of people called Manu and

Sapta Rishis. Secondly, it shows that the *Varna* was for a period after which a change was made by Manu. According to ancient tradition as embodied in the Puranas, the period for which the *Varna* of a person was fixed by Manu and *Saptarshi* was a period of four years and was called *Yug*. At the end of the period of four years, there occurred the *Manwantar* whereby every fourth year, the list was revised. Under the revision, some changed their old *Varna*, some retained it, some lost it, and some gained it.

The original system seems to have under contemplation the determination of the *Varna* of adults. It was not based on prior training or close scrutiny of bias and aptitude. Manu and Sapta Rishis were a sort of a Board of Interviews that determined the *Varna* of a person based on how he struck them at the interview. The determination of the *Varna* was done in a rough-and-tumble manner. This system seems to have gone into abeyance. A new system grew up in its place. It was known as the Gurukul system. The Gurukul was a school maintained by a Guru (teacher), also called Acharya (learned man). All children went to this Gurukul for their education. The period of education extended for twelve years. The child, while at Gurukul, was known as Brahmachari. After the period of education was over, the Upanayana ceremony was performed at the Gurukul by the Acharya. The Upanayana ceremony was the most important ceremony. It was a ceremony at which the Acharya determined the *Varna* of the student and sent him out into the world to perform the duties of that *Varna*. Upanayana by the Acharyas was the new method of determining *Varna*, which came into vogue in place of the method of determination by Manu and Sapta Rishis. The new method was undoubtedly superior to the old method. It retained the true feature of the old method, namely, that the *Varna* should be determined by a disinterested and independent body. But it added a new feature, namely, training, as a prerequisite for the assignment of *Varna*. On the ground that training alone developes the individual in the makeup of a person, and the only safe way to determine the *Varna* of a person is to know his individuality, the addition of this new feature was undoubtedly a great improvement.

With the introduction of the Acharya Gurukul system, the duration of the *Varna* came to be altered. *Varna*, instead of being *Varna* for a period, became *Varna* for life. But it was not hereditary.

Evidently, Brahmanism was dissatisfied with this system. The reason for dissatisfaction was quite obvious. Under the system, as it was prevalent, there was every chance of the Acharya declaring the child of a Brahmin as fitting only to be a Shudra. Brahmanism was naturally most anxious to avoid this result. It wanted the *Varna* to be hereditary. Only by making the *Varna* hereditary could it save the children of the Brahmins from being declared Shudra. To achieve this, Brahmanism proceeded in the most audacious manner one can think of.

III

Brahmanism made three radical changes in the system of determining the *Varna* of the child. In the first place, the system of Gurukul as the place where training was given to the child and its *Varna* was determined by the Guru at the end of the training period was abolished. Manu is quite aware of the Gurukul and refers to Guruvas—i.e., training and residence in the Gurukul under the Guru—but does not refer to it at all in connection with the *Upanayana*. He abolishes the Guru as an authority competent to perform *Upanayana* by omitting to make even the remotest reference to him in connection with *Upanayana*. In place of the Guru, Manu allows the *Upanayana* of the child to be performed by its father at home. Secondly, *Upanayana* was made into a *Sanskara* i.e., a sacrament. In olden times, *Upanayana* was like a convocation ceremony held by the Guru to confer degrees obtained by students in his Gurukul, in which certificates of proficiency in the duties of a particular *Varna* were granted. In Manu's law, this was a complete change in the meaning and purpose of this most important institution. Thirdly, the relation of training to *Upanayana* was totally reversed. In the olden system training came before *Upanayan*.

Under Brahmanism, *Upanayana* came before training. Manu directs that a child should be sent to the Guru for training, but only after *Upanayana,* i.e., after his *Varna* is determined by his father.

The principal change made by Brahmanism was the transfer of authority from the Guru to the father in the matter of performing *Upanayana*. The result was that the father, having the right to perform the *Upanayana* of his child, gave his own *Varna* to the child and thus made it hereditary. It is by divesting the Guru of his authority to determine the *Varna* and vesting it in the father that Brahmanism ultimately converted the *Varna* into caste.

Such is the story of the transformation of *Varna* into caste. The story of the transition from one to the other is, of course, reconstructed. For the reasons already given, it may not be quite as accurate as one would wish it to be in all its details. But I have no doubt that the stages and the ways by which *Varna* ceased to exist. Caste came into being must be similar to what has been suggested in the foregoing discussion of the subject.

What object Brahmanism could have had in converting *Varna* into caste is not difficult to imagine. The object was to make the high status enjoyed by the Brahmins from ancient times the privilege of every Brahmin and his progeny without reference to merit or qualifications. To put it differently, the object was to elevate and ennoble every Brahmin, however mean and worthless he may be, to the high status occupied by some of them on account of the virtue. It was an attempt to ennoble the whole Brahmin community without exception.

That this was the object of Brahmanism is clear from Manu's ordinances. Manu knew that by making *Varna* hereditary, even the most ignorant Brahmin would be elevated to the status occupied by the most learned Brahmin. He feared that the former might not be respected as much as the most latter, which was the object of this attempt at the ennoblement of the whole class of Brahmins. Manu is very much concerned about the ignorant Brahmin—a new phenomenon—and warns people against being disrespectful to an ignorant and mean Brahmin.

IX. 317. A Brahmin, whether learned or ignorant, is a powerful divinity, even as fire is a powerful divinity, whether consecrated or popular.

IX. 319. Thus, although Brahmins employ themselves in all sorts of menial ocupations, they must invariably be honoured, for they are something transcendently divine.

Such a warning was unnecessary if the object ennobled the whole Brahmin class. Here is a case where vice refuses to pay to virtue, even the homage of hypocrisy. Can there be greater moral degeneracy than what is shown by Manu in insisting upon the worship of the Brahmin, even if he is mean and ignorant?

So much for the object of change from *Varna* to caste. What have been the consequences of this change?

From the spiritual point of view, the consequences have been too harmful to be contemplated with equanimity. The harm done may perhaps be better realised by comparing the position of the Brahmin as a priest, resulting from the law of Manu, with that of the law of the clergy under the Church of England. There, the clergy is subject to the criminal law as every citizen is. However, in addition to that, he is always subject to Church Discipline Act. Under criminal law, he would be punished if he officiated as clergy without being qualified for it. Under the Church Discipline Act, he would be liable to be disqualified as clergy for conduct which would be deemed to be morally wrong, although it did not amount to a crime. This double check on the clergy is held justifiable because learning and morality are deemed to be quite essential for the profession of the clergy, who are supposed to administer to the spiritual needs of the people. Under Brahmanism, the Brahmin, who alone can be the clergy, need not possess learning or morality. Yet he is in sole charge of the spiritual affairs of the people! On the value of a creed that permits this, the comment is unnecessary.

From the secular point of view, the consequences of this transformation of *Varna* into caste have introduced a most pernicious mentality among the Hindus. It is to disregard merit and have regard only to birth. If one is descended from the high he has respect, although he may be utterly devoid of merit or worth. One who is of high birth will be superior to one who is of low birth, although the latter may be superior to the former in terms of worth. Under Brahmanism, it is the birth that always wins, whether it is birth or against worth. Merit by itself can win no meeds. This is entirely due to the dissociation of merits from status, which is the work of Brahmanism. Nothing could be better calculated to produce an unprogressive society which sacrifices the rights of intelligence on the altar of aristocratic privilege.

Now, the third deed in the catalogue of deeds done by Brahmanism after its triumphs over Buddhism. It was to separate the Brahmins from the result of the Non-Brahmin population and to sever the different social strata of the Non-Brahmin population.

Pushyamitra's Brahmanic Revolution was undertaken for the purpose of restoring the ancient social system of *Chaturvarna*, which under the Buddhist regime was put into the melting pot. But when Brahmanism triumphed over Buddhism it did not content itself with merely restoring *Charutvarna* as it was in its original form. The *Chaturvarna* system of the Pre-Buddhist days was a flexible and open system. This was because the *Varna* system had no connection with the marriage system. While *Chaturvarna* recognised the existence of four different classes, it did not prohibit intermarriage between them. A male of one *Varna* could lawfully marry a female of another *Varna*. There are numerous illustrations in support of this view. I give below some instances which refer to well-known and respectable individuals who have acquired a name and fame in the sacred lore of the Hindus.

	Husband	*His Varna*	*Wife*	*Her Varna*
1.	Shantanu	Kshatriya	Ganga	Shudra (Anamik)
2.	Shantanu	Kshatriya	Matsyagandha	Shudra (Fisher)
3.	Parashara	Brahmin	Matsyagandha	Shudra (Fisher)
4.	Vishwamitra	Kshatriya	Menaka	Apsara
5.	Yayati	Kshatriya	Devayani	Brahmin
6.	Yayati	Kshatriya	Sharmishta	Asuri (non-Aryan)
7.	Jaratkaru	Brahmin	Jaratkaru	Nag (non-Aryan)

Should anybody retain doubt on the question that the division of society into classes did not prohibit intermarriages between the four *Varnas* let him consider the genealogy of the family of the great Brahmin sage Vyasa.

Genealogy of Vyasa

Varuna and Mitra + Urvashi
|
Vasishtha + Arundhati
|
Shakti + Adrushyanti
|
Parashara + Matsyagandha
|
Vyasa

Brahmanism, with the ferocity of an outraged brute, proceeded to put a stop to intermarriages between the different *Varnas*. A new law was proclaimed by Manu. It is in the following terms:

III. 12. For the first marriage of twice-born men wives of equal caste are recommended.

III. 13. It is declared that a Shudra woman alone can be the wife of a Shudra.

III. 14. A Shudra woman is not mentioned even in any ancient story as the first wife of a Brahmin or of a Kshatriya, though they lived in the greatest distress.

III. 15. Twice-born men who, in their folly, wed wives of the low Shudra caste soon degrade their families and their children to the state of Shudras.

III. 16. According to Atri and Gautama, the son of Utathya, he who weds a Shudra woman becomes an outcast. According to Saunaka, the birth of a son, and according to Bhrigu, he who has male offspring from a Shudra female alone.

III. 17. A Brahmin who takes a Shudra wife to his bed will after death sink into hell; if he begets a child by her, he will lose the rank of a Brahmin.

III. 18. The manes and the gods will not eat the offerings of that man who performs the rites in honour of the gods, the manes, and guests chiefly with a Shudra wife's assistance, and such a man will not go to heaven.

III. 19. For him, who drinks the moisture of a Shudra's lips, who is tainted by her breath, and who begets a son on her, no expiation is prescribed.

Brahmanism, was not satisfied with the prohibition of intermarriage. Brahmanism went further and prohibited interdining.

Manu lays down certain interdicts on food. Some are hygenic while others are social. Of the social, the following are worthy of attention:

IV. 218. Food given by a king impairs his manly vigour; by one of the servile class, his divine light, and by goldsmiths, his life; by leathers cutters, his good name.

IV. 219. Given by cooks and the like mean artisans, it destroys his offspring, by a washerman, his muscular strength.

IV. 221. That of all others, mentioned in the order, whose food must never be tasted, is held equal by the wise to the skin, bones, and hair of the head.

IV. 222. Having unknowingly swallowed the food of any such people, he must fast for three days. But having eaten it knowingly, he must perform the same harsh penance as if he had tasted any seminal impurity, ordure, or urine.

I said that Brahmanism acted with the ferocity of an outraged brute in undertaking the task of prohibiting intermarriage and interdining. Those who have doubts about this matter ponder over the language of Manu.

Mark the disgust Manu shows concerning the Shudra woman. Mark what Manu states about the food of the Shudra. He says it is as impure as semen or urine.

These two laws have produced the caste system. Prohibition of intermarriage and prohibition against interdining are the two pillars on which it rests. The caste system and the rules relating to intermarriage and interdining are related to each other as ends to means. Indeed, by no other means could the end be realised.

The forging of these means shows that the creation of the caste system was the end and aim of Brahmanism. Brahmanism enacted the prohibitions against intemarriage and interdining. But Brahmanism introduced other changes in the social system, and if the purposes underlying these changes are those which I suggest them to be, then it must be admitted that Brahmanism was so keen on sustaining the caste system that it did not mind whether the ways and means employed were fair or unfair, moral or immoral. I refer to the laws contained in the Code of Manu regarding the marriage of girls and the life of widows.

See the law that Manu promulgates regarding the marriage of females:

IX. 4. Reprehensible is the father who does not give daughter in marriage at the proper time.

IX. 88. To a distinguished, handsome suitor of equal caste should a father give his daughter following the prescribed rule, though she may not have attained the proper age, i.e., although she may not have reached puberty.

By this rule, Manu enjoins that a girl should be married even though she may not have reached the age of puberty, i.e., even when she is a child. Now, about to widows, Manu promulgates the following rule:

XI. 157. At her pleasure, let her, i.e., widow emaciate her body by living voluntarily on pure flowers, roots, and fruits; but let her not, when her lord is deceased, even pronounce the name of another man.

XII. 161. But a widow, who, from a wish to bear children, slights her deceased husband by marrying again, brings disgrace on herself here below and shall be excluded from the seat of her lord in heaven.

V. 162. Offspring begotten on a woman by any other than her husband is here declared to be no progeny of hers; no more than a child begotten on the wife of another man belongs to the begetter; nor is a second husband anywhere prescribed for a virtuous woman.

This is the rule of enforced widowhood for a woman. A reference may also be made to *Sati* or a widow who burns herself on the funeral pyre of her husband and thus puts an end to her life. Manu is silent about it.

Yajnavalkya an authority nearly as great as Manu, says she must not live separately or alone.

86. When deprived of her husband, she must not remain away from her father, mother, son, brother, mother-in-law, or maternal uncle; otherwise, she might become liable to censure.

Here again, *Yajnavalkya* does not suggest that a widow become a *Sati*. But Vijnaneshwar, the author of *Mitakshara* a commentary on *Yajnavalkya Smriti*, makes the following observation in commenting on the above Shloka.

"This is in the case of the alternative of leading a celibate life, vide the text of Vishnu: 'After the death of the husband, either celibacy or ascending the cremation pile after him.'"

Vijnaneshwar adds, in his opinion, that "there is great merit in ascending the funeral pyre after him."

From this, one can very easily see how the rule of *Sati* came to be forged. Manu's rule was that a widow was not to remarry. But it appears from the statement by Vijnaneshwar that from the time of the *Vishnu Smriti* a different interpretation began to be put on the ordinance of Manu. According to this new interpretation, Manu's rule was explained to be offering the widow a choice between two alternatives: (1) either burn yourself on your husband's funeral pyre or (2) if you do not, remain unmarried. This, of course, is a false interpretation, quite unwarranted by Manu's clear words. Somehow, it came to be accepted. The date of the *Vishnu Smriti* is somewhere the 3rd or 4th century. It can, therefore, be said that rule of *Sati* dates from this period.

One thing is certain: these were new rules. The rule of Manu that a girl should be married before she has reached puberty is a new rule. In Pre-Buddhist Brahmanism, marriages were performed not only after puberty but also when girls had reached an age when they could be called grown up. Of this, there is ample evidence. Similarly, the rule that a woman, once she had lost her husband, must not remarry is a new rule. In Pre-Buddhist Brahmanism, there was no prohibition on widow remarriage. The fact that the Sanskrit language contains words such as *Punarbhu* (woman who has undergone a second marriage ceremony) and *Punarbhav* (second husband) shows that such marriages were quite common under Pre-Buddhist Brahmanism. With regard to *Sati* the position as to when it arose it still debated. There is evidence to suggest that it existed in ancient times. However, there is also evidence that it had died out and was revived after Brahmanism, under *Pushyamitra* obtained its victory over Buddhism, although it was sometime later than Manu.

The question is this: why were these changes made by the triumphant Brahmanism? What did Brahmanism want to achieve by having girls married before they had become pubescent, by denying the widow the right to marry again, and by telling her to put herself to death by immolating herself on the funeral pyre of her deceased husband? No explanations are forthcoming for these changes. Mr. C. V. Vaidya, who explains girl marriage, says that girl marriage was introduced to prevent girls from joining the Buddhist order of nuns. This explanation does not satisfy me. Mr. Vaidya omits considering another rule laid down by Manu—namely, the rule relating to suitable age for marriage. According to that rule:

IX. 94. A man aged thirty shall marry a maiden of twelve who pleases him, or a man of twenty-four a girl of eight years of age.

The question is not why girl marriage was introduced. The question is why Manu allowed so much discrepancy in the ages of the bride and the bridegroom.

Mr. Kane has attempted an explanation of *Sati*. He explains that there is nothing new in it. It existed in India in ancient times as it did in other parts of the world. This, again, does not satisfy the world. If it existed outside India, it would not been practised on such an enormous scale as it was in India. Secondly, if traces of it are found in Ancient India among the Kshatriyas, why was it revived? Why was it not universalised? There is no satisfactory explanation. Mr. Kane's explanation regarding the prevalence of *Sati* by reference to inheritance laws does not appear to be very convincing. It may be that because under the Hindu Law of inheritance, as it prevailed in Bengal, women got a share in property. Thus, the kins of her deceased husband pressed her to the become a *Sati* to get rid of a share. This may explain why *Sati* was Practised on such as large scale in Bengal. But it does not explain how it arose nor how it came into practice in other parts of India.

Again, with regard to the prohibition of widow remarriage, there is no explanation whatsoever. Why was the widow, contrary to established practice, prohibited from marrying? Why was she required to lead a life of misery? Why was she disfigured?

My explanation for girl marriage, enforced widowhood and *Sati* is quite different, and I offer it for what it is worth.

"Thus, the superposition of endogamy over exogamy means the creation of caste. But this is not an easy affair. Let us take in consideration an imaginary group that desire to make itself into a caste and analyse what means it will have to adopt to make itself endogamous. If a group desires to make itself endogamous, a formal injunction against intermarriage with outside groups will be of no avail, especially if prior to the introduction of endogamy, exogamy was to be the rule in all matrimonial relations. Again, there is a tendency in all groups living in close contact with one another to assimilate and amalgamate and thus consolidate into a homogeneous society. For this tendency to be strongly counteracted in the interest of caste formation, it is absolutely necessary to circumscribe a circle within which people should not contract marriages."

"Nevertheless, this encircling to prevent marriages from without creates problems from within which are not very easy to solve. Roughly speaking, in a normal group, the two sexes are more or less evenly distributed, and generally speaking, there is an equality between those of the same age. However, this equality was never quite realised in actual societies. While, to the group that is desirous of making itself into a caste, the maintenance of this equality between the sexes becomes the ultimate goal, for without this, endogamy can no longer subsist. In other words, if endogamy is to be preserved, conjugal rights from within have to be provided for, otherwise, members of the group will be driven out of the circle to take care of themselves in any way they please. However, for the conjugal rights to be provided for from within, it is absolutely necessary to maintain a numerical equality between the marriageable units of the two sexes within the group desirous of making itself into a caste. It is only through the maintenance of this equality that the necessary endogamy of the group could be kept intact, and a very large disparity is sure to break it."

"The problem of caste then ultimately resolves itself into one repairing the disparity between the marriageable units of the two sexes within it. The much-needed parity between the units could be realised only when a couple dies simultaneously. But this is a rare contingency. The husband may die before the wife and create a surplus woman who must be disposed of, otherwise through intermarriage she will violate the endogamy of the group. In like manner, the wife may die before her husband and create a surplus man within the group. While may sympathize with the surplus man for his sad bereavement, he has to be the group disposed of, or else he will marry outside the caste and break the endogamy. Thus, both the surplus man and the surplus woman constitute a menace to the caste if not taken care of. For, if suitable partners are not found inside their prescribed circle (and often they cannot find any, for there are just enough pairs to go around), then very likely they will transgress the boundary, marry outside, and import a population that is foreign to the caste. Let us see what our imaginary group is likely to do with this surplus man and surplus woman. We will first take up the case of the surplus woman. She can be disposed of in two different ways to preserve the endogamy of the caste."

"First, burn her on the funeral pyre of her deceased husband and get rid of her. This, however, is rather an impracticable way of solving the problem of sex disparity. In some cases, it may work; in others, it may not. Consequently, every surplus woman cannot thus be disposed of because it is an easy solution but a hard realisation. However, the surplus woman (widow), if not disposed of, remains in the group, but in her very existence lies a double danger. She may marry outside the caste and violate to endogamy, or she may marry within the caste, and through competition, encroach upon the chances of marriage that must be reserved for the potential brides in the caste. She, therefore, is a menace in any case, and something must be done to her if she cannot be burned along with her deceased husband."

"The second remedy is to enforce widowhood on a woman for the rest of her life. So far as the objective results are concerned, burning is a better solution than enforcing widowhood. Burning the widow eliminates all the three evils that a surplus woman is fraught with. Being dead and gone, she creates no problem of remarriage either inside or outside the caste. But compulsory widowhood is superior to burning because it is more practicable. Besides being comparatively humane, it also guards against the evils of remarriage, as does burning, but it fails to guard the morals of the group. No doubt under compulsory widowhood, the woman remains, and just because she is deprived of her natural right of being a legitimate wife in the future, the incentive to bad moral conduct is increased. But this is by no means an insuperable difficulty. She can be degraded to a condition where she could no longer be a source of allurement."

"The problem of the surplus man (widower) is much more important and much more difficult than that of the surplus woman in a group that desires to make itself into a caste. From time immemorial men, as compared with women, have had the upper hand. Men are dominant figures in every group, and of the two sexes, has greater prestige. With this traditional superiority of men over women, their wishes have always been consulted. Women, on the other hand, have been easy prey to all kinds of iniquitous injunctions—religious, social, or economic. But men, as the maker of injunctions are most often above them all. Such being the case, you cannot accord the same kind of treatment to a surplus man as you can to a surplus woman in a caste."

The project of burning man with his deceased wife is hazardous in two ways: first of all, it cannot be done just because he is a man. Secondly, if done, a sturdy soul is lost to the caste. There remain, then, only two solutions which can conveniently dispose of him. I say conveniently, because he is an asset to the group.

Important as man is to the group, endogamy is still more important, and the solution must assure both these ends. Under these circumstances, may be forced–or I should say induced, after the manner of the widow—to remain a widower for the rest of his life. This solution is not altogether difficult, for without there being any compulsion, some are so disposed of as to enjoy self-imposed celibacy or may even take a further step of their own accord to renounce the world and its joys. But, given human nature as it is, this solution can hardly be expected to be realised. On the other hand, as is very likely to be the case, if he remains in the group as an active participant in group activities, he is a danger to the morals of the group. Looked from a different viewpoint, celibacy—though easy in cases where it succeeds—is not so advantageous even then to the material prospects of the caste. If he observes genuine celibacy and renounces the world, he would not be a menace to the preservation of caste endogamy or caste morals as the undoubtedly would be if he remained a secular person. But as an ascetic celibate, he is as good as burned so far as the material well-being of his caste is concerned. For a caste to be large enough to afford a vigorous communal life, it must maintained at a certain numerical strength. But to hope for this and to proclaim celibacy is the same as trying to cure atrophy by bleeding."

"Imposing celibacy on the surplus man in the group, therefore, fails theoretically and practically. It is in the interest of the caste to keep him as a Grihastha (one who raises a family), using Sanskrit technicality. But the problem is to provide him with a wife from within the caste. At the outset, this is not possible, for the ruling ratio in a caste has to be one man to one woman, and none can have two chances of marriage, for in a caste thoroughly self-enclosed, there are always just enough marriageable women to go around for the marriageable men. Under these circumstances, the surplus man can only be provided with a wife by recruiting a bride from the ranks of those not yet marriageable to tie him down to the group. It is certainly the best of the possible solutions in the case of the surplus man. By this, he is kept within the caste. By this, the numerical depletion through constant outflow is guarded against, and endogamy and morals are preserved."

"It will now be seen that the four means by which numerical disparity between the two sexes is conveniently maintained are : (1) Burning the widow with her deceased husband; (2) Compulsory widowhood—a milder form of burning; (3) Imposing celibacy on the widower; and (4) Wedding him to a girl not yet marriageable. Though, as I said above, burning the widow and imposing celibacy on the widower are of doubtful service to the group in its endeavour to preserve its endogamy, all of them operate as means. But means such as force, when liberated or set in motion, creates an end. What, then, is the end that these means create? They create and perpetuate endogamy, while caste and endogamy, according to our analysis of the various definitions of caste, are the same thing. Thus, the existence of these means means caste, and caste involves these means."

"This, in my opinion, is the general mechanism of a caste in a system of castes. Let us now turn to the castes in Hindu society and inquire into their mechanism. I need hardly promise that there are many pitfalls in the path of those who try to unfold the past, and caste in India, to be sure, is a very ancient institution. It is especially true where there exist no authentic or written history or records or where the people, like the Hindus, are so constituted that to them writing history is a folly, for the world is an illusion. However, institutions do live, though for a long time they may remain unrecorded, and as often as not, customs and morals are like fossils that tell their own history. If this is true, our task will be amply rewarded if we scrutinize the solution the Hindus arrived at to meet the problems of the surplus man and surplus woman."

"Complex though it may be in its general working, the Hindu society, even to a superficial observer, presents three singular uxorial customs, namely:

(i) *Sati* i.e., the burning of the widow on the funeral pyre of her deceased husband.

(ii) Enforced widowhood, i.e., a widow is not allowed to remarry.

(iii) Girl marriage."

In addition to these, one also notes a great hankering after *Sannyasa* (renunciation) on the part of the widower, but it may, in some cases, be due purely to psychic disposition.

"So far as I know, no scientific explanation of the origin of these customs is forthcoming even today. We have plenty of philosophy to tell us why these customs were honoured. (Cf. A. K. Coomaraswamy— '*Sati*: A Defence of the Eastern Woman' in the British Sociological Review Vol. VI 1913.) Because it is as a 'proof of the perfect unity of body and soul' between husband and wife and of 'devotion beyond the grave', because it embodied the ideal of wifehood, which is well expressed by Uma when she said, 'Devotion to her Lord is woman's honour, it is her eternal heaven. And O Maheshwara,' she adds with a most touching human cry, 'I desire not paradise itself if thou art not satisfied with me!' Why compulsory widowhood is honoured, I know not, nor have I yet met with anyone who sang in praise of it, though there are a great many who adhere to it. The eulogy in honour of girl marriage is reported by Dr. Ketkar to be as follows. 'A faithful man or woman ought not to feel affection for a woman or a man other than the one with whom he or she is united. Such purity is compulsory not only after marriage but even before marriage, for that is the only correct ideal of chastity. No maiden could be considered pure if she feels love for a man other than to whom she might get married. As she does not know whom she is going to get married to, she must not feel affection for any man at all before marriage. If she does so, it is a sin. So a girl should know whom she has to love before any sexual consciousness has been awakened in her'. Hence, girl marriage."

"This high-flown and ingenious sophistry indicates why these institutions were honoured but does not tell us why they were practised. My own interpretation is that they were honoured because they were practised. Anyone slightly acquainted with, the rise of individualism in the 18th century will appreciate my remark. At all times, it is the movement that is most important, and the philosophies grow around it long afterwards to justify it and give it a moral support. In like manner, I urge that the very fact that these customs were so highly eulogized proves that they needed eulogy for their prevalence. Regarding the question of why they arose, I submit that they were needed to create the structure of caste, and the philosophies in honour of them were intended to popularize them or to gild the pill, as we might say, for they must have been so abominable and shocking to the sense of the unsophisticated that they needed a great deal of sweetening. These customs are essentially of the nature of means, though they are represented as ideals. But this should not blind us from understanding the results that flow from them. One might safely say that the idealization of means is necessary and, in this particular case, was perhaps motivated to endow them with greater efficacy. Calling means an end does not harm, except that it disguises its real character, but it does not deprive it of its real nature, that of a means. You may pass a law that all cats are dogs, just as you can call a means to an end. But you can no more change the nature of means thereby than you can turn cats into dogs. Consequently I am justified in holding that, regarding them as ends or as means. *Sati*, enforced widowhood, and girl marriage are customs that were primarily intended to solve the problem of the surplus man and surplus woman in a caste and to maintain its endogamy. Strict endogamy could not be preserved without these customs, while caste without endogamy is fake." In my view, girl marriage enforced widowhood, and *Sati* practice had no other purpose than supporting the caste system, which Brahmanism was seeking to establish by prohibiting intermarriage. It is difficult to stop intermarriage. Members of different castes are likely to go out of their caste either for love or for necessity. It is to provide against necessity that Brahmanism made these rules. This is my explanation of these new rules made by Brahmanism. That explanation may not be acceptable to all. However, there can be no doubt that Brahmanism was taking all means possible to prevent intermarriages between the different classes.

Another illustration of this desire on the part of Brahmanism is found in the rule regarding excommunication promulgated by Manu.

Manu says that a person excommunicated by his caste is an outcast. According to Manu, an outcast is to be treated as though he was actually dead. Manu ordains that his obsequies should be performed and lays down the mode and manner of performing these obsequies of the outcast.

XI. 183. The *Sapindas* and *Samanodakas* of an outcast must offer a libation of water to him, as if he were dead outside the village, on an inauspicious day, in the evening and in the presence of the relatives, officiating priests, and teachers.

XI. 184. A female slave shall upset with her foot a pot filled with water as if it were for a dead person his *Sapindas* and the *Samanodakas* shall be impure for a day and a night.

Manu, however, allows the outcast to return to caste on performing penance, as will be seen from the following rules:

XI. 187. But when he has performed his penance, they shall bathe with him in a holy pool and throw down a new pot filled with water.

XI. 188. But he shall throw that pot into water, enter his house, and perform, as before, all the duties incumbent on a relative.

XI. 189. Let him follow the same rule in the case of female outcasts, but clothes, food, and drink shall be given to them, and they shall live close to the family house.

But if the outcast was recalcitrant and impenitent, Manu provides for his punishment.

Manu will not allow the outcast to live in the family house. Manu enjoins that:

XI. 189 Clothes, food, and drink shall be given to them, i.e., the outcast members of the family, and they shall live close to the family house.

III. 92. Let him, i.e., the householder gently place on the ground some food for dogs, outcasts, chandals, those afflicted with diseases that are punishments for former sins, crows, and insects.

Manu declares that having social intercourse with an outcast is a sin. He warns the Snataka:

IV. 79. Not to stay together with outcasts.

IV. 213. Not to eat food given by outcasts.

To the householder, Manu says:

III. 151. Let him, i.e., the householder not entertain an outcast at a Shradha.

III. 157. A person who forsakes his mother, his father, or a teacher without an adequate reason, or he who has contracted an alliance with outcasts either through the Vedas or through a marriage.

Manu ordains a social boycott of the outcast by penalizing those who associate with him:

XI. 181. He who associates himself for one year with an outcast himself becomes an outcast, not by sacrificing, reading the Vedas, or contracting affinity with him, since by those acts he loses his class immediately, but even by using the same carriage or seat, or by taking his food at the same board.

XII. 182. He who associates with any of those outcasts must perform, to atone for such intercourse, the penance prescribed for that sinner.

Then, there are penalties against an outcast who defies his caste and chooses to remain an outcast. Manu tells him what will be his penalty in the next world.

XIII. 60. He who has associated with outcasts will become *Brahmarakshas*, i.e., an evil spirit. Manu, however, was not prepared to leave the outcast with just this. He proceeds to enact penalties, the severity of which cannot be doubted. The following are the penal sections of *Manusmriti* against an outcast.

III. 150. Those Brahmins who are outcasts or atheists are unworthy to partake of oblations to the gods and manes.

IX. 201. An outcast receives no share in inheritance.

XI. 185. But thenceforward, i.e. after the obsequies of the outcast have been performed it shall be forbidden to converse with him, to sit with him, to give him a share of the inheritance, and to hold with him such intercourse as is usual among men.

XI. 186. And if the outcast is the eldest his right of primogeniture shall be withheld, as well as the additional share due to the eldest son; in his stead, a younger brother excelling in virtue i.e., one who observes the rule of caste shall obtain the share of the eldest.

Such is the law of Manu against an outcast. The severity of the penalties prescribed against him is quite obvious. Its effect is to exclude him from all social intercourse, to suspend him from every civil function, to disqualify him for all offices, and to disable him from inheriting any property. Under these pains and penalties, the outcast might as well be dead, which indeed Manu considers him to be, directing libations to be offered to the manes as though he had died naturally. This system of privations and mortifications was enforced by prescribing a similar fate to anyone who endeavoured to associate with an outcast. The penalty was not confined to the outcast, nor was it restricted to males. Males and females were both subject to the law of the outcast. Even their progeny was subject to penalty. The law was extended to the son of the outcast. Born before excommunication, the son was entitled to inherit immediately, as though his father were dead. Born after excommunication, he lost his right to inherit, i.e., he became an outcast along with his father.

The laws of Manu regarding the outcast are, of course, devoid of justice and humanity. Some might think that there is nothing very strange about them. That is because these laws are very similar to the laws against apostasy and heresy found in all religious codes. It is, unfortunately, a fact that religions—except Buddhism—have used or misued the laws of inheritance to enforce adhesion and conformity to their codes. The conversion of a Christian to Judaism, paganism, or any other religion was punished by the Emperors Constantine and Julian.

Theodosius and Valentinian added capital punishment, in cases where the Emperors endeavoured to pervert others to the same inequity. This was apopted by all the European countries', which maintained a similar system of penalties to enforce the Christian faith.

Such a view of the law of the outcast would be quite superficial. First of all, the outcast is a creation of Brahmanism. It is a necessary coefficient of caste. Indeed, once Brahmanism was determined to create the caste system, the law against the outcast became essential. It is only by punishing the outcast that the caste system can be maintained. Secondly, there is a difference between the Christian or Mohammedan law of apostasy and the Brahmanic law of caste. The disqualification under the Christian or Mohammedan law of apostasy was restricted to the want of religious belief or the profession of wrong religious belief. Under the Brahmanic law, the disqualification had no connection with belief or lack of belief. It was connected with the sanctity of a certain form of social organization, namely caste. It is an act of going out of one's caste that was made punishable. It is a very important difference.

The Brahmanic law of the outcast, as compared with the law of apostasy in other religions, shows that a belief in God is not essential to Brahmanism; that a belief in life after death is not essential to Brahmanism; that a belief in salvation either by good deeds or by a belief in a prophet is not essential to Brahmanism; and that a belief in the sacredness of the Vedas is essential to Brahmanism. It is only thing essential to Brahmanism, for it is only the breach of caste that is penalized. All else is left to violation.

Those who are not blind to these forces of integration will admit that this act of Brahmanism in prohibiting intermarriage and interdining is nothing short of a complete dismemberment of society. It is a death knell to unity, an effective bar to united action. As will be shown hereafter, Brahmanism was keen on preventing united action by non-Brahmins to overthrow Brahmanism, and that is why Brahmanism brought about this segmentation of Indian society. But the fatal effects of a poison can never be confined to the limits of the original intention of the perpetrator. The same thing has happened in the case of caste. Brahmanism intended to paralyse the non-Brahmins for action against Brahmins, it did not design that they, as a nation, should be paralysed for action against a foreign nation. But the result of the poison of caste has been they have become stricken for action against Brahmanism as well as against foreigners. In other words, Brahmanism, in instituting caste system, has put the greatest impediment to the growth of nationalism.

It is Despite of what others say, the Hindu will not admit that there is anything evil in the caste system, and from one point of view, he is right. There is love, unity, and mutual aid among family members. There is honour among thieves. A band of robbers has common interests concerning its members. Gangs are marked by fraternal feelings and intense loyalty to their ends, however opposed they may be to the other gangs. Following this up, one can say that a caste has all the praiseworthy characteristics which a society is supposed to have.

It has the virtues of a family since there is love, unity, and mutual aid. It has the honour known to prevail among thieves. It has the loyalty and fraternal feeling we encounter in gangs, and it also possesses that sense of common interests found among robbers.

A Hindu may take satisfaction in these praiseworthy characteristics of the caste and deny that there is anything evil in it. But he forgets that his thesis, that caste is an ideal form of social organization is supportable on the supposition that each caste is entitled to regard itself as an independent society, as an end in itself—as nations do. However, the theory breaks down when the consideration pertains to Hindu society and to the caste-system that goes with it.

Even in such a consideration of the subject, the Hindu will not admit that the caste system is evil. Charge Hinduism with the responsibility for the evils of the caste system, and the Hindu will at once retort, "What about the class system in Europe?" Up to a point, the retort is valid if it means that there exists nowhere an ideal society, as envisioned by philosophers, marked by organic unity, accompanied by praiseworthy community of purpose, mutuality of sympathy, loyalty to public ends and concern for general welfare. Nobody can have many quarrels if the Hindu, by way of analogy, were to say that in every society, there are families and classes marked by exclusiveness, suspicion, and jealousy toward outsiders: bands of robbers, gangs, narrow cliques, trade unions, Employees' Associations, Cartels. Chambers of Commerce, and political parties. Some of these are held together by interest and plunder, and others, while aspiring to serve the public, do not hesitate to prey upon it.

It may be conceded that everywhere, *di facto* society, whether in the past or present, is not a single whole but a collection of small groups devoted to diverse purposes as their immediate and particular objectives. But the Hindu cannot take shelter under this analogy between the Hindu caste system and the non-Hindu class system and rest there as though there is nothing more to be said about the subject. The fact is there is, a far bigger question that the Hindu still has to face. He must take note of the fact that although every society consists of groups, there are societies in which the groups are only non-social, while there are societies in which the groups are anti-social. The difference between a society with a class system and a society with a caste system lies just in this: the class system is merely non-social but the caste system is positively anti-soicial.

It may be important to realise why, in some societies, the group system produces only non-social feelings while in other the group system produces anti-social feelings. No better explanation of this difference can be given than the one provided by Professor John Dewey. According to him, everything depends on whether the groups are isolated or associated, whether there is reciprocity of interest between them or whether there is a lack of reciprocity of interest. If the groups are associated, if there is a reciprocity of interest between them the feeling between them will be non-social. If the groups are isolated, if there is no reciprocity between them, the feeling between them will be anti-social. To quote Professor Dewey:

"The isolation and exclusiveness of a gang or clique brings its anti-social spirit into relief. But this same spirit is found wherever one group has interests 'of its own', which shut it out from full interaction with other groups, so that its prevailing purpose is the protection of what it has got, instead of reorganization and progress through wider relationships. It marks nations in their isolation from one another, families which seclude their domestic concerns as if they had no connection with a larger life schools when separated from the interest of home and community and the divisions of rich and poor, learned and unlearned. The essential point is that isolation makes for rigidity and formal institutionalizing of life, for static and selfish ideals within the group."

The question to be asked is not whether there are groups in a society or whether the society is one single whole. The question to be asked is what degree of association, cooperative intercourse, and interaction exists among the different groups: how numerous and varied are the interests consciously shared by them, and how full and free is the interplay with other forms of association? A society is not to be condemned as body simply because there are groups in it. It is to be condemned if the groups are isolated, each leading an exclusive life of its own, because it is this isolation that produces the anti-social spirit, which makes cooperative effort so difficult to achieve.

This isolation among the classes is the work of Brahmanism. The principal steps taken were to abrogate the system of intermarriage and interdining that was prevalent among the four *Varnas* in olden times. It has already been discussed in an earlier section of this chapter. There is, however, one part of the story that remains to be told. I have said that *Varna* system had nothing to do with marriage. Males and females belonging to different *Varnas* could marry and did marry. Law did not come in the way of *inter-Varna* marriage. Social morality was not opposed to such marriages. Savarna marriage was neither required by law nor demanded by society. All marriages between different *Varnas,* irrespective of whether the bride was of a higher *Varna* than the bridegroom or whether the bridegroom was of the higher *Varna* and the bride of a lower *Varna*, were valid. Indeed, as Prof. Kane says, the distinction between *Anuloma* and *Pratiloma* marriage was quite unknown, and even the terms *Anuloma* and *Pratiloma* were not in existence. They are the creation of Brahmanism. Brahmanism put a stop to *Pratiloma* marriages, i.e., marriages between women of a higher *Varna* and men of a lower *Varna.* That was a step in the direction of closing the connection between the *Varnas* and creating in them an exclusive and anti-social spirit regarding one another. However, while the interconnecting gate of *Pratiloma* marriage was closed, the interconnecting gate of *Anuloma* marriage remained open. That was not closed. As pointed out in the section on graded inequality, *Anuloma* marriage, i.e., marriage between a male of the higher Varna and the female of the lower *Varna*, was allowed by Brahmanism to continue. The gate of *Anuloma* marriage was not very respectable and was a one-way gate only, but still, it was an interconnecting gate by which it was possible to prevent a complete isolation of the *Varnas*. However, even here, Brahmanism played what cannot help but be called a dirty trick. To show how dirty the trick was, it is necessary first to state the rules that prevailed for determining the status of the child. Under the rule existing from very ancient times, the status of the child was determined by the *Varna* of the father. The *Varna* of the mother was quite unimportant. The following illustrations will place the point beyond doubt:

	Father's Name	Varna of Father	Mother's Name	Varna of Mother	Child's Name	Varna of Child
1.	Shantanu	Kshatriya	Ganga	Shudra	Bhishma	Kshatriya
			(Anamik)			
2.	Shantanu	Kshatriya	Matsyagandha	Shudra (Fisher)	Vichitra Virya	Kshatriya
3.	Parashar	Brahmin	Matsyagandha	Shudra (Fisher)	Krishna-Dwaipayana	Brahmin
4.	Vishwamitra	Kshatriya	Menaka	Apsara	Shakuntala	Kshatriya
5.	Yayati	Kshatriya	Devayani	Brahmin	Yadu	Kshatriya
6.	Yayati	Kshatriya	Sharmishta	Asuri (Non-Aryan)	Druhya	Kshatriya
7.	Jaratkaru	Brahmin	Jaratkari	Nag. (Non-Aryan)	Asita	Brahmin

The rule was known as the rule of *Pitra Savarnya*. It would be interesting to consider the effect of this rule of *Pitra Savarnya* on the *Anuloma* and *Pratiloma* marriage systems.

The effect on *Pratiloma* marriage would be that the children of mothers of the higher *Varnas* would be dragged down to the level of the lower *Varnas* represented by their fathers. Its effect on *Anuloma* marriage would be just the contrary. The children of mothers of the lower *Varnas* would be raised and absorbed into the higher *Varnas* of their fathers.

Manu stopped *Pratiloma* marriages and thereby prevented the higher from being dragged to the status of the lower. However, regrettably, not much damage was done by it so long as the *Anuloma* marriage and the rule of *Pitra Savarnya* continued in operation. The two together formed a very useful system. The *Anuloma* marriage maintained the interconnection, and the *Pitra Savarnya* rule made the higher classes quite composite in their make-up, for they could not help but be drawn from mothers of different *Varnas*. Brahmanism did not want to keep this gate of intercommunication between the *Varnas* open. It was bent on closing it. But it did so in a manner which is disreputable.

The straightforward and honourable way was to stop *Anuloma* marriage. But Brahmanism did not do that. It allowed the system of *Anuloma* marriage to continue. What it did was to alter the rule of determining the status of the child. It replaced the rule of Pitra Savarnya with the rule of *Matra Savarnya,* by which the status of the child came to be determined by the status of the mother. Through this change, marriage ceased to be the means of inter-social communication, which it is principally. It relieved men of the higher *Varna* from the responsibility to their children simply because they were, born of a mother of lower *Varna*. It made *Anuloma* marriage a mere matter of sex, a humiliation and insult to the lower *Varnas* and a privilege for the higher classes to lawfully commit prostitution with women of the lower classes. And from a larger social point of view, it brought about complete isolation among the *Varnas* which has been the bane of Hindu society. Not with standing all this, the orthodox Hindu still believes that the caste system is an ideal system.

But why talk about the orthodox Hindus. They are among the enlightened politicians and historians. There are, of course, Indians, both politicians and historians, who vehemently deny that the caste system comes in the way of nationalism. They presume that India is a nation and feel very much offended if anybody, instead of speaking of the Indian nation, speaks of the people of India. This attitude is quite understandable. Most of the politicians and historians are Brahmins. They cannot be expected to have the courage to expose the misdeeds of their ancestors or admit the evils perpetrated by them. Ask anyone the question, "is India a nation". And all, in a chorus, say, "yes." Ask for reasons, and they will say that India is a nation, firstly because India has a geographical unity and secondly because of the fundamental unity of the culture. All this may be admitted for the sake of argument and yet it is true to say that to draw an inference from these facts that India is a nation is really to cherish a delusion. For what is a nation? A nation is not a country in the physical sense of the country, whatever degree of geographical unity it may posses. A nation is not people synthesized by a common culture derived from common language, common religion, or common race.

To recall what I have said in another place: "Nationality is a subjective psychological feeling. It is a feeling of a corporate sentiment of oneness that makes those charged with it feel that they are kith and kin. This national feeling is double-edged. It is at once a feeling of fellowship for one's kith and an anti-fellowship feeling for those who are not one's kith. It is a feeling of 'consciousness of kind' which binds together those within the limits of the kindred and severs them from those outside the limits of the kindred. It is a longing to belong to one's own group and not to belong to another group. It is the essence of what is called nationality and national feeling. This longing to belong to one's own kindred, as I said, is a subjective psychological feeling, and what is important is to bear in mind that the longing to belong to one's own kindred ,is quite independent of geography, culture, economic, or social conflict.

There may be geographical unity, yet there may be no 'longing to belong'. There may be no geographical unity, yet the feeling of 'longing to belong' may be very intense. There may be cultural unity, yet there may be no 'longing to belong'. There may be economical conflicts and class divisions, yet there may be an intense feeling of 'longing to belong'. The point is that nationality is not primarily a matter of geography, culture or."

In the declining days of the Vedic regime, the Shudras and women had come to occupy a very low position. The rising tide of Buddhism had brought about a great change in the status of both. To put it briefly, a Shudra under the Buddhist regime could acquire property, learn, and even become a king. Nay, he could even rise to the highest rung of the social ladder occupied by the Brahmin in the Vedic regime. The Buddhist order of Bhikshus was the counterpart of the Vedic order of Brahmins. The two orders, each within its own religious system, were on par in the matter of status and dignity. The Shudra could never aspire to be a Brahmin in the Vedic regime, but he could become a Bhikshu and occupy the same status and dignity as the Brahmin. For, while the Vedic order of Brahmins was closed to the Shudra, the Buddhist order of Bhikshus was open to him, and many Shudras who could not become Brahmins under the Vedic regime had become their peers by becoming Bhikshus under Buddhism. A similar change is noticeable in the case of women. Under the Buddhist regime, she became a free person. Marriage did not make her a slave, for marriage under Buddhist rule was a contract. Under the Buddhist regime, she could acquire property, learn, and all that was unique, she could become a member of the Buddhist order of Nuns and reach the same status and dignity as a Brahmin. The elevation of the status of the Shudras and women was the result of the gospel of Buddhism that Buddhism was called by its enemies as the Shudra religion, i.e. the religion of the low classes.

All this, of course, must have been very galling to the Brahmins. How very galling it must have been to them is shown by the Vandalic fury with which Brahmanism, after it triumphed over Buddhism proceeded to bring about a complete demolition of the high status to which the Shudras and women had been elevated by the revolutionary changes effected by the vivifying gospel of Buddhism.

Starting with this background, one shudders at the inhumanity and cruelty of the laws made by Manu against the Shudras. I quote a few of them, assembling them under certain general heads.

Manu asks the householders of the Brahmin, Kshatriya, and Vaishya class:

IV. 61. Let him not dwell in a country where the rulers are Shudras.

It cannot mean that Brahmin. Kshatriya and Vaishya should leave the country where the Shudra is a ruler. It can only mean that if a Shudra becomes a king, he should be killed. Not only is a

Shudra not to be recognised fitting to be a king, but he is also not to be deemed a respectable person. For Manu enacts that:

XI. 24. A Brahmin shall never beg from a Shudra property for performing a sacrifice, i.e., for religious purposes. All marriage ties with the Shudra were proscribed. A marriage with a woman belonging to any of the three higher classes was forbidden. A Shudra was not to have any connection with a woman of the higher classes, and an act of adultery committed by a Shudra with her was declared by Manu to be an offence involving capital punishment.

VIII. 374. A Shudra who has intercourse with a woman of the higher caste, guarded or unguarded, shall be punished in the following manner: if she was unguarded, he loses the offending part, and if she was guarded, then he should be put to death and his property confiscated.

Manu insists that a Shudra shall be servile, unfit for office, without education, without property, and as a contemptible person, his person and property shall always be liable to conscription. As to office, Manu prescribes:

VIII. 20. A Brahmin who is only a Brahmin by descent, i.e., one has neither studied nor performed any other act required by the Vedas, may, at the king's pleasure, interpret the law to him, i.e., act as the judge, but never a Shudra (however learned he may be).

VIII. 21. The kingdom of that monarch who looks on while a Shudra settles the law will sink low, like a cow in a morass.

VIII. 272. If a Shudra arrogantly presumes to preach religion to Brahmins, the king shall have burning oil poured in his mouth and ears.

In olden times, the study of the Vedas stood for education. Manu declares that the study of the Vedas was not a matter of right but a matter of privilege. Manu deprived the Shudras of the right to study *Vedas*. He made it a privilege for the three higher classes.

Not only did he debar the Shudras from the study of the Vedas, but he enacted penalties against those who might help the Shudras to acquire the knowledge of the Vedas. To a person who is privileged to study the Vedas, Manu ordains that:

IV. 99. He must never read the Vedas ... in the presence of the Shudras.

Manu prescribes that:

III. 156. He who instructs Shudra pupils and he whose teacher is a Shudra shall become disqualified tor being invited to Shradha.

Manu's successors went much beyond him in the cruelty of their punishment of the Shudra for studying the Vedas. For instance, Katyayana lays down that if a Shudra overheard the Vedas or ventured to utter a word of the Vedas, the king shall cut his tongue in twain and put hot molten lead in his ears.

As to property, Manu is both ruthless and shameless towards Shudras. According to the Code of Manu:

X. 129. No superfluous collection of wealth must be made by a Shudra, even though he has power to make it since a servile man who has amassed riches becomes proud and, by his insolence or neglect, gives pain to Brahmins.

The reason for the rule is more revolting than the rule itself. Manu was, of course, not sure that the prohibitory injunction would be enough to prevent the Shudra from acquiring wealth. To leave no room for the Shudra offend to the Brahmins by his accumulation of wealth, Manu added another section to his Code whereby he declared that:

VIII. 417. A Brahmin may seize, without hesitation, if he is distressed for his subsistence, the goods of his Shudra. Not only is the property of a Shudra liable to conscription but the labour of the Shudra, Manu declares, is liable to conscription. Compare the following provision in *Manusmriti*:

VIII. 413. A Brahmin may compel a Shudra, whether bought or unbought, to do servile work because he is created by the Creator to be the slave of a Brahmin.

A Shudra was required by Manu to be servile in his speech. How very servile he must be can be seen from the following provisions in *Manusmriti*:

VIII. 270. A Shudra who insults a twice-born man with gross invective shall have his tongue cut out because he is of low origin.

VIII. 271. If he mentions the names and castes of the twice-born with contumely, an iron nail, ten fingers long, shall be thrust red hot into his mouth.

Manu's objective was to make the Shudra not merely a servile person but an altogether contemptible person. Manu will not even allow a Shudra the comfort of having a high-sounding name. Had Manu not been there to furnish incontrovertible proof, it would be difficult to believe that Brahmanism could have been so relentless and pitiless in its persecution of the Shudra. Observe Manu's law regarding the names that the different classes can give to their children:

II. 31. Let the first part of a Brahmin's name denote something auspicious, a Kshatriya's be connected with power, and a Vaishya's with wealth, but a Shudra's shuld express something contemptible.

II. 32. The second part of a Brahmin's name shall be a word implying happiness, of a Kshatriya's a word implying protection, of a Vaishya's a term expressive of thriving, and of a Shudra's an expression denoting service.

The basis of all these inhuman laws is the theory enunciated by Manu regarding the Shudras. At the outset of his Code, Manu asserts it emphatically and without hesitation. He says:

I. 91. One occupation only that the Lord prescribed to the Shudra is to serve meekly these other three castes, namely Brahmin, Kshatriya, and Vaishya.

Holding that the Shudra was born to be servile, Manu made his laws accordingly to compel him to remain servile throughout his life. In the Buddhist regime, a Shudra could aspire to be a judge, a priest and even a king—the highest status one could ever aspire to. Compare with this ideal that Manu places before the Shudra, and one can get an idea of what his fate was to be under Brahmanism:

X. 121. If a Shudra, unable to subsist by serving Brahmins, seeks a livelihood by serving Kshartiyas or he may also seek to maintain himself by attending a wealthy Vaishya.

X. 122. But let a Shudra serve Brahmins, either for the sake of heaven or with a view to this life and the next. For he who is called the servant of a Brahmin thereby gains all his ends.

X. 123. The service of Brahmins alone is declared (to be) an excellent occupation for a Shudra. For whatever else besides this he may perform will bear him no fruit.

X. 124. They must allot to him, out of their own family property suitable maintenance after considering his ability, his industry, and the number of those whom he is bound to support.

X. 125. The remnants of their food must be given to him, along with their old household furniture.

Manu can hardly be said to be more tender to women than he was to the Shudras. He starts with a low opinion of women. Manu proclaims:

II. 213. It is the nature of women to seduce men in this world. For that reason, the wise men are never unguarded in the company of females.

II. 214. For women can lead astray in this world not only a fool, but even a learned man, and can make him a slave of desire and anger.

II. 215. One should not sit in a lonely place with one's mother sister, or daughter. For the senses are powerful, and master even a learned man.

IX. 14. Women do not care for beauty, nor is their attention fixed on age. Thinking, 'It is enough that he is a man', they give themselves to the handsome and the ugly alike.

IX. 15. Through their passion for men, through their mutable temper, through their natural heartlessness, women become disloyal towards their husbands, however carefully they may be guarded in this world.

IX. 16. Knowing their disposition, which the Lord of Creatures laid in them at creation, to be such, every man should most strenuously exert himself to guard them.

IX. 17. When creating them Manu, allotted to women a love of their bed, of their seat, and of ornament, impure desires, wrath, dishonesty, malice, and bad conduct.

The laws of Manu against women are consistent with this view. Women are not to be independent under any circumstances. In the opinion of Manu:

IX. 2. Day and night, women must be kept in dependence by the males of their families, and, if they attach themselves to sensual enjoyments, they must be kept under one's control.

IX. 3. Her father protects her in childhood, her husband protects her in youth, and her sons protect her in old age: a woman is never fit for independence.

IX. 5. Women must especially be guarded against evil inclinations, however trifling they may appear. For, if they are not guarded, they will bring sorrow to two families.

IX. 6. Considering that the highest duty of all castes, even weak husbands must strive to guard their wives.

V. 147. By a girl, by a young woman, or even by an aged one, nothing must be done independently, even in her own house.

V. 148. In childhood, a female must be subject to her father, in youth to her husband, when her lord is dead to her sons: a woman must never be independent.

V. 149. She must not seek to separate herself from her father, husband, or sons; by leaving them, she would make both (her own and her husband's) families contemptible. Women do not have a right to divorce.

IX. 45. The husband is declared to be one with the wife, indicating that there could be no separation once a woman is married. Many Hindus stop here as though this is the whole story regarding Manu's law of divorce and keep on idolizing it by comforting their conscience by holding on to the view that Manu regarded marriage as a sacrament and, therefore, did not allow divorce. This, of course, is far from the truth. His law against divorce had a very different motive. It was not to tie up a man to a woman, but it was to tie up the woman to a man and to leave the man free. Manu does not prevent a man from giving up his wife. Indeed, he not only allows him to abandon his wife but also permits him to sell her. But what he does is to prevent the wife from becoming free. See what Manu Says:

IX. 46. Neither by sale nor by repudiation is a wife released from her husband.

The meaning is that a wife, sold or repudiated by her husband, can never become the legitimate wife of another who may have bought or received her after she was repudiated. If this is not monstrous, nothing can be. But Manu was not worried by considerations of justice or injustice of his laws. He wanted to deprive women of the freedom they had under the Buddhist regime.

He knew, by their misuse of their liberty, by their willingness to marry the Shudras, that the system of the gradation of the *Varna* had been destroyed. Manu was outraged by her license and in putting a stop to it, he deprived women of their was liberty.

Manu reduced the wife to the same level of a slave in the matter of property.

IX. 146. A wife, a son, and a slave, these three are declared to have no property—the wealth which they earn is acquired for him to whom they belong.

When a woman becomes a widow, Manu allows her maintenance if her husband was joint and a widow's estate in the property of her husband if he was separate from his family. But Manu never allows her to have any dominion over property.

A woman under the laws of Manu is subject to corporal punishment, and Manu allows the husband the right to beat his wife.

VIII. 299. A wife, a son, a slave, a pupil, and a younger brother of the full blood who has committed faults may be beaten with a rope or Manu bamboo stick.

In other matters, reduced women to the same position as the Shudras.

The study of the Vedas was forbidden to women by Manu as it was to the Shudras.

II. 66. Even for a woman, the performance of the *Sanskaras* is necessary and should be performed. But they should be performed without uttering the *Veda Mantras*.

IX. 18. Women have no right to study the Vedas. That is why their *Sanskars* are performed without *Veda Mantras*. Women do not know about religion because they have no right to know the Vedas. The uttering of the *Veda Mantras* is useful for removing sin. As women cannot utter the *Veda Mantras*, they are as unclean as untruth is.

Offering sacrifices, according to Brahmanism formed the very soul of religion. Yet, Manu will not allow women to perform them. Manu ordains that:

XI. 36. A woman shall not perform the daily sacrifices prescribed by the Vedas.

XI. 37. If she does, she will go to hell.

To disable her from performing such sacrifices, Manu prevents her from getting the aid and services of a Brahmin priest.

IV. 205. A Brahmin must never eat food given at a sacrifice performed by a woman.

V. 206. Sacrifices performed by women are inauspicious and not acceptable to God. They should, therefore, be avoided. A woman was not to have any intellectual pursuits, free will, or freedom of thought. She was not to join any heretical sect such as Buddhism. If she continued to adhere to it till death she was not to be given the libation of water, as is done in the case of all the dead.

Finally, a word regarding the ideal of life that Manu has sought to place before a woman. It is better stated in his own words:

V. 151. Him to whom her father may give her, or her brother with the father's permission, she shall obey as long as he lives, and when he is dead, she must not insult his memory.

V. 154. Though destitute of virtue, or seeking pleasure elsewhere, or devoid of good qualities, a husband must be constantly worshipped as a god by a faithful wife.

V. 155. No sacrifice, no vow, no fast must be performed by women, apart from their husbands; if a wife obeys her husband, she will, for that reason alone, be exalted in heaven. Then comes the choicest texts, which forms the pith and marrow of this ideal that Manu prescribes for women:

V. 153. The husband who wedded her with sacred *Mantras* is always a source of happiness to his wife, both in and out of season, in this world and the next.

X. 150. She must always be cheerful, clever in the management of her household affairs, careful in cleaning her utensils, and economical in expenditure.

The Hindus regard this as a very lofty ideal for a woman! The severity of these laws against Shudras and women shows that the phenomenal rise of these classes during the Buddhist regime not only offended the Brahmins but became intolerable to them. It was a complete reversal of their sacred social order—from top to bottom. The first had become last, and the last had become first. The laws of Manu also explain the determined way in which the Brahmins proceeded to use their political power to degrade the Shudras and women back to their old status. The triumphant Brahmanism began its onslaught on both the Shudras and women in pursuit of the old ideal of servility, and Brahmanism did succeed in making the Shudras and women the servile classes—Shudras, the serfs to the three higher classes, and women, the serfs to their husbands. Of the black deeds committed by Brahmanism, after it triumphs over Buddhism, this one is the blackest. There is no parallel in history for such foul deeds of degradation committed by a class of usurpers in the interest of class domination. The colossal character of this deed of degradation perpetrated by Brahmanism is unfortunately not fully realised. It is concealed by those small monosyllablic words, *Stri* and Shudra. Let those who wish to get an idea of the enormity of this deed think of the numbers behind these two terms. What part of the population do they apply to? Women represents one-half of the population. Of the balance, the Shudra represents not less than two-thirds. Together, they make up about 75% of the total population. It is this huge mass of people that has been doomed by Brahmanism to eternal servility and eternal degradation. It is because of the colossal scale of degradation, whereby 75% of her people were deprived of their right to life, liberty and pursuit of happiness, that India became a decaying if not a dead, nation.

The principle of graded inequality runs through the whole of the *Manusmriti*. There is no department of life in which Manu has not introduced this principle of graded inequality. To provide a complete and thorough exposition, it would be necessary to reproduce the entirety of *Manusmriti*. I will take only a few departments to illustrate how, in the hands of Manu, the principle of graded inequality became embedded in the social life. Take the field of marriage, for instance. Observe the rule of Manu:

III. 13. It is declared that a Shudra woman alone can be the wife of a Shudra. She, along with a woman can be of his own caste, of a Vaishya. Those two, along with a woman of his own caste, the wives of a Kshatriya. Those three, of his own caste, wives of a Brahmin.

Now, take the rules of Manu regarding the treatment of guests:

III. 110. But a Kshatriya who comes to the house of a Brahmin is not considered a guest (*Atithi*), nor a Vaisya, nor a Shudra, nor a personal friend, nor a relative, nor even the teacher.

III. 111. But a Kshatriya comes to the house of a Brahmin as a guest, the householder may feed him according to his desire after Brahmins have eaten.

III. 112. Even a Vaishya and a Shudra who have approached a Brahmin's house as a guest, he may be allowed to eat with his servants, thereby showing his compassionate disposition. In the house of a Brahmin. nobody except a Brahmin is to have the honour of being a guest. If the Kshatriya comes as a guest to the house of a Brahmin he is to be fed after all the Brahmins are fed, and if the Vaishyas and Shudras come as guests, they are to be fed after everybody else and only in the company of servants.

Take the rules of Manu regarding *Sanskaras*:

X. 126. A Shudra has no right to receive the sacraments.

X. 68. The law prescribes that neither of the two that is, those who belong to mixed castes, shall receive the sacraments—the first being excluded on account of the lowness of their and the second because the birth origin of his parents was against the order of the castes.

II. 66. The whole series of sacraments must be performed for females also to sanctify the body at the proper time and in the proper order, but without the recitaion of sacred Vedic Mantras.

Manu further lays down that:

VI. 1. A twice-born *Snataka*, who has thus lived according to the law in the order of householders, may, taking a firm resolution and keeping his organs in subjection, dwell in the forest, duly observing the rules given below.

VI. 33. Having thus passed the third part of a man's natural term of life in the forest, he may live as an ascetic during the fourth part of his existence after abandoning all attachment to worldly objects.

Even in law, Manu introduces the principle of graded inequality. To take only two illustrations, the laws of defamation, abuse, and assault:

VIII. 267. A Kshatriya, having defamed a Brahmin, shall be fined one hundred panas; a Vaishya, one hundred and fifty or two hundred panas; and a Shudra shall suffer corporal punishment.

VIII. 268. A Brahmin shall be fined fifty panas for defaming a Kshatriya; in the case of a Vaishya, the fine shall be twenty-five panas; in the case of a Shudra, twelve panas.

VIII. 269. For offences of twice-born men against those of equal caste (*Varna*), the fine shall also be twelve panas for speeches that ought not to be uttered, and every fine shall be double.

VIII. 276. For mutual abuse by a Brahmin and a Kshatriya, a fine must be imposed by a discerning king, with the Brahmin receiving the lowest amercement but the Kshatriya receiving the middlemost.

VIII. 277. A Vaishya and a Shudra must be punished exactly in the same manner according to their respective castes, but the tongue of the Shudra shall not be cut out: that is the decision.

VIII. 279. With whatever limb a man of a low caste does harm to a man of the three highest castes, even that limb shall be cut off: that is the teaching of Manu.

VIII. 280. He who raises his hand or a stick shall have his hand cut off; he who in anger kicks with his foot shall have his foot cut off.

Everywhere, the principle of graded inequality is evident. So it had become ingrained in the social system that the successors of Manu were careful to introduce it even where he had failed to give effect to it. For instance, Manu had recognised the system of slavery but failed to prescribe whether the system of slavery was subject to the principle of graded order of insubordination.

Lest it be misunderstood that the law of graded inequality did not apply to slavery and that a Brahmin could be a slave of the Shudra, Yajnavalkya immediately to cleard the doubt. He expressly laid down that:

"Slavery is in the descending order of the *Varnas* and not in the ascending order" (XIV. 183).

Vijnaneshwar, in his commentary on Yajnavalkya, makes this concept concrete with illustrations when he says:

"Of the *Varnas* such as the Brahmin and the rest, a state of slavery shall exist *Anulomyena,* in the descending order. Thus, of a Brahmin, a Kshatriya and the rest may become a slave; of a Kshatriya, the Vaishya and the Shudra; and of a Vaishya, the Shudra. Thus, the state of slavery shall operate in the descending order." Stated in the language of equality and inequality, this means that the Brahmin is the highest because he can be the slave of nobody but is entitled to keep a person of any class as his slave. The Shudra is the lowest because everybody can keep him as a slave, but he can keep no one as his slave except another Shudra. The place assigned to the Kshatriya and the Vaishya introduces the system of graded inequality. A Kshatriya, while being inferior to the Brahmin (as he can be a slave of the Brahmin), is superior to the Vaishya and the Shudra because he can keep them as his slaves. The Vaishyas and the Shudras have no right to keep a Kshartiya as their slave. Similarly, a Vaishya, while being inferior to the Brahmins and the Kshatriyas, (as they can keep him as a slave and he cannot keep any one of them as his slave), is proud that he is at least superior to the Shudra because he can keep the Shudra as his slave, whereas the Shudra cannot keep the Vaishya as his slave.

Such is the principle of graded inequality that Brahmanism injected into the very bone and marrow of the people. Nothing worse to paralyze society and overthrow of inequity could have been done.

Although its effects have not been clearly noticed, there can be no doubt that because of it, the Hindus have been stricken with palsy. Students of social organization have been content with noting the difference between equality and inequality. None have realised that, in addition to equality and inequality, there is such a thing as graded inequality. Yet inequality is not half so dangerous as graded inequality. Inequality carries within itself the seeds of its own destruction. Inequality does not last long. Under pure and simple inequality, two things happen. It creates general discontent which forms the seed of revolution. Secondly, it makes the sufferers combine against a common foe and on a common grievance. However, the nature and circumstances of the system of graded inequality leave no room for either of these two things to happen. The system of graded inequality prevents the rise of general discontent against inequity. It cannot, therefore, become the storm centre of revolution. Secondly, with sufferers under inequality becoming unequal both in terms of the benefit and the burden, there is no possibility of a general combination of all classes to overthrow the inequity. To make things concrete, the Brahmanic law of marriage is full of inequity. The right of a Brahmin to take a woman from the classes below him but not to give a woman to them is inequity. But the Kshatriya, Vaishya, and Shudra will not combine to destroy it. The Kshatriya resents this right of the Brahmin, but he will not combine with the Vaishya or the Shudra, and that for two reasons. Firstly, because he is satisfied that if the Brahmin has the right to take the women of three communities, the Kshatriya has the right to appropriate the women of two communities. He does not suffer as much as the other two. Secondly, if he joins in a general revolution against this marriage inequity, in one way, he will rise to the level of the Brahmins. However, in another way, all will be equal, which to him means that the Vaishyas and the Shudras will rise to his level they will claim Kshatriya women, which means he will fall to their level. That is, take any other inequity and think of a revolt against it. The same social psychology will show that a general rebellion against it is impossible.

One of the reasons why there has been no revolution against Brahmanism and its inequities is due entirely to the principle of graded inequality. It is a system of permitting a share in the spoils to enlist the support of others for the spoils system. It is a system full of low cunning that no man could have invented to perpetuate inequity and to profit by it. It is nothing else but inviting people to share in inequity so that they may all be supporters of inequity.

There now remains to lift the curtain from the last act of this drama of Brahmanism.

Brahmanism inherited from the Vedic past that system of *Chaturvarna*. The system of *Chaturvarna*, which the Hindus regard as the unique creation of their Aryan ancestors, is in no sense unique. There is nothing original about it. The whole ancient world had stumbled into it. The Egyptians had it, and the ancient Persians had it. Plato was so convinced about its excellence that he presented it as the ideal form of social organization. The idea of the *Chaturvarna* is faulty. The lumping together of individuals into a few sharply marked-off classes is a very superficial view of man and his powers. The Ancient Aryans, as well as Plato, had no conception of the uniqueness of every individual, of his incommensurability with others, and of each individual forming a class of his own. They had no recognition of the infinite diversity of active tendencies and combinations of tendencies of which an individual is capable. To them, there were types of faculties or powers in the individual constitution, and all that is necessary for social organization is to classify them. All this is demonstrably wrong. Modern science has shown that the lumping together of individuals into a few sharply marked-off classes, each confined to one particular sphere, does injustice both to the individual and society. The stratification of society by classes and occupations is incompatible with the fullest utilization of the qualities which is so necessary for social advancement. It is also incompatible with the safety and security of the individual and society in general.

There is another mistake which the ancient Hindus, including Plato, made. There is probably some truth in saying that there is among human beings a dimorphism or polyformism, as there is among insects. Although in the former, it is only psychological while, in the latter, it is both physical and psychological. But assuming that there is such a thing as psychological dimorphism or polyformism among human beings, it is wrong to separate them into those who are born to do one thing and others to do another—some born to command, i.e., to be masters, and some born to obey, i.e., to be slaves. It is wrong to suppose that in a given person, some qualities are present and others are absent. On the contrary, the truth is that all qualities are present in every person, and this truth is not diminished in any way by the fact that some tendency predominates to the extent of being the only one that is apparent. So well established is this truth that a tendency which may be dominant in a man at one time may be quite different from, and even the direct opposite of, the tendency that may be dominant at another time. As Prof. Bergson in speaking of the Nietzsche's false antithesis of 'men' and 'slaves', observes:

"We have a clear vision of this falsity in times of revolution. Unassuming citizens, up to that moment humble and obedient, wake up one fine day with pretentions to be leaders of men." The cases of Mussolini and Hitler are a complete disproof of the theory of the Aryans and Plato.

This Vedic system of *Chaturvarna*, far from being an ideal system, was made positively worse by the changes that Brahmanism made and which have already been described. Every one of these changes were mischievous in character; this is beyond question. The Buddhist order of Bhikshus and the Vedic order of Brahmins were designed to serve the same purpose. They formed the elite of their society whose function was to lead and guide society along the right road. Although designed to discharge the same function, the Buddhist Bhikshu was better placed to discharge it than the Brahmin. It is because Buddha recognised what nobody, either before him or after him, has done. Buddha realised that for a person to give a true lead to society and be its trustworthy guide, he must be intellectually free. Further, and more importantly, to be intellectually free, he must not have private property. An elite charged with the care of private property must fail to discharge his duty of leading and guiding society along the right road. Buddha, therefore, took care to include in the code of discipline for the Bhikshus a rule prohibiting a Bhikshu from holding private property. In the Vedic order of Brahmins, there was no such prohibition. A Brahmin was free to hold property. This difference produced a profound difference in the character and outlook of the Buddhist Bhikshu and the Vedic Brahmin. The Bhikshus formed an intellectual class whereas the Brahmins, on the other hand, merely formal an educated class. There is a great difference between an intellectual class and an educated class. An intellectual class has no limitations arising out of any affiliations to any class or interest. An educated class, on the other hand, is not an intellectual class, although it has cultivated its intellect. The reason is that its range of vision and its sympathy for a new ideology is circumscribed by its being identified with the interest of the class with which it is affiliated.

The Brahmins, from the very beginning, were inclined to be a purely educated class enlightened but selfish. This evil in the Vedic order of Brahmins was exacerbated by the changes made in the old Vedic System. The right of the Brahmins to rule and the grant of special privileges and immunities made them more selfish and induced in them the desire to use their education not for the advancement of learning but for the use of their community and against the advancement of society.

All their energy and their education have been spent on maintaining their privileges against the good of the public. Many Hindu authors have boasted that the civilization of India is the most ancient civilization in the world. They will insist that there was no branch of knowledge in which their ancestors were not the pioneers. Open a book like *The Positive Background of Hindu Sociology* by Prof. Benoy Kumar Sarkar, or a book like *The Positive Sciences of the Ancient Hindus* by Dr. Brajendranath Seal and one is overwhelmed with data touching upon the knowledge their ancestors had about various scientific subjects. From these books, it would appear that the ancient Indians knew astronomy, astrology, biology, chemistry, mathematics, medicine, mineralogy, physics, and, in the view of the masses even aviation. All this may be very true. The important question is not how the ancient Indians discovered these positive sciences. The important question is why the ancient Indians ceased to make any progress in the sciences in which they were the pioneers. This sudden arrest in the progress of science in ancient India is as astounding as it is deplorable. In the scientific world, India occupies a position which—even if it be first among the primitive—is certainly last among the civilized nation. How did it happen that a person who began the work of scientific progress stopped, halted on the way, and left in an inchoate and incomplete condition? This is a question that needs to be considered and answered, not what the ancient Indians knew.

There is only one answer to the question, and it is a very simple answer. In ancient India, the Brahmins were the only educated class. They were also the class that claimed to be above all others.

Buddha disputed their claim for supremacy and declared war on the Brahmins. The Brahmins acted as an educated class—as distinguished from an intellectual class—would act under the circumstances. They abandoned all pursuits and engaged themselves in defending their claim of supremacy and the social, economic, and political interests of their class. Instead of writing books on science, the Brahmins undertook to write *Smritis*. Here is an explanation why the progress of science in India became arrested: the Brahmins found it more imperative to write *Smritis* to repel the Buddhist doctrine of social equality.

How many *Smritis* did the Brahmins write? Mr. Kane, a great authority on *Smriti* literature, has computed their number to be 128. And what for? The Smritis are called lawbooks, which, of course, hide their, nature. They are really treatises expounding the supremacy of the Brahmins and their rights to special privileges. The defence of Brahmanism was more important than the progress of science. Brahmanism not only defended its privileges but set about extending them in a manner that would cover every decent man with shame. The Brahmins started particularly to expand the meaning of certain privileges granted to them by Manu.

Manu had given the Brahmins the right to *dana* (gift). The *dana* was always intended to be money or chattel. But over time, the concept of *dana* was expanded to include the gift of a woman whom a Brahmin could keep as his mistress or who could be released by the Brahmin on commutation for money payment.

Manu designated the Brahmins as Bhudevas, Lords of the Earth. The Brahmins enlarged the scope of this statement and began to claim the right to sexual intercourse with women of other classes. Even queens were not exempt from this claim. Ludovico di Varthema, who came to India as a traveller in about 1502 A.D., records the following about the Brahmins of Calicut:

"It is a proper, and at the same time pleasant, thing to know who these Brahmins are. You must know that they are the chief people of the faith, as priests are among us. And when the king takes a wife, he selects the most worthy and the most honoured of these Brahmins and makes him sleep the first night with his wife so that he may deflower her." Similarly, Hamilton another writer says:

"When the Zamorin marries, he must not cohabit with his bride until the Nambudiri Brahmin, or chief priest, has enjoyed her, and if he pleases, he may have three nights of her company because the first fruits of her nuptials must be an holy oblation to the god she worships."

In the Bombay Presidency, the priests of the Vaishnava sect claimed the right to deflower the women of their sect. It gave rise to the famous Maharaja Libel case brought by the chief priest of the sect against one Karsandas Mulji in the High Court of Bombay in the year 1869, which shows that the right to claim the benefit of the first night was certainly effective till then.

When such a right to sexual cohabitation for the first night could be extended against the generality of the lower classes, the Brahmins did not hesitate to extend it. This they did particularly in Malabar. There, Manu designated the Brahmins as Bhudevas, Lords of the Earth. The Brahmins enlarged the scope of this statement and began to claim the right of promiscuous sexual intercourse with the womenfolk of the other classes. It happened particularly in Malabar. There:

"The Brahmin castes follow the Makatyam system—the system by which the child belongs to its father's family. They contract within their own caste regular marriages, with all the ordinary legal and religious sanctions and incidents. But the Brahmin men are also in the habit of entering into Sambandham unions with women of the lower castes." This is not all. Observe further what the writer has to say:

"Neither party of a Sambandham union becomes thereby a member of the other family; and the offsprings of the union belong to their mother's *tharwad* (family) and have no sort of claim, so far as the law goes, to a share of their father's property or maintenance therefrom."

Speaking of the origin of this practice, the author of the *Gazetteer* observes that the origin of this institution:

"Is found in the claim of the Bhudevas or 'Earth Gods' (that the Brahmins) and on a lower plane of the Kshatriyas or the ruling classes, to the first fruits of lower Caste Womanhood, a right akin to the medieval droit de Seigneurie."

It is an understatement to say that it is only a right to first fruits as the 'right to the first night' was called in the Middle Ages in Europe. It is more than that. It is a general right of the Brahmin against the lower caste to claim any woman of that class for mere prostitution, for the mere satisfaction of sexual appetite, without burdening the Brahmin with any of the obligations of marriage.

Such were the rights which the Brahmins, the spiritual preceptors, claimed against the laity! The Borgese Popes have been run down in history as the most debauched race of spiritual preceptors who ascended the throne of Peter. One wonders whether they were really worse than the Brahmins of India.

A purely intellectual class, free to consider general good and having no interest of a class to consider, such as the one contemplated by Buddha, is not to be found anywhere. Limitations resulting from the property on the freedom of intellect of the elite have not been generally recognised until very recently. But this want of an intellectual class has been made good in other countries by the fact that in those countries, each strata of society has its educated class. There is safety, if not definite guidance, in the multiplicity of views expressed by different educated classes drawn from different strata of society. In such a multiplicity of views, there is no danger of society being misguided or misdirected by the views of one single, educated class drawn from one single class of society, which is naturally bound to place the interests of its class before the interests of the country. By the changes made by Brahmanism, India ceased to have the safe and sure guidance of an intellectual class. But what is worse is that the Hindus lost the safety and security which other peoples have, which arises from the multiplicity of views expressed by various educated classes drawn from different strata of society.

By the denial of education to the Shudras, by diverting the Kshatriyas to military persuits and the Vaishyas to trade, and by reserving education to themselves, the Brahmins alone could become the educated class—free to misdirect and misguide the whole society. By converting *Varna* into caste, they declared that mere birth was a real and final measure of the worth of a man. Caste and graded inequality made disunity and discord a matter of course.

All this disfigurement of the original *Varna* system would have been tolerable if it had remained a mere matter of social practice. But Brahmanism was not content to leave the matter there. It wanted to give the *Chaturvarna* to its changed and perverted form the force of law. This new *Chaturvarna*, the making of Brahmanism, occupies in the *Manusmriti* as the Law of People and the Law of Family. Nobody can mistake it. Manu made it an offence for a person of a lower caste to arrogate to himself the status of a higher caste or to pass off as a member of the higher caste.

X. 96. A man of low caste who, through covetousness, lives by the occupations of a higher one, the king shall deprive of his property and banish.

XI. 56. Falsely attributing to oneself high birth, giving information to the king regarding a crime, and falsely accusing one's teacher are offences equal to slaying a Brahmin.

Here, there are two offences: general impersonation (X. 96) and impersonation by the Shudra (XI. 56). Note also how severe the punishments are. For the first, the punishment is confiscation of property and banishment. For the second, the punishment is the same as the punishment for causing the death of a Brahmin.

The offence of personation is not unknown in modern jurisprudence, and the Indian Penal Code recognises it in Section

419. But what is the punishment the Indian Penal Code prescribes for cheating by personation? A fine, and, if imprisonment, then three years or both. Manu must be turning in his grave to find the British Government making so light of his law of caste.

Manu next proceeds to direct the king that he should execute this law. In the first place, he appeals to the king in the name of his pious duty:

VIII. 172. By preventing the confusion of castes the, power of the king grows, and he prospers in this world and after death.

Manu perhaps knows that the law relating to the confusion of *Varna* may not be quite agreeable to the conscience of the king, and he avoids enforcement. Consequently, Manu tells the king how, in the matter of the execution of the laws, the king should act:

VIII. 177. Therefore, let the king, not heeding his likes and dislikes, behave exactly like Yama, i.e., he should be as impartial as Yama, the Judge of the Dead.

Manu, however, does not wish to leave the matter to the king as a mere matter of pious duty. Manu makes it a matter of obligation upon the king. Accordingly, Manu lays down as a matter of obligation that:

VIII. 410. The king should order a Vaishya to trade, to lend money, to cultivate the land, or to lend cattle, and the Shudra to serve the twice-born caste.

Again Manu reverts to the subject and says:

VIII. 418. The king should carefully compel Vaishyas and Shudras to perform the work prescribed for them, for if these two castes swerved from their duties, they would throw this whole world into confusion.

What if the kings do not act up to this obligation? This law of *Chaturvarna* is so supreme in the eyes of Manu that he will not allow himself to be thwarted by a king who does not keep his obligation to maintain this law. Boldly, Manu forges a new law that such a king shall be disposed. One can imagine how dear *Chaturvarna* was to Manu and Brahmanism.

As I have said, the *Chaturvarna* of the Vedic system, though better than caste system, was not very favourable to the creation of a society that could be regarded as one single whole, possessing the unity of the ideal society. By its very theory the *Chaturvarna* give birth to four classes. These four classes were far from friendly. Often, they were quarrelling, and their quarrels were so bitter that they cannot help but be designated as class wars. All the same, this old *Chaturvarna* had two saving features, which Brahmanism most selfishly removed. Firstly, there was no isolation among the *Varnas*. Intermarriage and interdining, the two strongest bonds for unity, had full play. There was no room for the different *Varnas* to develop that anti-social feeling which destroys the very basis of society. While the Kshatriyas fought against the Brahmins and the Brahmins fought against the Kshatriyas, there was no wanting Kshatriyas who fought against the Kshatriyas for the sake of Brahmins, and there was no wanting Brahmins who joined hands with Kshatriyas to put down the Brahmins.

Secondly, this old *Chaturvarna* was conventional. It was the ideal of the society, but it was not the law of the State. Brahmanism isolated the *Varnas* and sowed the seed of antagonism. Brahmanism made legal what was only conventional. By giving it a legal basis, it perpetrated the mischief. The *Vedic Chaturvarna*, if it were an evil, would have died out by force of time and circumstances. By giving it the force of law Brahmanism has made it eternal. It is probably the greatest mischief that Brahmanism has done to Hindu society.

In considering this question, one cannot fail to notice that the obligation imposed upon the king for the maintenance of the law of *Chaturvarna* which is another name for the system of graded inequality, does not require the king to enforce it against the Brahmins and the Kshatriyas. The obligation is limited to the enforcement of the law against the Vaishyas and the Shudras.

Having regard to the fact that Brahmanism was so intent on giving the system the force of law, the result has been very awkward, to say the least about it. Notwithstanding this attempt at legalization, the system remained half legal and half conventional—legal as to the Vaishyas and the Shudras and merely conventional as to the Brahmins and the Kshatriyas.

This difference needs to be accounted for. Was Brahmanism honest in its attempt to give the system the force of law? Did it wish that each of the four *Varnas* be bound by it? The fact that Brahmanism would not bind the Brahmins and the Kshatriyas through laws it made shows that in this business, Brahmanism was far from honest. If it believed in the system as ideal, it could not have failed to make it an universal binding force.

But there is more than dishonesty in this foul game. One can quite understand why the Brahmins were left free and untrammelled by the shackles of the law. Manu called them gods on earth, and gods must be above the law. But why were the Kshatriyas left free in the same way as the Brahmins? He knows that the Kshatriyas will not humble themselves before the Brahmins. He then proceeds to warn them how the Brahmins can punish them if the Kshatriyas show arrogance and plan rebellion.

IX. 320 When the Kshatriyas become in any way overbearing towards the Brahmins, the Brahmins themselves shall duly restrain them; for the Kshatriyas sprang from the Brahmins.

IX. 321. Fire sprang from water, Kshatriya from Brahmins, iron from stone; the all-penetrating force of those three has no effect on that whence they were produced.

One might think that the reason why Manu does not impose an obligation upon the king to enforce the law against the Kshatriyas is that the Brahmins felt themselves quite capable of dealing with Kshatriyas by their own prowess and without the aid of the king and that they meant to put their sanctions against the Kshatriyas when the time came and without fear of consequences. All this could not have been meant by Manu. After uttering these vows of vengeance, threats, and imprecations, Manu suddenly comes down and begins to plead with the Kshatriyas for cooperation and a common front with the Brahmins. In a verse next, after the verse in which he utters the threats and imprecations against the Kshatriyas, Manu pleads:

IX. 323. But a king who feels his end drawing nigh shall bestow all his wealth, accumulated from fines, on Brahmins, hand over his kingdom to his son, and then seek death in battle.

From imprecations to supplication is a very queer cry. What is the explanation of this anti-climax in the attitude of this strange behaviour of Manu towards the Kshatriyas? What is the object of this cooperation between Brahmins and Kshatriyas? Against whom is this common front to be? Manu does not explain. A whole history of a thousand years must be told before this puzzle is solved and the questions satisfactorily answered.

The history which furnishes the clue to the solution of this puzzle is the history of the class wars between the Brahmins and the Kshatriyas.

Most of the orthodox Hindus are repelled by the doctrine of Class War, which was propounded by Karl Marx and would be certainly be shocked if they were told that the history of their own ancestors probably furnishes the most cogent evidence that Marx was searching for in support of his theory. Indeed, there have been numerous class wars between Brahmins and Kshatriyas, and only the most important of them have been recorded in ancient Hindu literature. We have a record of the conflict between the Brahmins and the kings, who were all Kshatriyas. The first of these conflicts was a conflict with king Vena, the second with Pururavas, the third with Nahusha, the fourth with Nimi, and the fifth with Sumukha. There is a record of a conflict between Vashishtha, a Brahmin, and Vishwamitra, an ordinary Kshatriya and not a king. Then, we have the record of the wholesale massacre of the Brahmins of the Bhrigu clan by the Kshatriya decendants of Kratavirya. Lastly, we have the record of the whole class of Kshatriyas being exterminated by Parashurama, acting on behalf of the Brahmins. The issues that brought them in conflict extended over a wide range and show how bitter and strained the feelings between Brahmins and Kshatriyas. There were conflicts over whether the Kshatriya had a right to become a Brahmin. There were conflicts over the question of whether the

Brahmins were subject to the authority of Kshatriyas or not. There were conflicts over who should salute first and who should give way to whom. The wars were wars of authority, status, and dignity.

The results of these wars could not help but be obvious to the Brahmins. Notwithstanding their boastful utterances, they must have realised that they could not crush the Kshatriyas and that, notwithstanding the wars of extermination, the Kshatriyas survived in sufficient numbers to plague the Brahmins. One need not pay any attention to the filthy story told by the Brahmins and alluded to by Manu that the Kshatriyas of Manu's day were not the original Kshatriyas but a race of new Kshatriyas begotten by the Brahmins upon the widows of the old Kshatriyas who were massacred by Parashurama. Blackmailing is one of the means that Brahmanism is never ashamed of using to advance its purposes. The fight of Brahmanism against the Kshatriyas was, from the very beginning, a fight between a fool and a bully. Brahmins were fighting against the Kshatriyas for the maintenance of the *Chaturvarna*. Now, it is this very *Chaturvarna* which allowed bayonets to the Kshatriyas and denied them to the Brahmins. How, under this theory, could the Brahmin fight with the Kshatriya with any hope of success? It could not have taken long for the Brahmins to realise the truth—which Tallyrand told Napoleon—that it is easy to give bayonets. However, it is very difficult to sit on them, and as Kshatriyas had bayonets and Brahmins none, war with the Kshatriya was the way to ruin. These were the direct consequences of these wars between the Brahmins and the Kshatriyas. But there were others which could not have escaped the attention of the Brahmins. While the Brahmins and Kshatriyas were fighting among themselves, nobody was left to check and keep the Vaishyas and the Shudras under control. They were on the road to social equality, almost nearing the status of the Brahmins and Kshatriyas. To Brahmanism, the possibility of suppressing the Kshatriya was very remote, and the danger of being overtaken by Vaishyas and Shudras was real and imminent. Should the Brahmin continue to fight the Kshatriya and ignore the danger posed by the Vaishyas and the Shudras? Or should the Brahmin give up the hopeless struggle against the Kshatriya, befriend him, and make a common cause to suppress the growing menace of the Vaishyas and Shudras? Brahmanism, after being exhausted in the wars with the Kshatriyas, chose the second alternative. It sought to befriend their worthwhile enemies the Kshatriyas, to work for a new ideal—namely, to enslave and exploit the two classes below them, namely the Vaishyas and the Shudras. This new ideal must have taken shape sometime when the *Shatapatha Brahmin* came to be composed. It is in the *Shatapatha Brahmin* that we find the new ideal expressed and well-established. The language in which it is expressed and the subject to which it is applied, are so telling that I feel it should be quoted in its original terms. Says the author of the *Shatapatha*:

"They then make the beast return to the *Ahavaniya*; the he-goat goes first of them, then the ass, then the horse. Now, in going away from this *Ahavaniya*, the horse goes first, then the ass, then the he-goat—for the horse corresponds to the Kshatriya (nobility), the ass to the Vaishya and Shudra, and the he-goat to the Brahmin since in going from here, the horse goes first, therefore the Kshatriya, going first, is followed by the three others castes; and in-as-much as, in returning from here, the he-goat goes first, therefore the Brahmin, going first, is followed by the three other castes. And since the ass does not go first, either in going back from here or in coming back from there, therefore the Brahmin and Kshatriya never go behind the Vaishya and Shudra; hence they walk thus to avoid a confusion between good and bad. And, moreover, he thus encloses those two castes (the Vaishyas and Sudra) on both sides by the priesthood and the nobility and makes them submissive."

Here is the explanation of the puzzling attitude of Manu towards the Kshatriyas, attitude of willing to wound but afraid to strike, of wishing to dictate but preferring to befriend.

It is these wars and the compromise that had taught Manu that it was no use trying to coerce the Kshatriyas to submit to the domination of the Brahmin. It may be an ideal to be kept up. But as practical politics it was an impossible ideal. Like Bismark.. Manu knew that politics was the game of the possible. What was possible was to make a common cause and to build up a common front between the Brhamins and the Kshatriyas against the Vaishyas and the Shudras and this is what Manu did. The pity of it is that it was done in the name of religion. This need not shock anybody who has studied the soul and spirit of Brahmanism. With Brahmanism religion is a cloak to cover and hide its acquisitive politics.

❑

Part III

Chapter 8
The Morals of the House

This is 61-page typed manuscript. This is a second copy, but it has corrections and modifications done by Dr. Ambedkar himself. It is reproduced here, taking all the corrections into account. There is one separate file entitled 'Manusmriti or the Gospel of Counter-Revolution.' In that copy, notes on Manusmriti under various categories have been drawn. However, all these notes are incorporated in this essay, 'The Morals of the House.' It is felt that printing of these notes would be a mere repetition of this essay. Hence, the said copy is not separately printed.

– Editors

I

The morals of the Hindus and their religious creed are prescribed by the *Smritis,* which form a part of the sacred literature of the Hindus. It is to the *Smritis* that one must go to understand the ethics and religion of the Hindus. The *Smritis* are by no means few in number. A conservative estimate gives the total number of *Smritis* as 108. The large number of *Smritis* cannot, however, make our problem difficult. Though the *Smritis* are numerous, they do not differ in essentials. Indeed, they repeat one another so closely that reading the *Smritis* creates the most monotonous task. They are all derived from one common source.

That source is the *Smriti* of Manu, otherwise known as *Manava Dharma Shastra*. The other *Smritis* are faithful repetitions of the *Manusmriti*. A study of the *Manusmriti* is, therefore, quite sufficient to obtain an adequate conception of the moral standards and religious notions of the Hindus.

It may be said that *Manusmriti*—and the same is true of the other *Smritis*—is a Code of Laws. It is not a book of Ethics, nor a book of Religion, and to take a book of Laws and treat it as though it is a book of Ethics and Religion is to confound Ethics, Religion, and Law.

In the first place, it is only in modern times that law has been separated from religion. In all ancient societies, law and religion were one. As Prof. Max Muller points out:

"Law seems naturally to be the foundation of society and the bond that binds a nation together. Those who look below the surface have quickly perceived that law itself, at least ancient law, derives its authority, force, and very life from religion. The belief that the lawgiver enjoyed some closer intimacy with the Deity than ordinary mortals pervades the ancient traditions of many nations. According to a well-known passage in *Diodorus Siculus*, the Egyptians believed their laws to have been communicated to Menvis by Hermes; the Cretans held that Minos received his laws from Zeus and the Lacedaemonians that Lykurgus received his laws from Apollon. According to the Arians, their lawgiver Zarathustra had received his laws from the Good Spirit. According to the Stoe, Zamolxis received his laws from the goddess Hestia; and according to the Jews, Moses received his laws from the God."

No one has pointed out more forcibly than Sir Henry Maine that, in ancient times, religion as a divine influence was underlying and supporting every relation of life and every social institution when he speaks of religion as:

"A supernatural presidency (which) is supposed to consecrate and keep together all the cardinal institutions of those times—the State, the Race, and the Family."

From this supernatural presidency of religion, law did not succeed in finding an escape until a later time when law finally broke away from religion, but not without leaving many traces to show the link it had with religion at the very beginning of human history.

Again, it is only in modern times that a difference is being made between Religion and Ethics. Religion and Ethics are inextricably and indissolubly bound together. Morality and Ethics are essentially practical. As Prof. Jacks insists, the problem of Ethics is not merely getting the Good understood but realised, not merely getting the Right placed on a scientific basis but done. Morality is more than merely defining what is good and what is right. Prof. Jacks rightly says:

"Whenever we embark on the study of morality without interest in its application, I cannot help but think that it is not morality we are studying. Morality does not arise until the point of application is reached. The effect of a moral theory launched upon the world is next to nothing unless the application of it can be reinforced by powerful motives. The good life, as Aristotle pointed out, is a very difficult affair. Difficult even when it goes no further than conformity to existing conventions. But when the good life demands that existing standards must be transcended, how can this be effected without an immense liberation of power? Mere information regarding why men should do the right thing has no effect against their natural tendencies to do wrong—it is no match for the difficulties that beset good life."

Unless some motive force comes to its aid, morality remains inert. There can be no doubt that what gives motive force to morality is religion. It is a propelling force that creates, to use again, the language of Principal Jacks:

"Motives which are strong enough to overcome the enormous difficulties involved in living the good life, even in its simpler forms, and adequate to maintain that continuous improvement of the moral ideal."

Religion as a motive force reinforces the moral will in various ways. Sometimes, it takes the form of sanctions by laying down a scheme of rewards and punishments after death; sometimes, it makes rules of morality as the commandments of God; sometimes, it invests these rules with sanctity, which evokes willing obedience. However, these are only different ways in which motive power generated by religion helps to sustain moral life in action. Religion is the dynamics which move the wheels of morality.

If Ethics and Morality are duties, then there can be no doubt that *Manusmriti* is a book of Ethics. Anyone who takes the trouble to read the *Smriti* of Manu will have to admit that if there is any subject which figures prominently in the book, it is that of duties. Manu was the first to systematize and codify the duties to which a Hindu was bound. He distinguishes between *Varnashrama dharmas* and *Sadharana dharmas.* The *Varnashrama dharmas* are the specific duties relating to one's station in life, i.e., one's station as determined by one's Varna or caste and one's *Ashrama* or particular stage of life. The *Sadharana dharmas* are duties irrespective of one's age, caste, or creed, i.e., duties obligatory on man as a man and not as a member of a particular community or social class or as being at a particular stage or period of life. The whole book deals with duties and with nothing else.

Manusmriti is thus a book of Law, Religion, and Ethics rolled into one. It is Ethics because it deals with the duties of men. It is a Religion because it deals with caste, which is the soul of Hinduism. It is Law because it prescribes penalties for the breach of duties. In this view, there is nothing wrong in going to *Manusmriti* to ascertain the moral standards and religious notions of the Hindus.

That *Manusmriti* is a book of Religion may not be quite obvious. That is because Hinduism is a very elusive term. Different writers have defined it in various ways. Sir D. Ibbetson defines Hinduism as:

"A hereditary sacerdotalism with Brahmins for its devices, the vitality of which is preserved by the social institution of caste and which includes all shades and diversities of religion native to India, as distinct from foreign importations of Christianity and Islam, and from the later outgrowths of Buddhism, more doubtfully of Sikhism and still more doubtfully of Jainism." Sir J. A. Baines defined Hinduism as:

"The large residuum that is not Sikh, or Jain, or Buddhist, or professedly Animistic, or included in one of the foreign religions such as Islam, Mazdaism, Christianity, or Hebraism." To Sir Edward Gait, Hinduism:

"...is a complex congeries of creeds and doctrines. It shelters within its portals monotheists, polytheists, and pantheists; worshippers of the great God Shiva and Vishnu, or of their female counterparts, as well as worshippers of the divine mothers, of the spirits of trees, rocks, and streams, and of the tutelary village deities; people who propitiate their deity by all manner of bloody sacrifices, and people who will not only kill no living creature but who must not even use the word "cut"; those whose ritual consists mainly of prayers and hymns, and those who indulge in unspeakable orgies in the name of religion."

This description of complexity is thorough but still incomplete. To the list must be added those who revere the cow and those who eat it, those who worship natural forces, and those who worship a single God, and those who are worshippers of idols, demons, ghosts, ancestors, saints, and heroes.

Such are the answers given by the three Census Commissioners to the simple question: What is Hinduism? Others have not found it less difficult to answer the question. Consider how Sir A. Lyall has fared in answering it. In his *"Rede Lecture"*, delivered at Cambridge in 1891, he said:

"And if I were asked for a definition of Hinduism, I could give no precise answer. I could not define it concisely by giving its central doctrines and essential articles of faith, as I might do in describing any of the great historical religions. The word 'Hindu' is not exclusively a religious denomination; it also denotes a country and, to a certain degree, a race. When we speak of a Christian, a Muslim, or a Buddhist, we mean a particular religious community, in the widest sense, without distinction of race or place. When we speak of a Russian or a Persian, we indicate country or parentage without distinction of creed. But when a person tells me that he is a Hindu, I know that he means all three things together—Religion, Parentage, and Country."

Speaking of Hinduism as a religion, Sir Alfred Lyall said that:

"Hinduism was a tangled muddle of disorderly superstitions, a collection of rites, worships, beliefs, traditions, and mythologies that are sanctioned by the sacred books and ordinances of the Brahmins and are propagated by Brahmanic teachings." Lastly, I will quote the definition given by a Hindu, Mr. G. P. Sen, who is not merely a Hindu but also a student of Hinduism. In his book called *'Introduction to the Study of Hinduism'*, Mr. Sen says:—

"Hinduism is what the Hindus, or a major portion of them in a Hindu community, do."

Is there then no principle in Hinduism to which all Hindus, no matter what their other differences are, feel bound to render willing obedience? It seems to me there is, and that principle is the principle of caste. There may be a difference of opinion as to which matters constitute matters of essence so far as Hinduism is concerned. But there can be no doubt that caste is an essential and integral part of Hinduism. Every Hindu—if he is not merely a statutory Hindu—believes in caste, and every Hindu—even one who prides himself on being a statutory Hindu—has a caste. A Hindu is as much born into caste as he is born into Hinduism. Indeed, a person cannot be born into Hinduism unless he is born into a caste. Caste and Hinduism are inseparable. As Prof. Max Muller observes:

"Modern Hinduism rests on the system of caste as on a rock which no arguments can shake."

It follows that in so far as Manu lays down the creed of the caste, and in so far as Hinduism at its core is the creed of caste, the *Manusmriti* must be accepted as the Book of Religion.

II

What are the ethical and religious norms prescribed by Manu for Hindus to observe and follow?

To begin with, Manu divides Hindus into four Varnas or social orders. He not only divides Hindus into four orders, but he also grades them. The following is his scheme of gradation:

X. 3. On account of his pre-eminence, on account of the superiority of his origin, on account of his observance of (particular) restrictive rules, and on account of his specific sanctification, the Brahmin is the Lord of (all) *Varnas*.

He proceeds to amplify his reasons and does so in the following characteristic manner:

I. 93. As the Brahmin sprang from Prajapati's, i.e. God's mouth, as he was first-born, and as he possesses the Vedas, he is by right the Lord of This whole creation.

I. 94. For the self-existent (Swayambhu, i.e., God), having performed austerities, produced him first from His own mouth so that the offerings might be conveyed to the gods and manes and that this universe might be preserved.

I. 95. What created being can surpass him, through whose mouth the gods continually consume the sacrificial viands and the manes the offerings to the dead?

I. 96. Of created beings, the most excellent are said to be animated; of the animated, those who subsist by intelligence, of the intelligent, mankind; and of the men, the Brahmins.

Besides the reasons given by Manu, the Brahmin is first in rank because he was produced by God from His mouth so that the offerings might be conveyed to the gods and manes. Manu gives another reason for the supremacy of the Brahmins. He says:

I. 98. The very birth of a Brahmin is an eternal incarnation of the sacred Law (Vedas), for he is born to fulfil the sacred Law and become one with Brahma (God).

I. 99. A Brahmin, coming into existence, is born as the highest on earth, the Lord of All Created Beings, for the protection of the treasury of the Law.

Manu concludes by saying that:

I. 101. The Brahmin eats but his own food, wears but his own apparel, and bestows but his own alms; other mortals subsist through the benevolence of the Brahmin.

According to Manu:

I. 100. Whatever exists in the world is the property of the Brahmin; on account of the excellence of his origin, the Brahmin is, indeed, entitled to it all.

It is an understatement to say that according to Manu, the Brahmin is a Lord of All Creation. Manu gives a warning to the effect that:

IX. 317. A Brahmin, be he ignorant or learned, is a great divinity, just as the fire, whether carried forth (for the performance of a burnt oblation) or not carried forth, is a great divinity.

IX. 319. Thus, though the Brahmins employ themselves in all sorts of menial occupations, they must be honoured in every way, for each of them is a very great deity.

Being a deity, the Brahmin is above the law and the king. Manu directs:

VII. 37. Let the king, after rising early in the morning, worship Brahmins who are well-versed in the threefold sacred science and learned in polity and follow their advice.

VII. 38. Let him worship daily the aged Brahmins who know the Vedas and are pure.

Finally Manu says:

XI. 35. The Brahmin is thus declared to be the creator of the world, the punisher, the teacher, and a benefactor of all created beings; to him, let no man say anything unpropitious nor use any harsh words.

In the Code of Manu, there are rules regarding the different occupations which the different orders are required to follow:

I. 88. To Brahmins, he (Swayambhu Manu) assigned the duties of reading the Vedas, of teaching it, of sacrificing, of assisting others to sacrifice, of giving alms, if they the rich, and if indigent, of receiving gifts.

I. 89. To defend the people, to give alms, to sacrifice, to read the Vedas, to shun the allurements of sensual gratifiction are, in a few words, the duties of a Kshatriya.

I. 90. To keep herds of cattle, to bestow largeness, to sacrifice, to read the scriptures, to carry on trade, to lend at interest, and to cultivate land are prescribed or permitted to a Vaishya.

I. 91. One principal duty the Supreme Ruler assigns to a Shudra, namely, to serve the aforementioned classes without depreciating their worth.

X. 74. Let such Brahmins who are intent on the means of attaining the Supreme Godhead and firm in their duties completely perform, in order, the six following acts:

X. 75. Reading the Vedas, teaching others to read them, sacrificing, and assisting others to sacrifice, giving to the poor if they have enough, and accepting gifts from the virtuous if they are poor are the six prescribed acts of the first-born class.

X. 76. But, among those six acts of a Brahmin, three are his means of susbsistence: assisting with sacrifice, teaching the Vedas, and receiving gifts from a pure-handed giver.

X. 77. Three acts of duty cease with the Brahmin and belong not to the Kshatriya: teaching the Vedas, officiating at a sacrifice, and, thirdly, receiving presents.

X. 78. Those three are also (by the fixed rule of law) forbidden to the Vaishya since Manu, the Lord of All Men, prescribed not those acts to the two classes: military and commercial.

X. 79. The means of subsistence, peculiar to the Kshatriya, are bearing arms, either held for striking or missile, to the Vaishya, merchandise, attending on cattle, and agriculture. But with a view to the next life, the duties of both are almsgiving, reading, and sacrificing.

Besides prescribing rank and occupation, Manu grants privileges to certain orders and imposes penalties on others. As to privileges, those relating to marriage may be referred to first. Manu says:

III. 12. For the first marriage of the twice-born classes, a woman of the same class is recommended. But for such as are impelled by an inclination to marry again, women in the direct order of the classes are to be preferred:

III. 13. A Shudra woman must be the wife of a Shudra only; she and a Vaishya, of a Vaishya; they two and a Kshatriya, of a Kshatriya; those three and a Brahmini of a Brahmin.

Then, there are privileges relating to occupations. These privileges stand out quite prominently when Manu deals with the question of what a person is to do when he is in distress.

X. 81. Yet a Brahmin, unable to subsist by his duties just mentioned, may live by the duty of a soldier, for that is the next in rank.

X. 82. If asked how he must live, should he be unable to get a subsistence by either of those employments, the answer is that he may subsist as a mercantile man, applying himself in person to tillage and attendance on cattle.

X. 83. But a Brahmin and a Kshatriya, obliged to subsist by the acts of a Vaishya, must avoid with care, if they can live by keeping herds, the business of tillage, which gives great pain to sentient creatures, and is dependent on the labour of others, such as bulls and so forth.

X. 84. Some think that agriculture is excellent, but it is a mode of subsistence which the benevolent greatly blame for the iron-mouthed pieces of wood not only wound the earth, but also the creatures dwelling in it.

X. 85. If, through want of a virtuous livelihood, they cannot follow laudable occupations, they may then gain a competence of wealth by selling commodities usually sold by merchants, avoiding what ought to be avoided.

X. 86. They must avoid selling liquids of all sorts, dressed grains, seeds of *tila*, stones, salt, cattle, and human creatures.

X. 87. All woven cloth dyed red, cloth made of *sana*, of *cshuma*-bark, and of wool, even though not red; fruit, roots, and medicinal plants.

X. 88. Water, iron, poison, flesh meat, the moon plant, and perfumes of any sort; milk, honey, buttermilk, clarified butter, oil of *tila*, wax, sugar, and blades of *kusha* grass.

X. 89. All beasts of the forest, such as deer and the like, ravenous beasts, birds, and fish; spirituous liquors, *nili*, or indigo, and *lascha*, or lac; and all beasts with uncloven hoofs.

X. 90. But the Brahmin-husbandman may at pleasure sell pure *tila* seeds for holy rites, provided he does not keep them long with a hope of more gain and shall have produced them by his own cultivation.

X. 91. If he applies seeds of *tila* to any purpose other than food, anointing, and sacred oblations, he shall be plunged, in the shape of a worm, together with his parents, into the ordure of dogs.

X. 92. By selling flesh meat, lac, or salt, a Brahmin immediately sinks low; and by selling milk three days, he falls to a level with a Shudra.

X. 93. By selling the other forbidden commodities of his own free will, he assumes in this world, after seven nights, the nature of a mere Vaishya.

X. 94. Fluid things may, however, be bartered for other fluids, but not salt for anything liquid; likewise, dressed grains for grains undressed, and *tila* seeds for grains in the husk, equal weights or measures being given and taken.

X. 102. The Brahmin, having fallen into distress, may receive gifts from any person whatsoever, for by no sacred rule can it be shown that his absolute purity can be sullied.

X. 103. From interpreting the Vedas, officiating at sacrifices, or taking presents, though in modes generally disapproved, no sin is committed by priests in distress, for they are as pure as fire or water.

Compare what Manu states regarding what the other *Varnas* can do in an emergency Manu says:

X. 96. A man of the lowest class, who, through covetousness, lives by the acts of the highest, should be stripped of all his wealth and instantly banished by the king.

X. 97. His own duties, though defectively performed, is preferable to that of another, even if performed completely, for he who, without necessity, discharges the duties of another class immediately forfeits his own.

X. 98. A mercantile man, unable to subsist by his duties, may descend even to the servile acts of a Shudra, taking care never to do what ought never to be done; but, when he has gained a competence, let him depart from service.

X. 99. A man of the fourth class, not finding employment by waiting on the twice-born while his wife and son are tormented with hunger, may subsist by handicrafts.

X. 121. If a Shudra wants a subsistence and cannot attend a priest, he may serve a Kshatriya; or, if he cannot wait on a soldier by birth, he may gain his livelihood by serving an opulent Vaishya.

X. 122. To him, who serves Brahmins with a view to a heavenly reward, or even with a view to both this life and the next, the union of the word Brahmin with his name of a servant will assuredly bring success.

X. 123. Attendance on Brahmins is pronounced the best work of Shudra; whatever else he may perform will comparatively avail him nothing.

X. 124. They must allot him a fitting maintenance according to their circumstances after considering his ability, his exertions, and the number of those he must provide with nourishment.

X. 125. What remains of their dressed rice must be given to him, along with apparel which they have worn, the refuse of their grain, and their old household furniture.

X. 126. There is no guilt in a man of the servile class who eats leeks and other forbidden vegetables; he must not have the sacred investiture, nor he is concerned with the duty of making oblations to fire and the like, but there is no prohibition against his offering dressed grain as a sacrifice, by way of discharging his duty.

X. 127. Even Shudras, who are anxious to perform their entire duty and, knowing what they should perform, imitate the practice of good men in the household sacraments but without any holy text—except those containing praise and salutations—are so far from sinning that they acquire just applause.

X. 128. As a Shudra, without injuring another man, performs the lawful acts of the twice-born, even thus, without being censured, he gains exaltation in this world and the next.

X. 129. No superfluous collection of wealth must be made by a Shudra, even though he has the power to make it, since a servile man who has amassed riches becomes proud and, by his insolence or neglect, gives pain even to Brahmins.

He concludes:

X. 130. Such, as have been fully declared, are the several duties of the four classes in distress for subsistence, and, if they perform them exactly, they shall attain the highest beatitude.

The privileges to some were not merely social—they were also financial, says Manu:

VIII. 35. From the man, who shall say with truth, "This property, which has been kept, belongs to me." The king may take a sixth or twelfth part for having it secured.

VIII. 36. But he, who shall say so falsely, may be fined either an eighth part of his property or else in some small proportion to the value of the goods falsely claimed, a just calcultion having been made.

VIII. 37. A learned Brahmin, having found a treasure formerly hidden, may take it without any deduction since he is the lord of all.

VIII. 38. But of a treasure anciently deposited underground, which any other subject or the king has discovered, the king may lay up half in his treasury, having given half to the Brahmins.

IX. 323. Should the king be near his end through some incurable disease, he must bestow on the priests all his riches and his kingdom to his son. Let him seek death in battle or, if there is no war, by abstaining from food.

VII. 127. Having ascertained the rates of purchase and sale, the length of the way, the expenses of food and condiments, the charges of securing the goods carried, and the net profits of trade, let the king oblige traders to pay taxes on their saleable commodities.

VII. 128. After full consideration, let a king so levy those taxes continually in his dominions that he and the merchant may receive a just compensation for their several acts.

VII. 129. As the leech, the suckling calf, and the bee take their natural food little by little, thus must a king draw from his dominions an annual revenue.

VII. 130. Of cattle, of gems, of gold and silver, added each year to the capital stock, a fiftieth part may be taken by the king; of grains, an eighth part, a sixth, or a twelfth, according to the difference of the soil, and the labour necessary to cultivate it.

VII. 131. He may also take a sixth part of the annual increase of trees, flesh meat, honey, clarified butter, perfumes, medical substances, liquids, flowers, roots, and fruits.

VII. 132. Of gathered leaves, pot herbs, grass, utensils made with leather or cane, earthen pots, and all things made of stone, a similar proportion may be taken as tax.

VII. 133. A king, even though dying with want, must not receive any tax from a Brahmin learned in the Vedas nor suffer such a Brahmin, residing in his territories, to be afflicted with hunger.

VII. 134. Of that king, in whose dominion a learned Brahmin is afflicted with hunger, the whole kingdom will, in a short time, be afflicted with famine.

VII. 137. Let the king order a mere trifle to be paid, in the name of the annual tax, by the meaner inhabitants of his kingdom, who subsist by petty traffic.

VII. 138. By low handicraftsmen, artificers, and servile men, who support themselves by labour, the king may cause work to be done for a day each month.

VIII. 394. Neither a blind man, nor an idiot, nor a cripple, nor a man full seventy years old, nor one who confers great benefits on priests of eminent learning, shall be compelled by any king to pay taxes.

X. 118. A military king who takes even a fourth part of the crops of his kingdom at a time of urgent necessity, such as war or invasion, and protects his people to the utmost of his power commits no sin.

X. 119. His peculiar duty is conquest, and he must not recede from battle so that, while he defends with arms the merchant and the husbandman, he may levy the legal tax as the price of protection.

X. 120. The tax on the mercantile class, which in times of prosperity must be only a twelfth part of their crops, and a fiftieth of their personal profits, maybe an eighth of their crops in a time of distress, or a sixth, which is the medium, or even a fourth in great public adversity. However, a twentieth of their gains on money and other moveables is the highest tax; serving men, artisans, and mechanics must assist by their labour but at no time pay taxes.

X. 187. To the nearest *sapinda*, male or female, after him in the third degree, the inheritance next belongs; then, on the failure of *sapindas* and of their issue, the *samanodaca*, or distant kinsman, shall be the heir, or the spiritual preceptor, or the pupil, or the fellow student, of the deceased.

IX.188. On failure of all those, the lawful heirs are such Brahmins who have read the three Vedas, are pure in body and mind, and have subdued their passions. They must consequently offer the cake, thus ensuring that the rites of obsequies cannot fail.

IX. 189. The property of a Brahmin shall never be taken as an escheat by the king; this is a fixed law. However, the wealth of the other classes, on failure of all heirs, can be taken by the king.

The terms on which the different social orders should conduct their associated life are defined by Manu in a set of rules that form a very important part of the morals of the Hindu house. Manu ordains that:

X. 3. From priority of birth, superiority of origin, a more exact knowledge of scripture, and a distinction in the sacrificial thread, the Brahmin is the Lord of All Classes.

IX. 317. A Brahmin, whether learned or ignorant, is a powerful divinity, even as fire is a powerful divinity, whether consecrated or popular.

IX. 319. Thus, although Brahmins may employ themselves in all sorts of menial occupations, they must invariably be honoured, for they are something transcendently divine.

VII. 35. A king was created as the protector of all those classes and orders who, from the first to the last, discharge their several duties.

VII. 36. And all that must be done by him for the protection of his people, with the assistance of good ministers, I will declare to you, as the law directs, in due order.

VII. 37. Let the king, having risen at early dawn, respectfully attend to Brahmins learned in the three Vedas and the science of ethics, and by their decision, let him abide.

VII. 38. Constantly must he show respect to Brahmins who have grown old, both in years and piety, who know the scriptures, and who in body and mind are pure; for he, who honours the aged will perpetually be honoured even by cruel demons.

IX. 313. Let him not, although in the greatest distress for money, provoke Brahmins to anger by taking their property. For they, once enraged, could immediately, through sacrifices and imprecations, destroy him with his troops, elephants, horses and Vehicle.

Such was to be the relationship in the field of political life. For ordinary social intercourse between the different *Varnas*, Manu lays down the following rules:

III. 68. A householder has five places of slaughter, or where small living creatures may be slain: his kitchen hearth, his grindstone, his broom, his pestle and mortar, and his water pot. By using these, he becomes bound to sin.

III. 69. For the sake of expiating offences committed unknowingly in those places mentioned in the order, the five great sacraments were appointed by eminent sages to be performed each day by such householders.

III. 70. Teaching and studying the scripture is the sacrament of the Vedas; offering cakes and water, the sacrament of the manes, an oblation to fire, the sacrament of the deities; giving rice or other food to living creatures, the sacrament of spirits; and receiving guests with honour is the sacrament of men.

III. 71. Whoever omits none of these and five great ceremonies, if he can perform them, is untainted by the sins of the five slaughtering places, even though he constantly resides at home.

III. 84. In his domestic fire, used for preparing the food of all the gods, after the prescribed ceremony, let a Brahmin make an oblation each day to the following divinities. After it is offered to the deities, Manu directs:

III. 92. The share of dogs, outcasts, dog-feeders, sinful men, punished with elephantiasis or consumption, crows, and reptiles, let him drop on the ground little by little.

Concerning the rules of hospitality, Manu directs the householder:

III. 102. A Brahmin, staying for one night as a guest, is called an *atithi*, since continuing so short a time, he is not even a sojourner for a whole *tithi*, or day of the moon.

III. 98. But an offering in the fire of a sacerdotal mouth, which richly blazes with true knowledge and piety, will release the giver from distress and even from deadly sin.

III. 107. To the highest guests in the best form, to the lowest in the worst, to the equal equally, let him offer seats, resting places, and couches, giving them proportionable attendance when they depart and honour as long as they stay.

III. 110. A military man is not denominated as a guest in the house of a Brahmin, nor is a man of the commercial or servile class, nor his familiar friend, nor his paternal kinsmen, nor his preceptor.

III. 111. But if a warrior comes to his house in the form of a guest, let food be prepared for him, according to his desire, after the aforementioned Brahmins have eaten.

III. 112. Even to a merchant or a labourer approaching his house in the form of guests, let him give food, showing marks of benevolence at the same time with his domestics.

On the social bearing of one class towards another, Manu has laid down some very interesting ordinances. He has an equation for social status:

II. 135. The student must consider a Brahmin, though ten years old, and a Kshatriya, though aged a hundred years, as father and son; as between those two, the young Brahmin is to be respected as the father.

II. 136. Wealth, kindred, age, moral conduct, and, fifthly, divine knowledge entitle men to respect, but that which is last mentioned in order, is the most respectable.

II. 137. Whatever man of the three highest classes possesses the most of those five attributes both in number and degree, that man is entitled to most respect—even a Shudra, if he has entered the tenth decade of his age.

II. 138. Way must be made for a man in a wheeled carriage, or above ninety years old, or afflicted with disease, or carrying a burden; for a woman; for a priest just returned from the mansion of his preceptor; for a prince, and a bridegroom.

II. 139. Among all these, if they are met at one time, the priest just returned home, and the prince is the most to be honoured. Of those two, the priest just returned should be treated with more respect than the prince.

As an illustration of the rules of social bearing, a reference may be made to rules regarding salutation:

II. 121. A youth who habitually greets and constantly reveres the aged obtains an increase of four things: life, knowledge, fame, and strength.

II. 122. After the words of salutation, a Brahmin must address an elder by saying, "I am such a one," pronouncing his name.

II. 123. If any person, through ignorance of the Sanskrit language, understand does not the import of his name, then a learned man should say to them, "It is I"; in that manner, he should address all classes of women.

II. 124. During the salutation, he should pronounce, after his name, the vocative particle '*bhoh*', for the particle '*bhoh*' is held by the wise to have the same property with names fully expressed.

II. 125. A Brahmin should thus be saluted in return: "May you live long, excellent man". At the end of his name, the vowel and preceding consonant should be lengthened, with an acute accent, to three syllabic moments or short vowels.

II. 126. That Brahmin, who does not know the form of returning a salutation, must not be saluted by a man of learning; he is just like a Shudra.

II. 127. Let a learned man ask a priest, when he meets him if his devotion prospers; a warrior, if he is unhurt; a merchant, if his wealth is secure; and one of the servile classes, if he enjoys good health—using respectively the words *Kusalam*, *anamayam, ksheman,* and *anarogyam*.

The provisions laid down by Manu about religion, religious sacraments, and sacrifice are noteworthy.

The ordinances of Manu relating to Sacraments and sacrifices are as follows:

III. 68. A householder has five places of slaughter, or where small living creatures may be slain: his kitchen hearth, his grindstone, his broom, his pestle and mortar, his water pot. By using these, he becomes in bondage to sin.

III. 69. For the sake of expiating offences committed unknowingly in those places mentioned in the order, the five great sacraments were appointed by eminent sages to be performed everyday by householders.

III. 70. Teaching and studying the scriptures is the sacrament of the Vedas; offering cakes and water, the sacrament of the manes; an oblation to fire, the sacrament of the deities; giving rice or other food to living creatures, the sacraments of spirits; receiving guests with honour, the sacrament of men.

III. 71. Whoever does not omit those five great ceremonies, if he can perform them, is untainted by the sins of the five slaughtering places, even though he constantly resides at home.

Manu then proceeds to lay down that all are not entitled to the benefits of the sacraments and do not have the same right to perform the sacrifices. He defines the position of women and Shudras in the matter of sacraments and sacrifices. As to women, Manu says:

II. 66. The same ceremonies, except that of the sacrificial thread, must be duly performed for women at the same age and in the same order so that the body may be made perfect, but without any text from the Vedas."

As to Shudras, Manu says:

X. 127. Even Shudras, who are anxious to perform their entire duty and, knowing what they should perform, imitate the practice of good men in the household sacraments, but without any holy text—except those containing praise and salutation—are so far from sinning, that they acquire just applause.

The investiture of a person with the sacred thread is a very important sacrament.

II. 36. In the eighth year from the conception of a Brahmin, in the eleventh from that of a Kshatriya, and in the twelfth from that of a Vaishya, let the father invest the child with the mark of his class.

II. 37. Should a Brahmin, or his father for him, be desirous of his advancement in sacred knowledge; a Kshatriya, of extending his power; or a Vaishya, of engaging in mercantile business; the investiture may be made in the fifth, sixth, or eighth years, respectively.

II. 38. The ceremony of investiture, hallowed by the *Gayatri,* must not be delayed, in the case of a priest, beyond the sixteenth year; nor in that of a soldier, beyond the twenty-second; nor in that of a merchant, beyond the twenty-fourth.

II. 39. After that, all youths of these three classes who have not been invested at the proper time become *vratyas*, or outcasts, degraded from the *Gayatri*, and condemned by the virtuous. As for the *Gayatri,* it is a *mantra,* and this is how Manu explains its importance:

II. 76. Brahma milked out, as it were, from the three Vedas, the letter A, the letter U, and the letter M, which form by their coalition the triliteral monosyllable, together with three mysterious words: *bhur*, *bhuvah*, and *svah* (earth, sky, and heaven).

II. 77. From the three Vedas, also, the Lord of Creatures, incomprehensibly exalted, successively milked out the three measures of that ineffable text, beginning with the word *tad*, and entitled *Savitri* or *Gayatri*.

II. 78. A priest who knows the Vedas, and shall pronounces to himself, both in morning and evening, that syllable and that holy texts, preceded by the three words, shall attain the sanctity which the Vedas confers.

II. 79. And a twice-born man, who shall a thousand times repeat those three (*Om*, the *Vyahritis*, and the *Gayatri*), apart from the multitude, shall be released in a month even from a great offence, as a snake is released from his slough.

II. 80. The priest, the soldier, and the merchant, who neglect these mysterious texts and fail to perform in due season their peculiar acts of piety, shall meet with contempt among the virtuous.

II. 81. The great immutable words, preceded by the triliteral syllable and followed by the *Gayatri,* which consists of three measures, must be considered as the mouth, or principal part, of the Vedas.

II. 82. Whoever shall repeat, day by day, for three years, without negligence, that sacred text shall hereafter approach the divine essence, move as freely as air, and assume an ethereal form.

II. 83. The triliteral monosyllable is an emblem of the Supreme; the suppressions of breath, with a mind fixed on God, are the highest devotion. But nothing is more exalted than the *Gayatri Mantra*. A declaration of truth is more excellent than silence.

II. 84. All rites ordained in the Vedas, oblations to fire, and solemn sacrifices pass away; but that which passes not away is declared to be the syllable '*Om*', thence called *akshara*, since it is a symbol of God, the Lord of Created Beings.

II. 85. The act of repeating His Holy Name is ten times better than the appointed sacrifice, a hundred times better when it is heard by no man, and a thousand times better when it is purely mental.

II. 86. The four domestic sacraments, accompanied by the appointed sacrifice, are not equal, though all be united, to a sixteenth part of the sacrifice performed by a repetition of the *Gayatri Mantra*. This investiture is equivalent to a new birth.

II. 147. Let a man consider that as a mere human birth, which his parents gave him for their mutual gratification and which he receives after lying in the womb.

II. 148. But that birth, which his principal *acharya*, who knows the whole Vedas, procures for him by his divine mother, the *Gayatri*, is a true birth; that birth is exempt from age and death.

II. 169. The first birth is from a natural mother; the second is from the ligation of the zone; the third is from the due performance of the sacrifice. Such are the births of him who is usually called twice-born, according to a text of the Vedas.

II. 170. Among them, his divine birth is that which is distinguished by the ligation of the zone and sacrificial cord; in that birth, the *Gayatri* is his mother, and the *Acharya* is his father. This sacrament is not permitted by Manu to Shudras and women.

II. 103. But he who stands not repeating it in the morning and sits not repeating it in the evening must be precluded, like a Shudra, from every sacred observance of the twice-born class. Manu has not forgotten to mention rules relating to education and learning. Manu has nothing to say about mass education. He does not see the utility of it, nor does he see the necessity of imposing any obligation upon the king or the state. He was merely concerned with the learning of the sacred and religious literature, namely the Vedas.

The Vedas must be learned from a preceptor and with his assent. No one can read and study the Vedas by himself. He will be guilty of theft if he does so.

II. 116. He who shall acquire knowledge of the Vedas without the assent of his preceptor incurs the guilt of stealing the scripture and shall sink to the region of torment. But others cannot study at all.

IX. 18. Women have no business with the texts of the Vedas; thus, it is lawfully settled. Having, therefore, no evidence of law and no knowledge of expiatory texts, sinful women must be as foul as falsehood itself, and this is a fixed rule.

IV. 99. He must never read the Vedas without accents and letters well pronounced, not even in the presence of Shudras; nor, having begun to read it in the late watch of the night, must he, though fatigued, sleep again.

This prohibition applies to *Vratyas* or outcasts from the three higher classes. For Manu says:

II. 40. With such impure men, let no Brahmin, even in distress for subsistence, ever form a connection in law either by the study of the Vedas, or by affinity.

Manu has prohibited teaching Vedas to disqualified people or performing sacrifices for disqualified people.

IV. 205. Never let a priest eat part of a sacrifice not begun with texts of the Vedas, nor of one performed by a common sacrificer, by a woman, or by an eunuch:

IV. 206. When those people offer the clarified butter, it brings misfortune to good men and raises aversion in the deities. Such oblations, therefore, he must carefully shun.

XI. 198. He, who has officiated at a sacrifice for outcasts, burned the corpse of a stranger, performed rites to destroy the innocent, or made the impure sacrifice called Ahinsa, may expiate his guilt by three Prajapatya penances.

Take equality before the Law.

When they come as witnesses, according to Manu, they are to be sworn as follows:

VIII. 87. In the forenoon, let the judge, being purified, severally call on the twice-born, being also purified, to declare the truth, in the presence of some image, a symbol of the divinity and of Brahmans, while the witnesses turn their faces either to the north or the east.

VIII. 88. To a Brahmin, he must begin by saying, "Declare;" to a Kshatriya, by saying, "Declare the truth;" to a Vaishya, by comparing perjury to the crime of stealing kine, grain, or gold; to a Shudra, with comparing it in some or all of the following sentences, to every crime that men can commit.

VIII. 113. Let the judge cause a priest to swear by his veracity; a soldier, by his horse or elephant and his weapons; a merchant, by his kine, grain, and gold; a mechanic or servile man, by imprecating on his own head, if he speak falsely, all possible crime.

Manu also deals with cases of witnesses giving false evidence. According to Manu, giving false evidence is a crime. Says Manu:

VIII. 122. Learned men have specified these punishments, which were ordained by sage legislators for perjured witnesses, with a view to prevent a failure of justice and to restrain iniquity.

VIII. 123. Let a just prince banish men of the three lower classes if they give false evidence, having first levied the fine, but a Brahmin, let him only be banish.

But Manu made one exception:

VIII. 112. To women, however, at a time of dalliance, or on a proposal of marriage, in the case of grass or fruit eaten by a cow, of wood taken for a sacrifice, or of a promise made for the preservation of a Brahmin, it is deadly sin to take a light oath.

As parties to proceedings, their position can be illustrated by quoting the ordinances of Manu relating to a few of the important criminal offences dealt with by Manu. Take the offence of defamation. Manu says:

VIII. 267. A soldier, defaming a priest, shall be fined ahundred panas a merchant, thus offending, an hundred and fifty, or two hundred : but, for such an offence, a mechanic or servile man shall be whipped.

VIII. 268. A priest shall be fined fifty panas if he slanders a soldier, twenty five panas if he slanders a merchant, and twelve panas if he slanders a man of the servile class.

Take the offence of insult. Manu says:

VIII. 270. A once-born man, who insults the twice-born with gross invectives, ought to have his tongue slit; for he sprang from the lowest part of Brahma.

VIII. 271. If he mention their names and classes with contumely, as if he say, "Oh Devadatta, thou refuse of Brahmin", a red-hot iron nail, ten fingers long, shall be thrust into his mouth.

VIII. 272. Should he, through pride, instruct priests concerning their duty, let the king order hot oil to be poured into his mouth and ear.

Take the offence of abuse. Manu says:

VIII. 276. For mutual abuse by a priest and a soldier, this fine must be imposed by a learned king; the lowest amercement on the priest and the middle-most on the soldier.

VIII. 277. Such exactly, as before mentioned, must be the punishment for a merchant and a mechanic, in respect of their several classes, except the slitting of the tongue; this is a fixed rule of punishment.

Take the offence of assault. Manu propounds:

VIII. 279. With whatever member of a low-born man shall assault or hurt a superior, even that member of his must be slit or cut more or less in proportion to the injury; this an ordinance of Manu.

VIII. 280. He who raises his hand or staff against another shall have his hand cut, and he who kicks another in wrath shall have an incision made in his foot.

Take the offence of arrogance. According to Manu:

VIII. 281. A man of the lowest class, who shall insolently place himself on the same seat with one of the highest, shall either be banished with a mark on his hinder parts, or the king shall order to cause a gash on his buttock.

VIII. 282. Should he spit on him through pride, the king shall order both his lips to be gashed; should he urine on him, his penis; should he break wind against him, his anus.

VIII. 283. If he seizes the Brahmin by the locks, the feet, the beard, the throat, or the scrotum, let the king without hesitation cause incisions to be made in his hands.

Take the offence of adultery. Says Manu:

VIII. 359. A man of the servile class who commits actual adultery with the wife of a priest ought to suffer death; the wives, indeed, of all the four classes must ever be most especially guarded.

VIII. 366. A low man who makes love to a damsel of high birth ought to be punished corporally. But he who addresses a maid of equal rank shall give the nuptial present and marry her if her father pleases.

VIII. 374. A mechanic or servile man, having an adulterous connection with a woman of a twice-born class, whether guarded at home or unguarded, shall thus be punished: if she was unguarded, he shall lose the offending part and his whole substance; if guarded, and a he shall lose, priestess everything, even his life.

VIII. 375. For adultery with a guarded priestess, a merchant shall forfeit all his wealth after imprisonment for a year. A soldier shall be fined a thousand panas and shaved with the urine of an ass.

VIII. 376. But, if a merchant or soldier commits adultery with a woman of the priestly class, whom her husband guards not at home, the king shall only fine the merchant five hundred panas and the soldier a thousand panas.

VIII. 377. Both of them, however, if they commit that offence with a priestess who was not only guarded but eminent with good qualities, shall be punished like men of the servile class or be burned in a fire of dry grass or reeds.

VIII. 382. If a merchant converses criminally with a guarded woman of the military class or a soldier with one of the mercantile class, they both deserve the same punishment as in the case of a priestess unguarded.

VIII. 383. But a Brahmin, who shall commit adultery with a guarded woman of those two classes, must be fined a thousand panas; and for the same offence with a guarded woman of the servile class, the fine for a soldier or merchant shall also be one thousand panas.

VIII. 384. For adultery with a woman of the military class, if unguarded, the fine for a merchant is five hundred. But a soldier, for the converse of that offence, must be shaved with urine or pay the fine just mentioned.

VIII. 385. A priest shall pay five hundred panas if he connects himself criminally with an unguarded woman of the military, commercial, or servile class, and a thousand for such a connection with a woman of vile mixed breed.

Upon turning to the punishment system for offences, Manu's scheme throws an interesting light on the subject. Consider the following ordinances:

VIII. 379. Ignominious tonsure is ordained, instead of capital punishment, for an adulterer of the priestly class, whereas the punishment for other classes may extend to loss of life.

VIII. 380. Never shall the king slay a Brahmin, though when convicted of all possible crimes: let him banish the offender from his kingdom, but with all his property secure and his body unhurt.

XI. 127. For killing intentionally a virtuous man of the military class, the penance must be a fourth part of that ordained for killing a priest; for killing a Vaishya, only an eighth; for killing a Shudra, who had been constant in discharging his duties, a sixteenth part.

XI. 128. But, if a Brahmin kills a Kshatriya without malice, he must, after a full performance of his religious rites, give the priests one bull together with a thousand cows.

XI. 129. Or he may perform for three years the penance for slaying a Brahmin, mortifying his organs of sensation and action, letting his hair grow long, and living remote from the town, with the root of a tree for his mansion.

XI. 130. If he kills without malice a Vaishya, who had a good moral character, he may perform the same penance for one year or give the priests a hundred cows and a bull.

XI. 131. For six months he must perform this whole penance if, without intention, he kills a Shudra, or he may give ten white cows and a bull to the priests.

VIII. 381. No greater crime is known on earth than slaying a Brahmin, and the king, therefore, must not even form in his mind an idea of killing a priest.

VIII. 126. Let the king, having considered and ascertained the frequency of a similar offence, the place and time, the ability of the criminal to pay or suffer, and the crime itself, cause punishment to fall on those alone who deserve it.

VIII. 124. Manu, son of the Self-existent, has named ten places of punishment, which are appropriate to the three lower classes, but a Brahmin must depart from the realm unhurt in any one of them.

VIII. 125. The part of generation, the belly, the tongue, the two hands, and, fifthly, the two feet, the eye, the nose, both ears, the property, and, in a capital case, the whole body.

On the point of rights and duties relating to religious Sacraments and Sacrifices, the views of Manu are noteworthy:

II. 28. By studying the Vedas, by religious observances, by oblations to fire, by the ceremony of *Traividya*, by offering to the gods and manes, by the procreation of children, by the five great sacraments, and by solemn sacrifices, this human body is rendered fit for a divine state.

III. 69. For the sake of expiating offences committed ignorantly in those places mentioned in the order, the five great sacraments were appointed by eminent sages to be performed every day by such as keep house.

III. 70. Teaching and studying the scripture is the sacrament of the Vedas; offering cakes and water, the sacrament of the manes; an oblation to fire, the sacrament of the deities; giving rice or other food to living creatures, the sacrament of spirits; receiving guests with honour, the sacrament of men.

III. 71. Whoever omits not those five great ceremonies, if he can perform them, is untained by the sins of the five slaughtering places, even though he constantly resides at home.

Such are the ordinances of Manu. Laws are never complete enough to cover every point. There are always moot questions. Manu was conscious of this and provided for such contingencies.

XII. 108. If asked how the law shall be ascertained when particular cases are not comprised under any general rules, the answer is this: "That which well-instructed Brahmins propound shall be held incontestable law."

XII. 109. Well-instructed Brahmins are they who can adduce ocular proof out of the scripture itself, having studied, as the law ordains, the Vedas and their extended branches, or Vedangas, Mimamsa, Nyaya, Dharma, Shastra, and Puranas.

XII. 113. Even the decision of one priest, if more cannot be assembled, who perfectly knows the principles of the Vedas, must be considered as law of the highest authority, not the opinion of myriads who have no sacred knowledge.

The Laws of Manu are eternal. Therefore, there is no question of considering how changes could be effected in them. The only question Manu had to consider was how to uphold and maintain the system. Manu has laid down several provisions with this purpose in mind.

As to the preservation of the Social Code, Manu has made it the duty of the king to uphold and maintain:

VIII. 410. The king should order each man of the mercantile class to practice trade, money lending, agriculture and attendance on cattle, and each man of the servile class to act in the service of the twice-born.

VIII. 418. With vigilant care should the king exert himself in compelling merchants and mechanics to perform their respective duties, for when such men swerve from their duty, they throw this world into confusion.

Failure to maintain was made an offense by the king, punishable by Law.

VIII. 335. Neither a father, nor a preceptor, nor a friend, nor a mother, nor a wife, nor a son, nor a domestic priest must be left unpunished by the king, if they adhere not with firmness to their duty.

VIII. 336. Where another man of lower birth would be fined one pana, the king shall be fined a thousand, and he shall give the fine to the priests or cast it into the river; this is a sacred rule.

Failure to uphold and maintain the system on the part of the king involved a forfeiture of his right to rule, for Manu allows the right to rebel against such a king.

VIII. 348. The twice-born may take up arms when their duty is obstructed by force and when, in some evil time, a disaster has struck the twice-born classes.

The right of rebellion is given to the three higher classes and not to the Shudras. It is very natural, because only the three upper classes would benefit from the maintenance of this system. But supposing the Kshatriyas joined the king in destroying the system—what is to be done? Manu gives the authority to the Brahmins to punish all, and particularly the Kshatriyas.

XI. 31. A priest who knows the laws well need not complain to the king of any grievous injury since, even by his own power, he may chastise those who injure him.

XI. 32. His own power, which depends on himself alone, is mightier than the royal power, which depends on other men; by his own might, therefore, may a Brahmin coerce his foes.

XI. 33. He may use, without hesitation, the powerful charms revealed to Atharvan and by him to Angiras, for speech is the weapon of a Brahmin, with that, he may destroy his oppressors.

IX. 320. Of a military man who raises his arm violently on all occasions against the priestly class, the priest himself shall be the chastiser since the soldier originally proceeded from the Brahmin.

How can the Brahmins punish the Kshatriyas unless they can take arms? Manu is aware of this and, therefore, allows the Brahmins to arm themselves to punish the Kshatriyas.

XII. 100. Command of armies, royal authority, power of inflicting punishment, and sovereign dominion over all nations—he alone truly deserves, who perfectly understands the Veda Shastra.

So intent is Manu on the maintenance of the system of *Chaturvarna* that he did not hesitate to make this fundamental change in it. Asking a Brahmin to take up arms is a fundamental change compared to the rule that was prevalent before Manu. The prohibition against Brahmins handling arms was very strict. In the *Apastamba Dharma Sutras,* which predates Manu, the rule is laid down in the following terms:

I. 10, 29, 6. A Brahmin shall not take up a weapon in his hand, though he is only desirous of examining it.

The successor of Manu—Baudhayana—improved upon this and laid down in his Code of Laws:

II. 24, 18. For the protection of the cows and Brahmins, or in the case of the confusion of Varnas, Brahmins, and Vaishyas (also) should take up arms, out of consideration for the Dharma, and maintain the system at any cost.

❑

Chapter 9

Essays on the Bhagavad Gita: Philosophic Defence of Counter-Revolution: Krishna and His Gita

The first page of 'Essays on the Bhagavad Gita' is autographed by Dr. Ambedkar. The next 42 pages consist of analytical notes on the Virata Parva and Udyoga Parva, including the table of contents on this subject. The table of contents is printed in the schemes. This file contains two typed copies of an essay entitled 'Philosophic Defence of Counter-Revolution: Krishna and His Gita'. The last sentence of this essay is left incomplete. The total number of typed pages of this essay is only 40. The notes on Virata Parva and Udyoga Parva are printed in the next chapters.

– Editors

What is the place of the Bhagavad Gita in the literature of ancient India? Is it a gospel of the Hindu Religion in the same way as the Bible is of the Christian Religion? The Hindus have come to regard it as their gospel. If it is a gospel, what does it really teach? What is the doctrine it stands for? The variety of answers given to this question by students competent to speak on the subject is bewildering. Bohtlingk says:

"The Gita contains, by the side of many high and beautiful thoughts, not only a few weak points; contradictions (which the commentators have tried to pass over as excusable), repetitions, exaggerations, absurdities, and loathsome points.'"

"Hopkins speaks of the *Bhagavad Gita* as a Characteristic work of the Hindu literature in its sublimity as in its puerilities, in its logic as in its want of it; an ill-assorted cabinet of primitive philosophical opinions." In his judgment:

"Despite its occasional power and musical exaltation, the Divine song in its present state as a poetical production is unsatisfactory. The same thing is repeated over again, and the contradictions in phraseology and meaning are as numerous as the repetitions, so one is not surprised to find it described as 'the wonderful song, which causes the hair to stand on end.'"

Holtzmann says:

"We have before us in the *Bhagavad Gita* a Vishnuite revision of a pantheistic poem."

Garbe observes:

"The whole character of the poem, in its design and execution, is preponderatingly theistic. A personal God, Krishna, stands forth as a human hero, expounds his doctrine, and enjoins, above all things, on his listener, along with the performance of his duties, loving faith in Him and self-surrender. And by the side of this God—who is delineated as personally as possible, and who dominates the whole poem—stands out frequently the impersonal, neutral Brahman, the Absolute, as the highest principle. At one time, Krishna says that He is the sole Highest God who has created the world and all beings and rules over it all; at another time, He expounds the Vedantic doctrine of Brahmin and *maya*—the Cosmic Illusion—and expounds as the highest goal of human being that he be freed from the World-Illusion and become Brahmin. These two doctrines—the theistic and the pantheistic—are mixed up with each other and follow each other, sometimes quite unconnected and sometimes loosely connected. And it is not the case that the one is represented as a lower, exoteric, and the other as the higher esoteric doctrine. It is nowhere taught that Theism is a preliminary step to the knowledge of the reality or its symbol, and that the pantheism of the *Vedanta* is the ultimate reality itself. However, the two beliefs are treated of almost throughout as though there was indeed no difference between them, either verbal or real." Mr. Telang says:

"There are several passages in the *Gita* that are not very easy to reconcile with one another, and no attempts have been made to harmonize them. Thus, for example, in stanza 16 of Chapter VII, Krishna divides his devotees into four classes, one of which consists of 'men of knowledge', whom Krishna says he considers 'as his own self'. It would probably be difficult to imagine any expression that indicates higher esteem. Yet, in stanza 46 of Chapter VI, we have it laid down that the devotee is superior not only to the mere performer of penances but even to the men of knowledge. The commentators betray their gnostic bias by interpreting 'men of knowledge' in this latter passage to mean those who have acquired erudition in the Shastras and their significations. It is not an interpretation to be necessarily rejected. But there is in it a certain twisting of words, which, under the circumstances here, I am not inclined to accept. On the other hand, it must not be forgotten that the implications fairly derivable from Chapter IV, stanza 39 (pp. 62, 63) would seem to be that knowledge is superior to devotion—is the higher stage to be reached through devotion as the stepping stone. In another passage again in *Gita*, Chapter XII, stanza 12, concentration is focused on knowledge, which also seems to me to be irreconcilable with Chapter VII, stanza 16. Take still another instance. In Gita, Chapter III, stanza 15, it is said that 'Lord receives the sin or merit of none.' Yet, in Chapter V, stanza 24, Krishna calls himself the Lord and 'enjoyer of all sacrifices and penances'. It may be well asked, can the Supreme Being 'enjoy that which he does not even receive?' Once more, in Chapter X, stanza 29, Krishna declares that 'none is hateful to me, none dear.' Yet the remarkable verse at the close of Chapter XII seems to stand in point-blank contradiction to that declaration. There, through a most elaborate series of stanzas, the burden of Krishna's eloquent sermon is, 'Such a one is dear to me.' And again, in those fine verses, where Krishna winds up his Divine Law, he tells Arjuna, that he, Arjuna, is 'dear' to Krishna. Krishna also speaks of that devotee as 'dear' to him who may publish the mystery of the *Gita* among those who reverence the Supreme Being. And yet again, how are we to reconcile the same passage about none being 'hateful or dear' to Krishna with his own words in Chapter XVI, stanza 18, and following stanzas? The language used in describing the 'demoniac' people there mentioned is not remarkable for sweetness towards them. However, Krishna says positively, 'I hurl down such people into demoniac wombs, whereby they go down into misery and the vilest condition.' These persons are scarcely characterized with accuracy 'as neither hateful nor dear' to Krishna. It seems to me that all these are real inconsistencies in the Gita—not such, perhaps, as might not be explained away, but such, I think, as indicate a mind making guesses at truth, as Professor Max Muller puts it, rather than a mind elaborating a complete and organized system of philosophy. There is not even a trace of consciousness on the part of the author that these inconsistencies exist. And the contexts of the various pasages indicate, in my judgment, that a half-truth is struck out here. Another half-truth there, with special reference to the special subject then under discussion, but no attempt is made to organize the various half-truths which are apparently incompatible into a symmetrical whole, where the apparent inconsistencies might possibly vanish altogether in the higher synthesis."

These are the views of what might be called modern scholars. Turning to the views of the orthodox Pandits, we again find a variety of views. One view is that the Bhagavad Gita is not a sectarian book. It pays equal respect to the three ways of salvation: (1) *Karma Marga* or the path of works, (2) *Bhakti Marga* or the path of devotion, and (3) *Jnana Marga* or the path of knowledge, and preaches the efficacy of all three as means of salvation. In support of their contention that the *Gita* respects all the three ways of salvation and accepts the efficacy of each one of them, the Pandits point out that of the 18 chapters of the *Bhagavad Gita*, Chapters I to VI are devoted to the preaching of the *Jnana Marga*, Chapters VII to XII to the preaching of *Karma Marga,* and Chapters XII to XVIII to the preaching of *Bhakti Marga,* and say that this equal distribution of its chapters shows that the *Gita* upholds all the three modes of salvation.

Quite contrary to the view of the Pandits is the view of Shankaracharya and Mr. Tilak, both of whom must be classed among orthodox writers. Shankaracharya believed that the *Bhagavad Gita* preached that the *Jnana Marga* was the only true way of salvation. Mr. Tilak does not agree with the views of any of the other scholars. He repudiates the view that the *Gita* is a bundle of inconsistencies. He does not agree with the Pandits, who say that the *Bhagavad Gita* recognises all the three ways of salvation. Like Shankaracharya, he insists that the *Bhagavad Gita* has a definite doctrine to preach. But he differs from Shankaracharya and holds that the *Gita* teaches *Karma Yoga* and not *Jnana Yoga*.

It cannot be a matter of great surprise to find such a variety of opinions as to the message that the *Bhagavad Gita* preaches. One is forced to ask why there should be such a divergence of opinion among scholars. My answer to this question is that scholars have gone on a false errand. They have gone on a search for the message of the *Bhagavad Gita* on the assumption that it is a gospel as the *Quoran*, the *Bible,* or the *Dhammapada* is. In my opinion, this assumption is quite a false assumption. The *Bhagavad Gita* is not a gospel, and it can, therefore, have no message, and it is futile to search for one. The question will no doubt be asked: What is the *Bhagavad Gita* if it is not a gospel? My answer is that the *Bhagavad Gita* is neither a book of religion nor a treatise on philosophy. What the *Bhagavad Gita* does is to defend certain dogmas of religion on philosophical grounds. If, on that account, anybody wants to call it a book of religion or a book of philosophy, he may please himself. But essentially, it is neither. It uses philosophy to defend religion. My opponents will not be satisfied with a bare statement of view. They would insist on my proving my thesis by reference to specific instances. It is not at all difficult. Indeed, it is the easiest task.

The first instance one comes across in reading the *Bhagavad Gita* is the justification of war. Arjuna had declared himself against the war, against killing people for the sake of property. Krishna offers a philosophical defence of war and killing in war. This philosophical defence of war will be found in Chapter II, verses 11 to 28. The philosophical defence of war offered by the *Bhagavad Gita* proceeds along two lines of argument. One line of argument is that, anyhow, the world is perishable, and man is mortal. Things are bound to come to an end. Man is bound to die. Why should it make any difference to the wise whether man dies a natural death or whether he is done to death as a result of violence? Life is unreal. Why shed tears because it has ceased to be? Death is inevitable. Why bother how it has resulted? The second line of argument in justification of war is that it is a mistake to think that the body and the soul are one. They are separate. Not only are the two quite distinct, but they differ since the body is perishable while the soul is eternal and imperishable. When death occurs, it is the body that dies. The soul never dies. Not only does it never die, but air cannot dry it, fire cannot burn it, and a weapon cannot cut it. It is, therefore, wrong to say that when a man is killed, his soul is killed. What happens is that his body dies. His soul discards the dead body as a person discards his old clothes—wears a new ones and carries on. As the soul is never killed, killing a person can never be a matter of any moment. War and killing, therefore, need to give no ground to remorse or shame, so argues the *Bhagavad Gita*.

Another dogma to which the *Bhagavad Gita* comes forward to offer a philosophical defence is Chaturvarnya. The *Bhagavad Gita*, no doubt, mentions that the *Chaturvarnya* is created by God and, therefore, sacrosanct. However, it does not make its validity dependent on it. It offers a philosophical basis to the theory of

Chaturvarnya by linking it to the theory of innate, inborn qualities in men. The fixing of the *Varna* of a man is not an arbitrary act, says the *Bhagavad Gita*, but it is fixed according to his innate, inborn qualities.

The third dogma for which the *Bhagavad Gita* offers a philosphical defence is the *Karma Marga*. By *Karma Marga,* the *Bhagavad Gita* means the performance of the observances, such as *Yagnas*, as a way to salvation. The *Bhagavad Gita* stands out most for the *Karma Marga* throughout and is a great upholder of it. The line it takes to defend *Karma Yoga* is by removing the excrescences which had grown upon it and which had made it appear quite ugly. The first excrescence was blind faith. The Gita tries to remove it by introducing the principle of *Buddhi Yoga* as a necessary condition for *Karma Yoga*. Sthitaprajna By becoming i.e., 'befitted with Buddhi'—there is nothing wrong in the performance of *Karma Kanda*. The second excrescence on the *Karma Kanda* was the selfishness that was the motive behind the performance of the *Karmas*. The *Bhagavad Gita* attempts to remove it by introducing the principle of *Anasakta* i.e., the performance of *Karma* without any attachment to the fruits of the *Karm*a. Founded in *Buddhi Yoga* and dissociated from selfish attachment to the fruits of *Karma,* what is wrong with the dogma of *Karma Kand*? This is how the *Bhagavad Gita* defends the *Karma Marga*. It would be quite possible to continue in this strain, pick up other dogmas and show how the *Gita* comes forward to offer a philosophical defence in their support where none existed before. But this could be done only if one were to write a treatise on the *Bhagavad Gita*. It is beyond the scope of a chapter, the main purpose of which is to assign to the *Bhagavad Gita* its proper place in the ancient Indian literature. I have, therefore, selected the most important dogmas just to illustrate my thesis.

Two other questions are sure to be asked about my thesis. Whose are the dogmas for which the *Bhagavad Gita* offers this philosophical defence? Why did it become necessary for the *Bhagavad Gita* to defend these dogmas?

To begin with the first question, the dogmas that the *Gita* defends are the dogmas of counter-revolution as put forth in the Bible of counter-revolution, namely, Jaimini's *Purva Mimamsa.* There ought to be no difficulty in accepting this proposition. If there is any, it is largely due to the wrong meaning attached to the word *Karma Yoga*. Most writers on the *Bhagavad Gita* translate the word *Karma Yoga* as 'action' and the word *Janga Yoga*, as 'knowledge' and proceed to discuss the *Bhagavad Gita* as though it was engaged in comparing and contrasting knowledge versus action in a generalized form. It is quite wrong. The *Bhagavad Gita* is not concerned with any general philosophical discussion of action versus knowledge. As a matter of fact, the *Gita* is concerned with the particular and not with the general. By *Karma Yoga* or action, the *Gita* means the dogmas contained in Jaimini's *Karma Kanda,* and by *Jnana Yoga* or knowledge, it means the dogmas contained in Badarayana's *Brahma Sutras*. That the Gita, while speaking of *Karma,* is not speaking of activity or inactivity, quietism or energism, in general terms, but religious acts and observances cannot be denied by anyone who has read the *Bhagavad Gita*. It is to life the *Gita* from the position of a party pamphlet engaged in a controversy on small, petty points and make it appear as though it was a general treatise on matters of high philosophy that this attempt is made to inflate the meaning of the words *Karma* and *Jnana* and make them words of general import. Mr. Tilak is largely to be blamed for this trick of patriotic Indians. The result has been that these false meanings have misled people into believing that the *Bhagavad Gita* is an independent, self-contained book and has no relation to the literature that has preceded it. But if one were to keep to the meaning of the word *Karma Yoga* as one finds it in the *Bhagavad Gita* itself, one would be convinced that in speaking of *Karma Yoga,* the *Bhagavad Gita* is referring to nothing but the dogmas of *Karma Kanda* as propounded by Jaimini, which it tries to renovate and strengthen.

To take up the second question: Why did the *Bhagavad Gita* feel it necessary to defend the dogmas of counter-revolution? To my mind, the answer is very clear. It was to save them from the attack of Buddhism that the *Bhagavad Gita* came into being. Buddha preached non-violence. He not only preached it, but the people at large—except the Brahmins—had accepted it as the way of life. They had acquired a repugnance to violence. Buddha preached against *Chaturvarnya.* He used some of the most offensive similes in attacking the theory of *Chaturvarnya.* The framework of *Chaturvarnya* had been broken. The order of *Chaturvarnya* had been turned upside down. Shudras and women could become *sannyasis*, a status which counter-revolution had denied them. Buddha had condemned the *Karma Kanda* and the Yagnas. He condemned them on the grounds of *hinsa* or violence. He condemned them too because the motive behind them was a selfish desire to obtain a bonus. What was the reply of the counter-revolutionaries to this attack? Only this: These things were ordained by the Vedas, and the Vedas were infallible. Therefore, the dogmas were not to be questioned. In the Buddhist age, which was the most enlightened and the most rationalistic age India has known, dogmas resting on such silly, arbitrary, irrational, and fragile foundations could hardly stand. People who had come to believe in non-violence as a principle of life and had gone so far as to make it a rule of life—how could they be expected to accept the dogma that the Kshatriya may kill without sinning because the Vedas say that it is his duty to kill? People who had accepted the gospel of social equality and who were remaking society based on each one according to his merits—how could they accept the Chaturvarnya theory of gradation and separation of man based on birth simply because the Vedas say so? People who had accepted the doctrine of Buddha that all misery in society is due to *Tanha* or what Tawny calls the acquisitive instinct—how could they accept a religion which deliberately invited people to obtain boons by sacrifices merely because there is behind it the authority of the Vedas? There is no doubt that, under the furious attack of Buddhism, Jaimini's counter-revolutionary dogmas were tottering and would have collapsed had they not received the support the *Bhagavad Gita* gave them. The philosophical defence of the counter-revolutionary doctrines given by the *Bhagwat Gita* is by no means impregnable. The philosophical defence offered by the *Bhagavad Gita* of the Kshatriya's duty to kill is, to say the least, puerile. To say that killing is no killing because what is killed is the body and not the soul is an unheard-of defence of murder. This is one of the doctrines that some people say that doctrines make one's hair stand on end. If Krishna were to appear as a lawyer acting for a client who is being tried for murder and pleaded the defence set out by him in the *Bhagavad Gita,* there is not the slightest doubt that he would be sent to the lunatic asylum. Similarly childish is the defence of the *Bhagavad Gita* for the dogma of *Chaturvarnya.* Krishna defends it based on the *Guna* theory of the Sankhya. But Krishna does not seem to have realised what a fool he has made of himself. In the *Chaturvarnya,* there are four *Varnas*. But the gunas according to the Sankhyas are only three. How can a system of four varnas be defended on the basis of a philosophy which does not recognise more than three varnas? The whole attempt of the *Bhagavad Gita* to offer a philosophical defence of the dogmas of counter-revolution is childish and does not deserve a moment's serious thought. Nonetheless, there is not the slightest doubt that without the help of the *Bhagavad Gita* the counter-revolution would have died out of sheer stupidity of its dogmas. Mischievous as it may seem to the revolutionaries, the part played by the *Bhagavad Gita* resuscitated the counter-revolution. If the counter-revolution lives even today, it is entirely due to the plausibility of the philosophical defence that it received from the *Bhagavad Gita*—anti-Veda and anti-Yagna. Nothing can be a greater mistake than this. As will appear from other portions of the *Bhagavad Gita,* it is not against the authority of the Vedas and Shastras (XVI, 23, 24: XVII, I I, 13, 24). Nor is it against the sanctity of the Yagnas (III. 915). It upholds the virtue of both.

There is, therefore, no difference between Jaimini's *Purva Mimamsa* and the *Bhagavad Gita.* If anything, the *Bhagavad Gita* is a more formidable supporter of counter-revolution than Jaimini's *Purva Mimamsa* could have ever been. It is formidable because it seeks to give to the doctrines of counter-revolution that philosophical and, therefore, permanent basis which they never had before and without which they would never have survived.

Particularly more formidable than Jaimini's *Purva Mimamsa* is the philosophical support that the *Bhagavad Gita* gives to the central doctrine of counter-revolution—namely, *Chaturvarnya*. The soul of the *Bhagavad Gita* seems to be the defence of *Chaturvarnya* and securing its observance in practice. Krishna does not merely rest content with saying that *Chaturvarnya* is based on *guna and karma*, but he goes further and issues two positive injunctions.

The first injunction is contained in Chapter III, verse 26. In this, Krishna says that a wise man should not, by counter-propaganda, create doubt in the mind of an ignorant person who is a follower of *Karma-kand* which, of course, includes the observance of the rules of *Chaturvarnya*. In other words, one must not agitate or excite people to rise in rebellion against the theory of *Karma-kand* and all that it includes. The second injunction is laid down in Chapter XVIII, verses 4148. In this, Krishna tells everyone to perform the duty prescribed for his Varna and no other and warns those who worship him and are his devotees that they will not obtain salvation by mere devotion but by devotion accompanied by the observance of duty laid down for their Varna. In short, a Shudra, however great he may be as a devotee, will not get salvation if he has transgressed the duty of the Shudra—namely, to live and die in the service of the higher classes. The second part of my thesis is that the essential function of the *Bhagavad Gita* to give new support to Jaimini—at least in those portions of it which offer a philosophical defence of Jaimini's doctrines—and, therefore, must have been written after Jaimini's *Purva Mimamsa* had been promulgated. The third part of my thesis is that this philosophical defence of the *Bhagavad Gita*, and of the doctrines of couter-revolution became necessary because of the attack to which they were subjected by the revolutionary and rationalistic thought of Buddhism.

I must now turn to the objections that are likely to be raised against the validity of my thesis. I see one looming large before me. I shall be told that I am assuming that the *Bhagavad Gita* is posterior in time to Buddhism and to Jaimini's *Purva Mimamsa* and that this assumption has no warrant behind it. I am aware of the fact that my thesis runs counter to the most cherished view of Indian scholars, all of whom seem to be more concerned with fixing a very ancient date for the composition of the *Bhagavad Gita,* far anterior to Buddhism and Jaimini, than in finding out what is the message of the *Bhagavad Gita* and what value it has as a guide to man's life. This is particularly the case with Mr.Telang and Mr.Tilak. But as Garbe observes: "To Telang, as to every Hindu—howsoever enlightened—it is an article of faith to believe in so high an antiquity of the *Bhagavad Gita* and where such necessities are powerful, criticism indeed comes to an end." In the words of Prof. Garbe:

"The task of assigning a date to the *Gita* has been recognised by everyone who has earnestly tried to solve the problem as being very difficult, and the difficulties grow all the more if the problem is presented twofold, viz., to determine as well the age of the original *Gita* as also of its revision. I am afraid that, generally speaking, we shall succeed in arriving, not at any certainties, but only at probabilities in this matter."

What are the probabilities? I have no doubt that the probabilities are in favour of my thesis. Indeed, so far as I can see, there is nothing against it. In examining this question, I propose first to advance direct evidence from the *Gita* itself, showing that it was composed after Jaimini's *Purva Mimamsa* and after Buddhism.

Chapter III, verses 9-13 of the *Bhagavad Gita* have a special significance. In this connection, it is true that the *Bhagavad Gita* does not refer to Jaimini by name, nor does it mention *Mimamsa* by name. But is there any doubt that in Chapter III, verses 9-18, the *Bhagavad Gita* is dealing with the doctrines formulated by Jaimini in his *Purva Mimamsa*? Even Mr. Tilak, who believes in the antiquity of the *Bhagavad Gita* has to admit that here, the *Gita* is engaged in the examination of the *Purva Mimamsa* doctrines. There is another way of presenting this argument. Jaimini preaches pure and simple *Karma Yoga*. The *Bhagavad Gita,* on the other hand, preaches *Anasakta Karma*. Thus the *Gita* preaches a doctrine which is fundamentally modified Not only does the *Bhagavad Gita* modify the *Karma Yoga,* but it also attacks the upholders of pure and simple *Karma Yoga* in somewhat severe terms. If the *Gita* is before Jaimini, one would expect Jaimini to take note of this attack on the *Bhagavad Gita* and reply to it. But we do not find any reference in Jaimini to this *Anasakta Karma Yoga* of the *Bhagavad Gita*.

Why? The only answer is that this modification came after Jaimini and not before—which is simply another way of saying that the *Bhagavad Gita* was composed after Jaimini's *Purva Mimamsa*.

The *Bhagavad Gita* does not mention *Purva Mimamsa,* but it does mention by name the *Brahma Sutras* of Badarayana. This reference to *Brahma Sutras* is a matter of great significance, for it furnishes direct evidence for the conclusion that the *Gita* is later than the *Brahma Sutras*.

Mr. Tilak admits that the reference to the *Brahma Sutras* is a clear and definite reference to the treatise of that name which we now have. It may be pointed out that Mr. Telang discusses the subject in a somewhat cavalier fashion by saying that the treatise *Brahma Sutras* referred to in the *Bhagavad Gita* is different from the present treatise which goes by that name. He gives no evidence for so extraordinary a proposition but relies on the conjectural statement of Mr. Weber—given in a footnote of his *Treatise in Indian Literature*, again without any evidence—that the mention of *Brahma Sutras* in the *Bhagavad Gita* "may be taken as an appellative rather than as a proper name." It would not be fair to attribute any particular motives to Mr. Telang for the view he has taken on this point. However, there is nothing unfair in saying that Mr. Telang shied from admitting the reference to the *Brahma Sutra* because he saw that Weber had on the authority of Winternitz, assigned 500 A.D. to the composition of the *Brahma Sutras*, which would have destroyed his cherished theory regarding the antiquity of the *Bhagavad Gita*. There is thus ample internal evidence to support the conclusion that the *Gita* was composed after Jaimini's *Purva Mimamsa* and Badarayana's *Brahma Sutras*.

Is the *Bhagavad Gita* anterior to Buddhism? The question was raised by Mr. Telang: "We come now to another point. What is the position of the *Gita* in regard to the great reform of Sakya Muni? The question is one of much interest, regarding particularly the remarkable coincidences between Buddhist doctrines and the doctrines of the *Gita* which we have drawn attention to in the footnotes of our translation. But the materials for deciding the question are unhappily not forthcoming. Professor Wilson, indeed, thought that there was an allusion to Buddhism in the *Gita.* but his idea was based on confusion between the Buddhists and the Charvakas or materialists. Failing that allusion, we have nothing tangible but the unsatisfactory 'negative argument' based on the mere non-mention of Buddhism in the *Gita.* That argument is not quite satisfactory to my mind, although, as I have elsewhere pointed out, some of the ground occupied by the *Gita* is common to it with Buddhism, and although various previous thinkers are alluded to directly or indirectly in the *Gita.* There is, however, one view of the facts of this question, which appears to me to corroborate the conclusion deducible through the negative argument here referred to. The main points on which Budddha's protest against Brahmanism rests seem to be the true authority of the Vedas and the true view of the differences of caste. On most points of doctrinal speculation, Buddhism is still but one aspect of the older Brahmanism. The various coincidences to which we have drawn attention show that if there is a need to show that. Well now, on both these points, the *Gita*, while it does not go the whole length which Buddha goes, itself embodies a protest against the views current about the time of its composition. The *Gita* does not, like Buddhism, absolutely reject the Vedas, but it shelves them. The *Gita* does not totally root out caste. It places caste on a less untenable basis. One of two *hypotheses,* therefore, presents itself as a rational theory of these facts: either the *Gita* and Buddhism were similar in the outward manifestation of the same spiritual upheaval which shook to its centre the current religion, the *Gita* being the earlier and less thoroughgoing form of it; or Buddhism, having already begun to tell on Brahmanism, the *Gita* was an attempt to bolster it up, so to say, at its least weak points, the weaker ones being altogether abandoned. I do not accept the latter alternative because I cannot see any indication in the *Gita* of an attempt to compromise with a powerful attack on the old Hindu system, while the fact that, though strictly orthodox, the author of the *Gita* still undermines the authority, as unwisely venerated, of the Vedic revelation; and the further fact that, in doing this, he is doing what others also had done before him or about his time—go, in my opinion, a considerable way towards fortifying the results of the negative argument already set forth. To me, Buddhism is perfectly intelligible as one outcome of that play of thought on high spiritual topics, which in its other, and as we may say, less thoroughgoing, manifestation we see in the Upanishads and the *Gita*."

I have quoted this passage in full because it is typical of all Hindu scholars. Every one of them is most reluctant to admit that the *Bhagavad Gita* is never any way influenced by Buddhism and is ready to deny that the *Gita* has borrowed anything from Buddhism. It is the attitude of Prof. Radhakrishnan and also of Tilak. When there is any similarity in thought between the *Bhagavad Gita* and Buddhism too strong and too close to be denied, the argument is that it is borrowed from the Upanishads. It is typical of the narrow-minded mentality of the counter-revolutionaries not to allow any credit to Buddhism on any account.

The absurdity of these views must shock all those who have made a comparative study of the *Bhagavad Gita* and the Buddhist Suttas. It is true to say that the *Gita* is saturated with Sankhya philosophy. It is far more true to say that the *Gita* is full of Buddhist ideas. The similarity between the two is not merely in ideas but also language. A few illustrations will show how true it is.

The *Bhagavad Gita* discusses *Brahma-nirvana*. The steps by which one reaches *Brahma-nirvana* are stated by the *Bhagavad Gita* to be (1) *Shraddha* (faith in oneself); (2) *Vyavasaya* (firm determination); (3) *Smriti* (remembrance of the goal); (4) *Samadhi* (earnest contemplation); and (5) *Prajna* (insight or true knowledge). From where has the *Gita* borrowed this *Nirvana* theory? Surely, it is not borrowed from the Upanishads, for no Upanishad even mentions the word *Nirvana*. The whole idea is peculiarly Buddhist and is borrowed from Buddhism. Anyone who has any doubt on the point may compare this *Brahma-nirvana* of the *Bhagavad Gita* with the Buddhist conception of *Nirvana* as set out in the *Mahaparinibbana Sutta*. It will be found that they are the same which the Gita has laid down for *Brahma-nirvana*. Is it not a fact that the *Bhagavad Gita* has borrowed the entire conception of *Brahma-nirvana* instead of *Nirvana* for no other reason except to conceal the fact of its having borrowed it from Buddhism?

Take another illustration. In Chapter VII, verses 13-20, there is a discussion regarding who is dear to Krishna: one who knows, one who performs *karma,* or one who is a devotee. Krishna says that the devotee is dear to him but adds that he must have the true marks of a devotee. What is the character of a true devotee? According to Krishna, the true devotee is one who practices (1) *Maitri* (loving-kindness), (2) *Karuna* (compassion), (3) *Mudita* (sympathetic joy), and (4) *Upeksa* (equanimity unconcernedness). From where has the *Bhagvate Gita* borrowed these qualifications of a perfect devotee? Here again, the source is Buddhism. Those who want proof may compare the *Mahapadana Sutta* and the *Tevijja Sutta* where Buddha has preached what *Bhavanas* (mental attitudes) are necessary to cherish for the training of the heart. This comparison will show that the whole ideology is borrowed from Buddhism and that too word for word.

Take a third illustration. In Chapter XIII, the *Bhagavad Gita* discusses the subject of *Kshetra and Kshetrajna*. In verses 7-11, Krishna points out what is knowledge and what is ignorance in the following language:

"Pridelessness (humility), unpretentiousness, non-injury or harmlessness, forgiveness, straightforwardness (uprightness), devotion to preceptor, purity, steadiness, self-restraint, desirelessness towards objects of sense, absence of egoism, reflection on the suffering and evil of birth, death, decrepitude, and disease, non-attachment, non-identification of oneself concerning son, wife, and home and the rest, constant even-mindedness on approach of both (what is) agreeable and (what is) disagreeable, unswerving devotion to Me with undivided meditation of Me, resort to sequestered spots (contemplation, concentration, in solitude), distaste for the society of worldly men, incessant application to the knowledge relating to self, perception or realisation of the true purport of the knowledge of the *Tattvas* (Samkhya philosophy)—all this is called 'knowledge'; what is *Ajnana* (ignorance) is the reverse thereof." Can anyone who knows anything of the Gospel of Buddha deny that the *Bhagavad Gita* has, in these stanzas, reproduced word for word the main doctrines of Buddhism?

In Chapter XIII, verses 5, 6, 18 and 19, the *Bhagavad Gita* gives a new metaphorical interpretation of *karmas* under various heads: (1) *Yagnas* (sacrifices); (2) *Dana* (gifts); (3) *Tapas* (penances); (4) Food; and (5) *Svadhyaya* (Vedic study). What is the source of this new interpretation of old ideas? Compare this with what Buddha is reported to have said in the Nikaya Majjhima I, 286, Sutta XVI. Can anyone doubt that what Krishna says in verses 5, 6, 18, and 19 of Chapter XVII is a verbatim reproduction of the words of Buddha?

These are only a few illustrations I have selected—those of major doctrinal importance. Those interested in pursuing the subject may refer to the similarities between the *Gita* and Buddhism noted by Telang in the footnotes to his edition of the *Bhagavad Gita* and satisfy their curiosity. But the illustrations I have given should be enough to show how greatly the *Bhagavad Gita* is permeated by Buddhistic ideology and how much the *Gita* has borrowed from Buddhism. To sum up, the *Bhagavad Gita* seems deliberately modelled on the Buddhists Suttas. The Buddhists Suttas are dialogues. So is the *Bhagavad Gita*. Buddha's religion offered salvation to women and Shudras. Krishna also comes forward to offer salvation to women and Shudras. Buddhists say, "I surrender to Buddha, Dhamma, and Sangha." So Krishna says, "Give up all religions and surrender unto Me." No parallel can be closer than what exists between Buddhism and the *Bhagavad Gita*.

IV

I have shown that the *Gita* came into existence later than *Purva Mimamsa* and even later than Buddhism. I could well stop here. But I feel I cannot, for there remains one argument against my thesis which requires an answer. It is the argument of Mr. Tilak. It is an ingenious argument. Mr. Tilak realises that there are many similarities in ideas and words between the *Bhagavad Gita* and Buddhism. Buddhism, being earlier than the *Bhagavad Gita*, leads to the obvious conclusion that the *Bhagavad Gita* is the debtor and Buddhism is the creditor. This obvious conclusion is not palatable to Mr. Tilak, or for that matter, to all upholders of counter-revolution. For them, it is a question of honour that counter-revolution should not be shown to be indebted to the revolution. To get over this difficulty, Mr. Tilak has struck a new line. He points out the distinction between *Hinayana* Buddhism and *Mahayana* Buddhism and says, that *Mahayana* Buddhism was later than *Bhagavad Gita.* Therefore, if there are any similarities between Buddhism and the *Bhagavad Gita*, it is due to the borrowing by the Mahayanists from the *Bhagavad Gita*. It raises two questions: What is the date of the origin of *Mahayana* Buddhism? What is the date of the composition of the *Bhagavad Gita*? The argument of Mr. Tilak is ingenious. But it has no substance. In the first place, it is not original. It is based on certain casual remarks made by Winternitz and by Kern in footnotes, which suggests that there are certain similarties between the *Bhagavad Gita* and Mahayana Buddhism and that these similarities are the result of *Mahayana* Buddhism borrowing its ideas from the *Bhagavad Gita*. Behind these remarks, there is no evidence of special research either on the part of Winternitz, Kern, or Mr. Tilak. All of them seem to be led away by the assumption that the *Bhagavad Gita* is earlier than *Mahayana* Buddhism.

It leads me to examine the question of the date of composition of the *Bhagavad Gita,* particularly with reference to the theory put forth by Mr. Tilak. Mr. Tilak is of the opinion that the *Gita* is part of the *Mahabharata* and that both have been written by one and the same author named Vyasa. Consequently, the date of composition of the *Mahabharata* must be the date of the *Bhagavad Gita*. The *Mahabharata*, Mr. Tilak argues, must have been written at least 500 years before the Saka Era on the ground that the stories contained in the *Mahabharata* were known to Megasthenes, who was in India about 300 B.C. as a Greek ambassador to the court of Chandragupta Maurya. The Saka Era began in 78 A.D. On this basis, it follows that the *Bhagavad Gita* must have been composed before 422 B.C. This is his view about the date of the composition of the present *Gita*. According to him, the original *Gita* must have been some centuries older than *Mahabharata* if reliance is placed on the tradition referred to in the *Bhagavad Gita* that the religion of the *Bhagavad Gita* was taught by Nara to Narayana in very ancient times. Mr. Tilak's theory as to the date of the composition of the *Mahabharata* is untenable. In the first place, it assumes that the whole of the *Bhagavad Gita* and the whole of the *Mahabharata* have been written in one stretch, at one time, and by one hand. There is no warrant for such an assumption, either in tradition or in the internal evidence of these two treatises. Confining the discussion to the *Mahabharata,* the assumption made by Mr. Tilak is quite opposed to well-known Indian traditions. This tradition divides the composition of the *Mahabharata* into three stages: (1) *Jaya* (2) *Bharata,* and (3) *Mahabharata*, and assigns each part to a different author. According to this tradition, Vyasa was the author of the first edition-so to say—of the *Mahabharata* called '*Jaya*'. The second edition called '*Bharata*', assigned to authorship of the Vaishampayana, white the third edition, called *Mahabharata,* to '*Sauti*'. That this tradition is well-founded has been confirmed by the research of Prof. Hopkins, based on the examination of internal evidence furnished by the *Mahabharata*. According to Prof. Hopkins, there have been several stages in the composition of the *Mahabharata*. As pointed out by Prof. Hopkins, in the first stage, it was just a Pandu Epic consisting of plays and legends about heroes who took part in the *Mahabharata* war without the masses of didactic material. Such a *Mahabharata*, says Prof. Hopkins, may have come into existence between 400-200 B.C. The second stage was the remaking of the epic with the inclusion of didactic matter and the addition of Puranic material. This was between 200 B.C. and 200 A.D. The third stage is marked by: (1) the last books being added to the composition as it stood at the end of the second stage with the introduction of the first book and (2) the swollen Anushasana Parva being separated from *Shanti Parva* and recognised as a separate book. This happened between 200 and 400 A.D. To these three stages, Prof. Hopkins adds a fourth or a final stage of occasional amplification, which started from 400 A.D. onwards. In coming to this conclusion, Prof. Hopkins has anticipated and dealt with all the arguments advanced by Mr. Tilak, such as the mention of the *Mahabharata* in Panini and in the *Grihya-sutras*. The only new pieces of evidence produced by Mr. Tilak that have not been considered by Prof. Hopkins are two. One such piece of evidence consists of the statements which are reported to have been recorded by Megasthenes, the Greek ambassador to the court of Chandragupta Maurya, and the other is the astronomical evidence in the *Adi Parva,* which refers to the *Uttarayan* starting with the Shravana constellation. The facts adduced by Mr. Tilak as coming from Megasthenes may not be denied and may prove that at the time of Megasthenes, i.e., about 300 B.C., a cult of Krishna worship had come into existence among the Sauraseni community. But how can this prove that the *Mahabharata* had then come into existence? It cannot. Nor can it prove that the legends and stories mentioned by Megasthenes were taken by him from the *Mahabharata*. There is nothing to militate against the view that these legends and stories were a floating mass of sagas that served as a reservoir both to the writer of the *Mahabharata* as well as to Greek ambassador.

Mr. Tilak's astronomical evidence may be quite sound. He is right in saying that "it is stated in the *Anugita* that Vishwamitra started the enumeration of the constellation with Shravana (Ma. Bha.Asva.44.2, and Adi.71.34). That has been interpreted by commentators as showing that the *Uttarayan* then started with the Shravana constellation, and no other interpretation is proper. At the date of the *Vedanga-Jyotisha*, the Uttarayan used to start with the Sun in the Dhanistha constellation. According to astronomical calculations, the date when the Uttarayan should start with the Sun in the Dhanistha constellation to about 1,500 years before the Saka era, and according to astronomical calculations, it takes about a thousand years for the Uttarayan to start one constellation earlier. According to this calculation, the date when the Uttarayan ought to start with the Sun in the Shravana constellation comes to about 500 years before the Saka era. This conclusion would have been proper if it were true that the *Mahabharata* was one whole piece, written at one time by one author. It has, however, been shown that there is no warrant for such an assumption. In view of this, Mr. Tilak's astronomical evidence cannot be used to determine the date of the *Mahabharata*. It can be used only to determine the date of that part of the *Mahabharata* affected by it—in this case, the *Adi Parva* of the *Mahabharata*. For these reasons, Mr. Tilak's theory as to the date of the composition of the *Mahabharata* must fall to the ground. Indeed, any attempt to fix a single date for a work like the *Mahabharata*, which is a serial story produced in parts at long intervals, must be regarded as futile. All that one can say is that the *Mahabharata* was composed between 400 B.C. to 400 A.D.—a conclusion too broad to be used for the purpose which Mr. Tilak has in view. Even this span seems to some scholars to be too narrow. It is contended that the reference to *Edukas* in the 190th Adhyaya of the Vana Parva has been wrongly interpreted to mean Buddhist Stupas when, as a matter of fact, it refers to the Idgahs created by the Muslim invaders for Muslim converts. If this interpretation is correct, it would show that parts of the *Mahabharata* were written about or after the invasions of Muhammad Ghori.

Let me now turn to examine Mr. Tilak's theory as to the date of the composition of the *Vana Parva Gita*. There are two propositions underlying his theory. The first is that the *Gita* is part of the *Mahabharata*, both are written at one time and are the handiwork of one man. His second proposition is that the *Bhagavad Gita* has been the same as it is today from the very beginning when it first came to be written. To avoid confusion, I propose to take them separately.

Mr. Tilak's object in linking the *Gita* with the *Mahabharata* in the matter of its composition is quite obvious. It is to use the date of composition of the *Mahabharata*, which he thinks is known, to determine the date of composition of the *Bhagavad Gita,* which is unknown. The basis on which Mr. Tilak has tried to establish an integral connection between the *Mahabharata* and the *Bhagavad Gita* is, unfortunately, the weakest part of his theory. To accept that the Gita is a part of the *Mahabharata* because the author of both is Vyasa—and this is the argument of Mr. Tilak—is to accept fiction for a fact. It assumes that Vyasa is the name of some particular individual capable of being identified. This is evident from the fact that we have Vyasa as the author of the *Mahabharata*, Vyasa as the author of the *Puranas*, Vyasa as the author of *Bhagavad Gita,* and Vyasa as the author of the *Brahma Sutras*. It cannot, therefore, be accepted as true that the same Vyasa is the author of all these works, separated as they are by a long period of time extending to several centuries. It is well-known how orthodox writers, wishing to hide their identity gain better authority for their works, used to adopt the revered name Vyasa as a *nom-de-plume* or pen name. If the author of the *Gita* is a Vyasa, he must be a different Vyasa. There is another argument which seems to militate against Mr. Tilak's theory of synchrony between the composition of the *Bhagavad Gita* and the *Mahabharata*. The *Mahabharata* consists of 18 Parvas. There are also 18 *Puranas*. It is curious to find that the *Bhagavad Gita* also has 18 Adhyayas. The question is: Why should there be this parallelism? The answer is that the ancient Indian writers regarded certain names and certain numbers as invested with great sanctity. The name Vyasa and the number 18 are illustrations of this fact. But there is more in the fixation of 18 as the chapters of the *Bhagavad Gita* than is apparent on the face of it. Who set 18 as the sacred number—the *Mahabharata* or the *Gita*? If it was the *Mahabharata*, then the *Gita* must have been written after the *Mahabharata*. If it was the *Bhagavad Gita*, then the *Mahabharata* must have been written after the *Gita*. In any case, the two could not have been written at the same time.

These considerations may not be accepted as decisive against Mr. Tilak's first proposition. However, there is one consideration which I think is decisive. I refer to the relative position of Krishna in the *Mahabharata* and the *Bhagavad Gita*. In the *Mahabharata*, Krishna is not represented as a God accepted by all. The *Mahabharata* itself shows that the people were not prepared even to give him the first place. When, at the time of the Rajasuya Yagna, Dharma offered to give Krishna priority in honouring the guest, Shishupala—the near relation of Krishna—protested and abused Krishna. He not only charged him with low origin but also with loose morals, calling him an intriguer who violated the rules of war for the sake of victory. So abhorrent, but so true, was this record of Krishna's foul deeds that when Duryodhana flung them in the face of Krishna, the *Mahabharata* itself, in the *Gada Parva*, records that the gods in heaven came out to listen to the charges made by Duryodhana against Krishna, and, after listening, showered flowers as a token of their view that the charges contained the whole truth and nothing but the truth. On the other hand, the *Bhagavad Gita* presents Krishna as God: omnipotent, omniscient, omnipresent, pure, loving, and the essence of goodness. Two such works, containing two quite contradictory estimates about one and the same personality could not have been written at the same time by the same author. It is a pity that Mr. Tilak, in his anxiety to give a pre-Buddhist date to the composition of the *Bhagavad Gita*, should have completely failed to take note of these important considerations.

The second proposition of Mr. Tilak is equally unsound. The attempt to fix a date for the composition of the *Bhagavad Gita* is nothing but the pursuit of a mirage. It is doomed to failure. The reason is that the *Bhagavad Gita* is not a single book written by a single author. It consists of different parts written at different times by different authors.

Prof. Garbe is the only scholar who has seen the necessity of following this line of inquiry. Prof. Garbe holds that there are two parts of the *Bhagavad Gita*—one original and one added. I am not satisfied with this statement. My reading of the *Bhagavad Gita* leads me to the conclusion that there have been four separate parts of the *Bhagavad Gita*. They are so distinct that, taking even the present treatise as it stands, they can be easily marked off.

(i) The original Gita was nothing more than a heroic tale told or a ballad recited by the bards of how Arjuna was not ready to fight, how Krishna forced him to engage in battle, how Arjuna yielded, and so on. It may have been a romantic story, but there was nothing religious or philosophical in it.

This original *Gita* will be found embedded in Chapter I, Chapter II, verses.... and Chapter XI, verses 32-33, in which Krishna is reported to have ended the argument:

"Be my tool, carry out my will, do not worry about sin and evil resulting from fighting, do as I tell you, do not be impudent". It is the argument which Krishna used to compel Arjuna to fight. And this argument of coercion and compulsion made Arjuna yield. Krishna probably threatened Arjuna with brute force if he did not actually use it. The assumption of Vishvarupa by Krishna is only a different way of describing the use of brute force. On that theory, it is possible that the chapter in the present *Bhagavad Gita* dealing with Vishvarupa may also be a part of the original *Bhagavad Gita*.

(ii) The first patch on the original *Bhagavad Gita* is the part where Krishna is spoken of as Ishwara, the God of the Bhagavata religion. This part of the *Gita* is embedded in verses of the present-day *Bhagavad Gita* which are devoted to Bhakti Yoga.

(iii) The second patch on the original *Bhagavad Gita* is the part which introduces the Sankhya and the Vedanta philosophy as a defence to the doctrines of *Purva Mimamsa,* which they did not have before. The *Gita* was originally only a historical saga, with the cult of Krishna interwoven into it. The Philosophical portion of the *Bhagavad Gita* was a later intrusion, which can be proved quite easily from the nature of the original dialogue and the sequence of it.

In Chapter I, verses 20-47, Arjuna mentions those difficulties. In Chapter II, Krishna attempts to meet the difficulties mentioned by Arjuna. There are arguments and counter-arguments. Krishna's first argument is contained in verse 2 and 3, in which Krishna tells Arjuna that his conduct is infamous, unbecoming of an Arya, and that he should not play the part of an effeminate person, which is unworthy of him. To this, Arjuna gives a reply, which is embodied in verses 4 to 8. In verses 4 to 5, he says, "How can I kill Bhishma and Drona, who are entitled to the highest reverence? It would be better to live by begging than to kill them. I do not wish to live to enjoy a kingdom won by killing old revered elders." In verses 6 to 8, Arjuna says, "I do not know which of the two is more meritorious, whether we should vanquish the Kauravas or whether we should be vanquished by them." Krishna's reply to this is contained in verses 11 to 39, in which he propounds: (i) that grief is unjustified because things are imperishable, (ii) that it is a false view that a man is killed when the *atman* is eternal, and (iii) that he must fight because it is a duty of the Kshatriya to fight. Any one who reads the dialogue will notice the following points:

(1) The questions posed by Arjuna are not philosophical. They are natural questions posed by a worldly man faced with worldly problems.

(2) Up to a point, Krishna treats them as natural questions and returns quite natural replies.

(3) The dialogue takes a new turn. Arjuna, after having informed Krishna positively and definitely that he will not fight, suddenly takes a new turn and expresses doubt whether it is good to kill the Kauravas or be killed by them. It is a deliberate departure designed to give Krishna a philosophical defence of war, uncalled for by anything said by Arjuna.

(4) Again, there is a drop in the tone of Krishna from verses 31 to 38. He treats the question as natural and tells him to fight because it is the duty of a Kshatriya to fight.

Anyone can see from this that the introduction of the Vedanta philosophy is quite unnatural and, therefore, a later intrusion.

concerning the introduction of the Sankhya philosophy, the case is quite obvious. Often, it is expounded without any question by Arjuna, and whenever it has been propounded in answer to a question, that question has nothing to do with the war. It shows that the philosophical parts of the *Bhagavad Gita* are not parts of the original *Gita* but have been added later on, and to find a place for them, new, appropriate and leading questions have been put in the mouth of Arjuna, which has nothing to do with the mundane problems of war.

(iv) The third patch on the original *Bhagavad Gita* consists of verses in which Krishna is elevated from the position of Ishwara to that of Parmeshwara. This patch can be easily detected in chapters X and XV. As I said, to go in for a precise date for the composition of the *Bhagavad Gita* is to go on a fool's errand If an attempt in that direction is to be of any value, effort must be directed to determine the date of each patch separately. Proceeding in this way, it is possible that what I have called the original unphilosophical *Bhagavad Gita* was part of the first edition of the *Mahabharata* called *Jaya*. The first patch on the original *Bhagavad Gita,* in which Krishna is depicted as Ishwara, must be placed on point of date sometimes later than Megasthenes when Krishna was only a tribal God. How much later it is not possible to say, but it must be considerably later. It must be remembered that the Brahmins were not friendly to Krishnaism in the beginning. In fact, they were opposed to it. It must have taken some time before the Brahmins could have become reconciled to Krishna worship.

The second patch on the original *Bhagavad Gita*, having reference to Sankhya and Vedanta, must, for reasons already given, be placed later than the Sutras of Jaimini and Badarayana. The question of the date of composition of these Sutras has been carefully examined by Prof. Jacobi. He concludes that these Sutras were composed sometime between 200 and 450 A.D.

The third patch on the original *Bhagavad Gita,* in which Krishna is raised into Parmeshwara, must be placed during the reign of the Gupta kings. The reason is obvious. The Gupta kings made Krishna-Vasudev their family deity, whereas their opponents the, Saka kings, had made Mahadeo their family deity. The Brahmins, to whom religion has been a trade and who were never devoted to one God but came forward to worship the deity of the ruling race, thought of pleasing their masters by making their family deity into a high and mighty Parmeshwara. If this is the correct explanation, then this patch on the original *Bhagavad Gita* must be placed between 400 and 464 A.D.

All this goes to confirm the view that the attempt to place the *Bhagavad Gita* prior, in point of time, to Buddhism cannot succeed. It is the result of wishful thinking on the part of those who have inherited a positive dislike to Buddha and his revolutionary gospel. History does not support it. History proves quite abnormally that, at any rate, those portions of the *Bhagavad Gita* which have any doctrinal value are considerably later, in point of time, to the Buddhist canon and the Sutras of Jaimini and Badarayana.

The discussion of the dates does not only prove that the *Bhagavad Gita* came into existence later than Hinayana Buddhism, but it also came later than Mahayana Buddhism. The impression prevails that Mahayana Buddhism is later in origin. It is supposed to have come into being after 100 A.D. when Kanishka held the third Buddhist Council to settle the dissension in the Buddhist Church. It is absolutely a mistake. It is not true that after the Council, a new creed of Buddhism came into existence. What happened is that new names of abuse came into existence for very parties. As Mr. Kimura has shown, the Mahayanist is simply another name for the sect of Buddhists known as Mahasanghikas. The sect of Mahasanghikas had come into existence much earlier than was supposed to be the case. If tradition be believed, the sect had come into existence at the time of the First Buddhist Council held at Pataliputra 236 years after the death of Buddha, i.e., 307 B.C for settling the Buddhist canon, and is said to have led the opposition to the Theravada sect of Buddhism, which later came to be stigmatized as Hinayana (which means those holding to the low path). There could hardly be any trace of the *Bhagavad Gita* when the Mahasanghikas, later known as Mahayanists, came into being.

Apart from this, what have the Mahayanists borrowed from the *Bhagavad Gita*? Indeed, what can they borrow from the *Bhagavad Gita*? As Mr. Kimura points out, the doctrine of every school of Buddhism is mainly concerned, at least, with three doctrines: (1) Those which deal with cosmic existence, (2) Those which deal with Buddhology, and (3) Those which deal with the conception of human life. Mahayana is no exception to this. Except probably on Buddhology, the Mahayanists could hardly draw upon the *Bhagavad Gita*. So different is the approach of the two on the other doctrines, and even this possibility is excluded by the factor of time.

The preceding discussion completely destroys the only argument that could be urged against my thesis—namely that the *Bhagavad Gita* is very ancient, pre-Buddhistic in origin, and therefore could not be related to Jaimini's *Purva Mimamsa* and treated as an attempt to give a philosophical defence of his counter-revolutionary doctrines.

To sum up, my thesis is threefold. In other words, it has three parts. The first is that the *Bhagavad Gita* is fundamentally a counter-revolutionary treatise of the same class as Jamini's *Purva Mimamsa*—the official Bible of counter-revolution. Some writers, relying on verses 40-46 of Chapter II, hold the view that the *Bhagavad Gita* is....

(In all the copies available with us, the essay has been left here incomplete, as is seen from the above sentence
–Editors)

❑

Chapter 10

Analytical Notes of Virata Parva and Udyoga Parva

Virata Parva

1. The spies sent by the Kauravas to search for the Pandavas, return to Duryodhana and tell him that they are unable to discover them. They ask his permission on what to do.—*Virata Parva*, Adhyaya. 25.

2. Duryodhana asks for advice from his advisers. Karna suggests sending other spies. Dushasana says they might have gone beyond the sea but insists on searching for them.—*Ibid,* Adhyaya. 26.

3. Drona says the Pandavas are not likely to be defeated or destroyed. They may be living as Tapasis. Therefore, send Siddhas and Brahmins as spies.—*Ibid,* Adhyaya 27.

4. Bhishma supports Drona.—*Ibid,* Adhyaya. 28.

5. Kripacharya supports Bhishma and adds: "The Pandavas are great enemies, but a wise man does not neglect even small enemies. While they are in Agnyatavasa, you should begin collecting armies from now".— *Ibid,* Adhyaya. 29.

6. Then Susharma, King of Trigartha, raises a different subject. He says, I hear that "*Kichaka,* who was the Senapati of King

Virat, is dead. King Virat may cause us great trouble. With Kichaka dead, Virat must have become very weak. Why not invade the Kingdom of Virat? This is the most opportune time". Karna also supports Susharma saying, Why worry about the Pandavas? They are without wealth, without an army, and have fallen. Why bother with them? They might even be dead by now. Give up the search and undertake the project of Susharma."—*Ibid,* Adhyaya. 30.

7. Susharma's invades Virat's kingdom. He carries away the cows of Virat. The cowherds go to inform king Virat, asking him to pursue Susharma and rescue the cows.—*Ibid,* Adhyaya. 31.

8. Virat Prepares for war. Meanwhile, *Shatanika,* the younger brother of Virat, suggests that instead of going alone, he should take Tantipala (Sahadeva) Kanka (Yudhishthira), Vallaba (Bhima), and Granthika (Nakula) to help him fight Susharma. Virat agrees, and they all go—*Ibid,* Adhyaya. 31.

9. The war between Susharma and Virat.—*Ibid,* Adhyaya. 32.

10. Yudhishthira rescues Virat.—*Ibid,* Adhyaya. 33.

11. The announcement in the Virat Nagari that their king is safe.— *Ibid,* Adhyaya. 34.

Entry in Virat Nagari by Kaurvas

12. While King Virat is going after Susharma, Duryodhana, along with Bhishma, Drona, Karna, Kripa, Ashwatthama, Shakuni, Dushasana, Vivinshati, Vikarna, Chitrasen, Durmukha, Dushala, and other warriors, enters Virat Nagari, captures the cows of Virat, and begins to leave. The cowherds come to the palace of King Virat and give the news. They do not find the King but instead find his son, Uttar, and give him the news.—*Ibid,* Adhyaya. 35.

13. Uttar begins boasting, saying he is superior to Arjuna and will the handle. But, he complains that there is no one to act his Sarathi. Draupadi approaches him and tells him that Brihannala was once the Sarathi of Arjuna, suggesting he

ask him. He admits he lacks courage and requests Draupadi to make the request. She suggests asking his younger sister, Manorama. So, Uttar instructs Manorama to bring Brihannala.—*Ibid,* Adhyaya. 36.

14. Manorama takes Brihannala to her brothers, and Uttara persuades him to be his Sarathi. Brihannala agrees and takes the chariot of Uttara in front of the Kauravas.—*Ibid,* Adhyaya. 37.

15. Upon seeing the Kauravas army, Uttara abandons the chariot and starts running away. Arjuna stops him. The Kauravas, seeing this, begin to suspect that the man might be Arjuna. Arjuna tells Uttar not to be afraid.—*Ibid,* Adhyaya. 38.

16. Arjuna takes the chariot to the Shami tree. Seeing this, Drona remarks that the man must be Arjuna. Hearing this the Kauravas are greatly upset. However, Duryodhana says that if Drona is right, it is good for them because, if the Pandavas are discovered before the thirteenth year they will have to suffer another twelve years of exile.—*Ibid,* Adhyaya. 39.

17. Arjuna asks Uttar to climb the Shami tree and to take down the weapons.—*Ibid,* Adhyaya. 40.

18. Uttar's expresses doubts about the corpse on the Shami tree.—*Ibid,* Adhyaya. 41.

19. Uttar becomes excited after seeing the weapons.—*Ibid,* Adhyaya. 42.

20. Arjuna describes the weapons.—*Ibid,* Adhyaya. 43.

21. Uttar inquires about the whereabouts of the Pandavas.—*Ibid,* Adhyaya. 44.

22. Uttar climbs down from the tree.—*Ibid,* Adhyaya. 45.

23. The chariot Rath with the Vanar symbol appearis and, Drona becomes sure that the man is Arjuna. Bad omens are seen by the army of the Kauravas.—*Ibid,* Adhyaya. 46.

24. Duryodhana encourages the soldiers, who are frightened by Drona's confirmation that the man was Arjuna. Karna

slanders Drona and proposes to Duryodhana to remove Drona as a Commander-in-Chief.—*Ibid,* Adhyaya. 47.

25. Karna boasts and Pledges to defeat Arjuna.—*Ibid,* Adhyaya. 48.

26. Kripacharya admonishes Karna not to brag and boast, reminding him that war is regarded as harmful by the Shastras.—*Ibid,* Adhyaya. 49.

27. Ashwatthama criticises Karna and Duryodhana for slandering Drona—*Ibid,* Adhyaya. 50.

28. Ashwatthama continues to berate Karna and Duryodhana for speaking ill of Drona. Karna replied, "after all, I am only a Suta." He addes that Arjuna has behaved as poorly as Rama did towards Vali.—*Ibid,* Adhyaya. 50.

29. Ashwatthama is pacified by Bhisma, Drona, and Kripa. Duryodhana and Karna apologise to Drona.—*Ibid,* Adhyaya. 51.

30. Bhishma declares that the Pandavas have completed their 13 years of exile.—*ibid,* Adhyaya. 52.

31. Arjuna defeats the army of the Kauravas.—*Ibid,* Adhyaya. 53.

32. Arjuna defeats Karna's brother. He also defeats Karna, who then runs away.—*Ibid,* Adhyaya. 54.

33. Arjuna destroys the army of the Kauravas and breaks the chariot of Kripacharya.—*Ibid*, Adhyaya. 55.

34. The gods appear in the heavens to witness the battle between Arjuna and the army of the Kauravas.—*Ibid,* Adhyaya. 56.

35. The battle between Kripa and Arjuna ends with Kripa fleeing the battlefield.—*Ibid,* Adhyaya. 57.

36. The battle between Drona and Arjuna also ends with Drona running away.—*Ibid,* Adhyaya. 58.

37. A fierce battle takes place between Ashwatthama and Arjuna.—*Ibid,* Adhyaya. 59.

38. The battle between Karna and Arjuna results in defeat of Karna.—*Ibid*, Adhyaya. 60.

39. Arjuna attacks on Bhishma.—*Ibid,* Adhyaya. 61.

40. Arjuna kills the Kaurava soldiers.—*Ibid,* Adhyaya. 62.

41. Bhishma is defeated and flees from the battle-field.—*Ibid,* Adhyaya. 64.

42. The Kaurava soldiers faint. Bhishma advises them to return home.—*Ibid,* Adhyaya. 66.

43. The Kaurava soldiers surrender to Arjuna and plead for safety. Uttar and Arjuna return to Virat Nagari.—I*bid,* Adhyaya. 67.

44. King Virat enters his capital and is honoured by him—people.—*Ibid,* Adhyaya. 68.

45. The Pandavas enter the king's assembly.—*Ibid,* Adhyaya. 69.

46. Arjuna introduces his other brothers to Virat.—*Ibid,* Adhyaya. 71.

47. A marriage takes place between Arjuna's son and the daughter of Virat.—*lbid,* Adhyaya. 72.

48. Thereafter, the Pandavas leave Virat Nagari and settle in Upaplavya Nagari.—*Ibid*, Adhyaya. 72.

49. Arjuna thereafter brings his son Abhimanyu, Vasudev, and the Yadavas from Anrut Desh.—*lbid,* Adhyaya. 72.

50. Friends of Yudhishthira, such as Kings Kashiraj and Shalya, come with two Akshauhini armies. Similarly, Yagyasena Drupadraj arrives with one Akshauhini. Draupads sons, Ajinkya, Shikhandi, and Dhrishtadyumna, also come.—*Ibid,* Adhyaya. 72.

Udyoga Parva

1. After the marriage of Abhimanyu, the Yadavas and the Pandavas gather in the Sabha of King Virat. Krishna addresses them, discussing what should be done for the future. He suggests they must do what is beneficial both for the Kauravas and Pandavas. He explains that Yudhishthira

will accept anything—even one village—if given by *Dharma.* However, even if Duryodhana gives him the whole kingdom, Dharma will not accept it. Until now, the Pandavas have adhered to Niti. But if the Kauravas act with Aniti, the Pandavas will not hesitate to kill them. Let nobody be afraid on account of the fact that the Pandavas are a minority. They have many friends who will come to their rescue. We must try to know the wishes of the Kauravas. I suggest that we should send a messanger to Duryodhana and ask him to give part of the Kingdom to the Pandavas.—Udyoga Parva, Adhyaya. 1.

2. Balarama supports the proposal of Krishna but added that it was the fault of Yudhishthira for contiming the gamble even after knowing that he was losing at the hands of Shakuni. Therefore, instead of fighting the Kauravas he advises to get what you can by negotiation.—*Ihid,* Adhyaya. 2.

3. Satyaki rises and condemns Balarama for his stance.— *Ibid,* Adhyaya. 3.

4. Drupada supports Satyaki. and agrees to send his Purohit as a messanger to the Kauravas.—*Ibid,* Adhyaya. 4.

5. Krishna supports Drupada's decision and returns to Dwarka. Kings invited by Drupad and Virat arrive, as do the kings invited by Duryodhana.—*Ihid,* Adhva. 5.

6. Drupada instructs his Purohit on how to speak in the assembly and deal with the issue.—*Ibid,* Adhyaya. 6.

7. Arjuna and Duryodhana both go to Dwarka to ask for Krishna's aid for the war. Krishna said there will help them both. He can give his army to one and he can join the other. They have to choose what they want. Duryodhana choose the army. Arjuna choose Krishna.—*Ibid,* Adhyaya. 7.

8. Shalya arrives at the Pandavas' camp with a large army. Duryodhana thinks him lower. The Pandavas meet Shalya and request Shalya to discourage Karna in the war. Agreement of Shalya.—*Ibid,* Adhyaya. 8.

9. Adhyaya. 9—Irrelevant.
10. Adhyaya. 10—Irrelevant.
11. Adhyaya. 11—Irrelevant.
12. Adhyaya. 12—Irrelevant.
13. Adhyaya. 13—Irrelevant.
14. Adhyaya. 14—Irrelevant.
15. Adhyaya. 15—Irrelevant.
16. Adhyaya. 16—Irrelevant.
17. Adhyaya. 17—Irrelevant.
18. Adhyaya. 18—Irrelevant.
19. Satyaki joins the Pandavas with his army, while Bhagadatta ioins to Duryodhana.—Adhyaya. 19.
20. The Purohit of Drupada enters the Kaurava Sabha. He tells them that the Pandvas are willing to forgive past evil deeds of the Kauravas and make a compromise. He also states that the Pandavas have a large army but still prefer to compromise.—Adhyaya. 20.
21. Bhishma supports the Purohit. Karna objects. A dispute between Bhishma and Karna. Dhritrarashtra suggests sending Sanjaya for negotiation on their behalf.—Adhyaya. 21.
22. Adhyaya. 22—Dhritrarashtra sends Sanjaya to the Pandavas, instructing him to give his blessings and say what he deems appropriate for the occasion, ensuring that it does not escalate enmity between the two sides.
23. Adhyaya. 23—Sanjaya departs to meet to the Pandavas.
24. Adhyaya. 24—Conversation between Sanjaya and Yudhishthira.
25. Adhyaya. 25—Sanjaya condemns the idea of war.
26. Adhyaya. 26—Dharma says 'I am prepared to compromise if the Kauravas give us our Kingdom of Indraprastha.

27. Adhyaya. 27—It is *Adharma* to kill *Gurujan* to obtain a kingdom. If the Kauravas refuse to cede any part of the kingdom without war, it is better to live by begging in the Kingdom of Vrishnis and Andhakas.

28. Adhyaya. 28—Says, Yudhishthira states, "Blame us, Sanjaya, if you think we have acted or are acting against *Dharma*. Sanjaya replies that he seeks either *Swadharma* or *Shama*.

29. Adhyaya. 29—Krishna's addresses Sanjaya, explaining why war is Justified and asks him to convey his views to Dhritarashtra.

30. Adhyaya. 30—Sanjaya returns to the Kauravas and tells Duryodhana to either return Indraprastha to the Pandavas or be prepared for war.

31. Adhyaya. 30—Sanjaya advises Duryodhana to live and let them live. If he cannot return Indraprastha, let him offer the Pandavas at least five villages.

32. Adhyaya. 31—Sanjaya reaches Dhritarashtra at night and tells him, "I will give you the message of Yudhishthira in the morning".

33. Adhyaya. 32—Dhritarashtra is uneasy and wants to know the message Sanjaya brought. So he sends for Sanjaya immediately. Sanjaya gives him the message and says settle the dispute by g:iving them their share of the Kingdom.

34. Adhyaya. 34—Dhratarashtra calls for Vidura and seeks his advice. Vidura advises that the Pandavas should receive their portion of the kingdom.

35. Adhyaya. 35—Irrelevant.

36. Adhyaya. 36—Irrelevant. Vidura suggests reconciling the two sides.

37. Adhyaya. 37—Irrelevant.

38. Adhyaya 38—Irrelevant.

39. Adhyaya. 39—Dhritarashtra tells Vidura that he cannot give up Duryodhana, even though he is misled.

40. Adhyaya. 40—Vidura describes the concept of *Chaturvarna*.

41. Adhyaya. 41—Dhritarashtra asks Vidur about Brahma. He says I can't because I am a Shudra. Then comes Sanat-Sujata.

42. Adhyaya. 42—Conversation between Dhritarashtra and Sanat Sujata on Brahma Vidya.

43. Adhyaya. 43—Dialogue between Sanat Sujata and Dhritarashtra continues on the same subject.

44. Adhyaya. 44—Sanat Sujata elaborates on Brahma Vidya.

45. Adhyaya. 45—Sanat Sujata preaches the principles of Yoga.

46. Adhyaya. 46—Sanat Sujata speaks on Atma.

47. Adhyaya. 47—The Kauravas come to the Sabha to hear the message brought by Sanjaya.

48. Adhyaya. 48—Sanjaya delivers the message, particularly that part which was conveyed by Arjuna.

49. Adhyaya. 49—Praise of Arjuna & Krishna by Bhishma. Karna gets angry. Drona supports Bhisma and advices compromise.

50. Adhyaya. 50—Dhritarashtra asks Sanjaya about the allies of the Pandavas and their strength. Sanjaya taunts Dhritarashtra and then answers.

51. Adhyaya. 51—Dhritarashtra reflects on the prowess of Bhisma and sighs.

52. Adhyaya. 52—Dhritarashtra reflects on the prowess of Arjuna and sighs.

53. Adhyaya. 53—Dhritarashtra reflects on the prowess of Yudhishthira and his allies. He advises his sons to compromise with the Pandavas.

54. Adhyaya. 54—Sanjaya predicts the defeat of the Kauravas.

55. Adhyaya. 55—Duryodhana argues that the Pandavas cannot defeat them because the Kauravas have greater forces.

56. Adhyaya. 56—Sanjaya describes the arrangements for the army made by the Pandavas.

57. Adhyaya. 57—Sanjaya explains how the Pandavas have designed a strategy to kill the warriors of the Kauravas. Duryodhana claims that mentions he is not afraid of the Pandvas defeating the Kauravas became they have a larger army.

58. Adhyaya. 58—Dhritarashtra advises Duryodhana not to fight. Duryodhana however, takes an oath not to back down from battle, which makes Dhritarashtra weep.

59. Adhyaya. 59—Dhritarashtra asks Sanjaya to recount the conversation between Krishna and Arjuna.

60. Adhyaya. 60—Dhritarashtra tells Duryodhana that the Devas will help the Pandavas and will ruin the Kauravas.

61. Adhyaya. 61—Duryodhana responds that he is not afraid of the divine assistance of the Pandavas.

62. Adhyaya. 62—Karna asserts that he alone is capable of killing Arjuna.

63. Adhyaya. 63—Duryodhana declares he is fighting relying on Karna & not on Bhishma, Drona etc.

64. Adhyaya. 64—Vidura urges Duryodhana to give up his enmity.

65. Adhyaya. 65—Dhritarashtra admonishes Duryodhana for his stubbornness.

66. Adhyaya. 66—Sanjaya conveys to Dhritarashtra the message of Arjuna.

67. Adhyaya. 67—The kings assembled in the hall of the Kauravas return to their homes. Vyasa and Gandhari arrive with Vidura. Vyasa instructs Sanjaya to inform Dhritarashtra about the real Swarupa of Krishna and Arjuna.

68. Adhyaya. 68—Sanjaya enlightens Dhritarashtra about Krishna's true form.

69. Adhyaya. 69—Dhritarashtra urges Duryodhana to surrender to Krishna, but Duryodhana refuses. Gandhari rebukes Duryodhana.

70. Adhyaya 70—The different names of Krishna and their origins.

71. Adhyaya 71—Dhritarashtra surrenders to Krishna.

72. Adhyaya. 72—Conversation between Yudhishthira and Krishna. Yudhishthira that Sanjaya advised him not to rely on Dhritarashtra. Yudhistir stresses the importance of property Speaks of (Kshatradharma) & the necessity of observing it Krishna proposes to go to the Kauravas. Yudhistir does not like the idea but says to what you think is the best.

73. Adhyaya. 73—Krishna tells Dharma the secret he has in mind. Don't use soft speech with the Pandvas tells Krishna to Dharma. There are plenty of reasons why you should not make any compromise with the Kauravas. Emphasizes how the Kauravas disgraced Draupadi. Therefore Oh; Dharma do not hesitate to kill them.

74. Adhyaya. 74—Bhishma advises Krishna to use soft speech with the Kauravas.

75. Adhyaya. 75—Krishna ridicules Bhima.

76. Adhyaya. 76—Bhima makes up his mind to fight.

77. Adhyaya. 77—Krishna explains to Bhima the difference between *Daiva* and *Paurush.*

78. Adhyaya. 78—Arjuna tells Krishna to adopt *Shama* (peaceful negotiation). He suggests that war can be considered obly if shama fails.

79. Adhyaya. 79—Krishna's talk to Arjun. I will try to bring about a settlement by peace. If that is not possible be ready for war. I will not communicate to Duryodhana Dharma's willingness to accept five villages.

80. Adhyaya. 80—Nakula advises Krishna to do what he thinks is best.

81. Adhyaya. 81—Sahadeva meets Krishna and tells him to bring about a war with the Kauravas. Satyaki expresses that all warriors assembled agree with the view of Sahadeva.

82. Adhyaya. 82—Draupadi meets Krishna and tells him she will not be satisfied unless Duryodhana is punished. Krishna gives her assurance.

83. Adhyaya. 83—Last meeting between Arjuna and Krishna. Arjuna makes his best effort to advocate for *Shama.* Yudhishthira tells Krishna to give assurances to Kunti. Krishna then starts on his mission.

84. Adhyaya. 84—Krishna encounters both good and bad omens on his way to Hastinapur.

85. Adhyaya. 85—Duryodhana creates resting places for Krishna's journey to Hastinapur. Krishna arrives in Hastinapur.

86. Adhyaya. 86—Dhritarashtra tells Vidura what gifts are to be offered to Krishna.

87. Adhyaya. 87—Vidura tells Dhritarashtra that he cannot separate Krishna from the Pandavas.

88. Adhyaya. 88—Duryodhana acknowledges that Krishna is worthy of worship, but he argues that this is not the time to worship him. Bhishma tells Duryodhana to make a compromise with the Pandavas. Duryodhana desires to meet Krishna, Bhishma strong by opposes him.

89. Adhyaya. 89—Krishna's entry into Hastinapur. He meets with Dhritarashtra and stays with Vidura.

90. Adhyaya. 90—Meeting between Kunti and Krishna—Kunti expresses her sorrow. Krishna consoles her. Kunti tells Krishna two things: (1) to tell her sons to fight for their kingdom and (2) to express here sorrow for Draupadi.

91. Adhyaya. 91—The Kauravas invite Krishna to dinner, but Krishna refuses and goes to Vidura's house for a meal.

92. Adhyaya. 92—Vidura tells Krishna that he does not like Krishna's going among the Kauravas.

93. Adhyaya. 93—Krishna reassures Vidura, saying that not all the Kauravas can hurt him. He adds that he has come only because *Shama* is Punnyakarak (beneficial and Virtuous).

94. Adhyaya. 94—Krishna enters the assembly hall of the Kauravas.

95. Adhyaya. 95—Krishna addresses the assembly. He informs them Pandavas are ready for both peace and war and asks them to give half of their kingdom.

96. Adhyaya. 96—Jamadagni narrates a story against arrogance.

97. Adhyaya. 97-105—Matali Akhyan.

98. Adhyaya. 106—Narada's advice to Duryodhana.

99. Adhyaya. 106-123— Galava Akhyan.

100. Adhyaya. 124—Dhritarashtra tells Krishna to advise Duryodhana.

101. Adhyaya. 125—Bhishma advises Duryodhana. Drona supports him. Vidura condemns Duryodhana. Dhritarashtra also offers his advise.

102. Adhyaya. 126—Bhishma and Drona advise Duryodhana a second time.

103. Adhyaya. 127—Duryodhana announces, that hs will not give anything to the Pandavas.

104. Adhyaya. 128—Krishna condemns Duryodhana. Duryodhana leaves the assembly. Dushasana speaks. Krishna warns Bhishma.

105. Adhyaya. 129—Dhritarashtra asks Vidura to bring Gandhari to the assembly. Duryodhana returns—Gandhari asks him to give half the kingdom to Pandavas.

106. Adhyaya. 130—Duryodhana leaves the assembly with the intention of killing Krishna. Satyaki informs Dhritarashtra of this secret plot. Krishna's speech follows. Dhritarashtra calls Duryodhana back to the assembly and warns him. Vidura condemns Duryodhana.

107. Adhyaya. 131—Bhagwan's Vishwarupa Darshan Dhritarashtra gains *Divya Chakshu.* Krishna leaves the assembly and goes to Kunti.

108. Adhyaya. 132—Krishna tells Kunti what happened in the assembly. Kunti tells Krishna that war is natural for Kshatriyas and there is no better Dharma than this.

109. Adhyaya. 133—Kunti narrates the story of Vidula Krishna to reinforce her point.
110. Adhyaya. 134—Vidula's story.
111. Adhyaya. 135—Vidula's story.
112. Adhyaya. 136—Vidula's story.
113. Adhyaya. 137—Kunti advises her sons. Krishna advises Karna and the he departs for Upapalavya Nagari.
114. Adhyaya. 138—Bhishma and Drona advise to Duryodhana.
115. Adhyaya. 139—Bhishma expresses sorrow. Drona advises Duryodhana again.
116. Adhyaya. 140—Conversation between Dhritarashtra and Sanjaya. Krishna advises Karna.
117. Adhyaya. 141—Karna's reply to Krishna.
118. Adhyaya. 142—Krishna assures Karna that the Pandavas will win.
119. Adhyaya. 143—Karna sees bad omens. He is determined to defeat the Pandavas and returns home.
120. Adhyaya. 144—Conversation between Vidura and Pritha. Vidura knows that Duryodhana is determined to fight. Kunti expresses her sorrow and wishes to reveal Karna origin. Kunti goes to the bank of the river.
121. Adhyaya. 145—Kunti meets Karna and tells him his origin, requesting him to join the Pandavas.
122. Adhyaya. 146—Surya supports the proposal of Kunti. Karna rejects it but promises to save all the Pandavas except Arjuna.
123. Adhyaya. 147—Krishna goes to the Pandavas. Yudhishthira asks what happened in the Kaurava Sabha.
124. Adhyaya. 147, 148, 149, 150—Krishna narrates the whole story.
125. Adhyaya. 151—Appointment of the Senapati for the Pandavas' army. Entry of the Pandavas army in Kurukshetra.

126. Adhyaya. 152—Description of the Pandavas' arrangement for supplying the army.

127. Adhyaya. 153—Arrangements on the Kaurava side. The Kaurava army must enter Kurukshetra tomorrow early morning.

128. Adhyaya. 154—Yudhisthira's fear of consoles from his moral rectitude by going to war. Krishna deviating him. Arjuna tells him they must fight.

129. Adhyaya. 155—Description of Duryodhana's army.

130. Adhyaya. 156—Bhishma is appointed as the Senapati of the Kaurava army. Karna is offended decides not to take command until Bhishma is dead. The Kaurava army enters Kurushetra.

131. Adhyaya. 157—Krishna becomes the commander of the Pandavas army.

132. Balarama goes on a pilgrimage, saying,—I do not want to see the Kauravas destroyed".

133. Adhyaya. 158—Rukmi, neither wanted by Arjuna nor by Duryodhana, goes home.

134. Adhyaya. 159—Conversation between Sanjaya and Dhritarashtra. Sanjaya blames Dhritarashtra.

135. Adhyaya. 160—The Pandavas' army reaches the bank of the Hiranyavati river. Duryodhana sends offensive messages to the Pandavas and Krishna, saying, "Fight if you can".

136. Adhyaya. 161—Uluka delivers the messages.

137. Adhyaya. 162—The angry Pandavas send back heated responses. They give the order that the war will start tomorrow.

❑

Chapter II

Brahmins vs. Kshatriyas

This manuscript consists of 43 foolscap-typed pages. All the loose pages are tagged. The original title, 'Brahmins and Kshatriyas and the Counter-Revolution' has been modified in Dr. Ambedkar's handwriting as 'Brahmins Versus Kshatriyas' on the title page. The essay seems to be complete.

—Editors

The sacred literature of the Hindus contains many cases of conflicts between the Brahmins and the Kshatriyas and even of sanguinary wars between the two.

The first case reported was that of the King Vena. Vena was a Kshatriya King. His conflict with the Brahmins has been referred to in various sources. The following account is taken from the *Harivansa*:

"There was formerly a Prajapati (Lord of Creatures), a protector of righteousness, called Anga, of the race of Atrai, and resembling him in power. His son was the Prajapati Vena, who was indifferently skilled in duty, and was born of Sunitha, the daughter of *Mrityu*. This son of the daughter of (Death), owing to the taint derived from his maternal grandfather, threw his duties behind his back and lived in covetousness under the influence of desire. This king established an irreligious system of conduct; transgressing the ordinances of the Veda, he was devoted to lawlessness. In his reign, men lived without the study of the sacred books and the Vashatkara, and the gods had no soma-libations to drink at sacrifices.

No sacrifice or oblation shall be offered—such was the ruthless determination of that Prajapati as the time of his destruction approached. 'I', he declared, 'am the object, the performer of sacrifice, and the sacrifice itself; it is to me that sacrifice should be presented and oblations offered.' This transgressor of the rules of duty, who arrogated to himself what was not his due, was then addressed by all the great Rishis, headed by Marichi: 'We are about to consecrate ourselves for a ceremony which shall last for many years; practise, not unrighteousness, O Vena; this is not the eternal rule of duty. Thou art in every deed a Prajapati of Atri's race, and thou hast engaged to protect thy subject.' The foolish Vena, ignorant of what was right, laughably answered those great Rishis who had so addressed him: 'Who but myself is the ordainer of duty? Or whom ought I to obey? Who on earth equals me in sacred knowledge, prowess, austere fervour, and truth? Ye who are deluded and senseless know not that I am the source of all beings and duties. Hesitate not to believe that I, if I will, could turn up the earth, deluge it with water, or close up heaven and earth.' When owing to his delusion and arrogance, Vena could not be governed, then the mighty Rishis, becoming incensed, seized the vigorous and struggling king and rubbed his left thigh. From this thigh, so rubbed, was produced a black man, very short in stature, who, being alarmed, stood with joined hands. Seeing that he was agitated, Atri said to him, 'Sit down' (Nishida). He became the founder of the race of the Nishadas and also progenitor of the Dhivaras (Fishermen), who sprang from the corruption of Vena.'"

The second case is that of Pururavas. Pururavas is another Kshatriya King, son of Ila and grandson of Manu Vaivasvata. He came into conflict with the Brahmins, the following account of which appears in the *Adi Parva* of the *Mahabharata*:

"Subsequently, the wise Pururavas was born of Ila, who, as we have heard, was both his father and mother. Ruling over thirteen islands of the ocean and surrounded by beings who were all superhuman, himself a man of great renown, Pururavas, intoxicated by his prowess, engaged in a conflict with the Brahmins and robbed them of their jewels, although they loudly remonstrated. Sanatkumara came from Brahma's heaven and addressed to him an admonition, which, however, he did not regard. Being then straightway cursed by the incensed Rishis, he perished—this covetous monarch, who, through pride of power, had lost his understanding."

The third and a somewhat serious conflict was that between King Nahusha and the Brahmins. Nahusha is the grandson of Pururavas. The story is told in two places in the *Mahabharata*, once in the *Vana Parva* and a second time in the Udyogaparvan. The following account is taken from the *Udyoga Parva* of the *Mahabharata*:

After his slaughter of the demon Vritta, Indra became alarmed at the idea of having taken the life of a Brahmin (for Vritta was regarded as such) and hid himself in the waters. As a consequence of the disappearance of the king of the gods, all affairs, celestial as well as terrestrial, fell into confusion. The Rishis and gods then appealed to Nahusha to be their king. After first excusing himself on the plea of lack of power, Nahusha, in compliance with their solicitations, at length, accepted the high position. Up to the period of his elevation, he had led a virtuous life still, he now became addicted to amusement and sensual pleasure and even aspired to possess Indrani, Indra's wife, whom he happened to see. The queen resorted to the Angiras Brihaspati, the preceptor of the gods, who engaged to protect her. Nahusha was greatly incensed on hearing of this interference, but the gods endeavoured to appease him and pointed out the immorality of appropriating another man's wife. Nahusha, however, would listen to no remonstrance and insisted that in his adulterous designs, he was no worse than Indra himself.

'The renowned Ahalya, a rishi's wife, was formerly corrupted by Indra in her husband's lifetime. Why was he not prevented by you? And many barbarous acts, unrighteous deeds, and frauds were perpetrated by Indra in the past. Why was he not prevented by you?' Urged by Nahusha, the gods then went to bring Indrani, but Brihaspati would not give her up. At his recommendation, however, she solicited Nahusha for some delay, untill she could ascertain what had become of her husband. This request was granted. Indrani now went in search of her husband, and with the help of Upasruti (the goddess of night and revealer of secrets) ,discovered him existing in a very subtle form in the stem of a lotus growing in a lake situated in a continent within an ocean north of the Himalayas. She made known to him the wicked intentions of Nahusha and entreated him to exert his power, rescue her from danger, and resume his dominion. Indra declined any immediate interposition on the plea of Nahusha's superior strength but suggested to his wife a device by which the usurper might be hurled from his position. She was recommended to say to Nahusha that 'if he would visit her on a celestial vehicle borne by Rishis, she would with pleasure submit herself to him.'

'I desire for thee, king of the gods, a vehicle hitherto unknown, such as neither Vishnu, nor Rudra, nor the Asuras, nor the Rakshasas employ. Let the eminent Rishis, all united, bear thee, lord, in a car: this idea pleases me.' Nahusha receives this appeal to his vanity favourably and, in the course of his reply, thus gives utterance to his self-congratulation: 'He is a personage of no mean prowess who makes the Munis his bearers. I am a fervid devotee of great might, lord of the past, the future, and the present. If I were angry, the world would no longer stand; on me, everything depends. Wherefore, O goddess, I shall, without doubt, carry out what you propose. The seven Rishis and all the Brahmin-Rishis shall carry me. Behold, beautiful goddess, my majesty and my prosperity.' The narrative goes on: 'Accordingly, this wicked being, irreligious, violent, intoxicated by the force of conceit, and arbitrary in his conduct, attached to his car the Rishis who submitted to his command, and compelled them to bear him.' Indrani then again resorts to Brihaspati, who assures her that vengeance will soon overtake Nahusha for his presumption and promises that he will himself perform a sacrifice with a view to the destruction of the oppressor and the discovery of Indra's lurking place. Agni is then sent to discover and bring Indra to Brihaspati, and the latter, on Indra's arrival, informs him of all that had occurred during his absence. While Indra, with Kuvera, Yama, Soma, and Varuna was devising means for the destruction of Nahusha, the sage Agastya came up, congratulated Indra on the fall of his rival, and proceeded to relate how it had occurred:

"Wearied with carrying the sinner Nahusha, the eminent divine Rishis and the spotless Brahmin-Rishis a asked that divine personage Nahusha to solve a difficulty: 'Dost thou, O Vasava, most excellent of conquerors, regard as authoritative or not those. Brahmana texts which are recited at the immolation of kine?' 'No', replied Nahusha, whose understanding was enveloped in darkness. The Rishis rejoined: 'Engaged in unrighteousness, thou attainest not unto righteousness. These texts, which were formerly uttered by great Rishis, are regarded by us as authoritative.' Then (proceeds Agastya) disputing with the Munis, Nahusha, impelled by unrighteousness, touched me on the head with his foot. In consequence of this, the king's glory was smitten, and his prosperity departed. When he had instantly become agitated and oppressed with fear, I said to him, 'Since thou, O fool, contemnest that sacred text, always held in honour, which has been composed by former sages and employed by Brahmin-Rishis, and has touched my head with thy foot, and employest the Brahma-like, the irresistible Rishis, as bearers to carry thee, therefore, shorn of thy lustre, and all thy merit exhausted, sink sinner, degraded from heaven to earth. For ten thousand years, thou shalt crawl in the form of a huge serpent. When that period is completed, thou shalt again ascend to heaven.' So fell that wicked wretch from the sovereignty of the gods. Happily, O Indra, we shall now prosper, for the enemy of the Brahmins has been smitten. Take possession of the three worlds, and protect their inhabitants, O husband of Shachi (Indrani) subduing thy senses, overcoming thine enemies, and celebrated by the great Rishis.

The fourth case is of King Nimi. Nimi was one of the sons of Ikshvaku. The facts of his conflict with the Brahmins are related in the *Vishnu Purana,* which says:

"Nimi had requested the Brahmin-Rishi Vashistha to officiate at a sacrifice which was to last a thousand years. Vashistha, in reply, pleaded a pre-engagement to Indra for five hundred years but promised to return at the end of that period. The king made no remark, and Vashistha went away, supposing that king had assented to his arrangement. Upon his return, however, the priest discovered that Nimi had retained Gautama (who was, equally with Vashistha, a Brahmin-Rishi) and others to perform the sacrifice, and being incensed at the neglect to give him notice of what was intended, he cursed the king, who was then asleep, to lose his corporeal form. When Nimi awoke and learnt that he had been cursed without any prior warning, he retorted by uttering a similar curse on Vashistha and then died. Nimi's body was embalmed. At the close of the sacrifice which he had begun, the gods, willing on the intercession of the priests, offered to restore him to life, but he declined the offer; and was placed by the deities, according to his desire, in the eyes of all living creatures. It is in consequence of this that they are always opening and shutting (nimisha means "The twinkling of the eye").

The fifth case relates to the conflict between Vashishtha and Vishwamitra. Vashishtha was a Brahmin priest. Vishavamitra was a Kshatriya. His great ambition was to become a Brahmin. The following episode reported from the Ramayana explains the reasons why he became anxious to become a Brahmin.

"There was formerly, we are told, a king called Kusha, son of Prajapati, who had a son called Kushanabha, who was the father of Gadhi, the father of Vishwamitra. The latter ruled the earth for many thousand years. On one occasion, when he was making a circuit of the earth, he came to Vashishtha's hermitage, the pleasant abode of many saints, sages, and holy devotees, where, after at first declining, he allowed himself to be hospitably entertained with his followers by the son of Brahma. Vishwamitra, however, coveting the wondrous cow, which had supplied all the dainties of the feast, first asked that she be given to him in exchange for a hundred thousand common cows, adding that 'she was a gem, that gems were the property of the king, and, therefore, the cow was his by right.' When this offer was refused, the king increased his offer immensely , but all without effect. He then proceeds—very ungratefully and tyrannically, it must be allowed—to have the cow removed by force. But the cow breaks away from his attendants and rushes back to her master, complaining that he was deserting her. He replies that he was not deserting her but that the king was much more powerful than he. She answers, 'Men do not ascribe strength to a Kshatriya: the Brahmins are stronger. The strength of Brahmins is divine and superior to that of Kshatriyas. Their strength is immeasurable. Vishwamitra, though of great vigour, is not more powerful than thou. Thy energy is invincible. Commission me, who have been acquired by thy Brahmanical power, and I will destroy the pride, force, and attempt of this wicked prince.' She accordingly, by her bellowing, creates hundreds of Pahalvas, who destroy the entire host of Vishwamitra but are slain by him in their turn. Sakas and Yavanas, of great power and valour and well-armed, were then produced, who consumed the king's soldiers but were routed by him. The cow then calls into existence, by her bellowing and from different parts of her body, other warriors of various tribes, who again destroyed Vishwamitra's entire army—foot soldiers, elephants, horses, chariots, and all. A hundred of the monarch's sons, armed with various weapons, then rushed in great fury on Vashishtha but were all reduced to ashes in a moment by the blast of that sage's mouth. Vishwamitra, being thus utterly vanquished and humbled, appointed one of his sons to be regent and travelled to the Himalaya, where he took up austerities and thereby obtained a vision of Mahadeva, who at his desire revealed to him the science of arms in all its branches, and gave him celestial weapons with which, elated and full of pride, he consumed the hermitage of Vashishtha and put its inhabitants to flight.

Vashishtha then threatens Vishwamitra and raises his Brahmanical mace. Vishwamitra, too, raises his fiery weapon and challenges his adversary to stand. Vashishtha tells him to demonstrate his strength and boasts that he will soon humble his pride. He asks: 'What comparison is there between a Kshatriya's might and the might of a Brahmin? Behold, thou contemptible Kshatriya, my divine Brahmanical power. The dreadful fiery weapon uplifted by the son of Gadhi was then extinguished by the rod of the Brahmin, as fire is by water. Many other celestial missiles, such as the nooses of Brahma, Kala (Time), and Varuna, the discus of Vishnu, and the trident of Shiva, were hurled by Vishwamitra at his antagonist. But the son of Brahma absorbed them up in his all-devouring mace. Finally, to the intense consternation of all the gods, the warrior shot off the terrifying weapon of Brahma. But this was equally ineffective against the Brahmanical sage. Vashishtha had now assumed a direful appearance. Jets of fire mingled with smoke darted from the pores of his body; the Brahmanical mace blazed in his hand like a smokeless mundane conflagration, or a second sceptre of Yama. Being appeased, however, by the Munis, who proclaimed his superiority to his rival, the sage stayed his vengeance and Vishwamitra exclaimed with a groan: 'Shame on a Kshatriya's strength: the strength of a Brahmin's might alone is true strength; by the single Brahmanical mace, all my weapons have been destroyed.'

No alternative remained to the humiliated monarch but either to acquiesce in this helpless inferiority or to work towards his elevation to the Brahmanical order. He embraces the latter alternative: "Having pondered well this defeat, I shall betake myself, with composed senses and mind, to strenuous austere fervour, which shall exalt me to the rank of a Brahmin." Intensely vexed and mortified, groaning and full of hatred against his enemy, he travelled with his queen to the south and carried out his resolution. At the end of a thousand years, Brahma appeared and announced that he had conquered the heaven of royal sages (Rajarshis). As result of his austere fervour, he was recognised as having attained that rank.

The conflict seems to have begun in the reign of King Sudas, who belonged to the line of Ikshvaku. Vashishtha was the hereditary priest of King Sudas. For some reason, which is not very clearly stated, Sudas appointed Vishwamitra as his family priest. This brought about a conflict between Vishwamitra and Vashishtha. This conflict, once started, raged on for a long time.

The conflict between the two took a peculiar turn. If Vishwamitra was involved in a dispute, Vashishtha would side with the opponent. If Vishwamitra was involved in a dispute, Vashishtha would side. with Vishwamitra as the opponent. It was a case of one persecuting the other."

The first such episode is that of Satyavrata, otherwise called Trishanku. The story, as told in the *Harivamsa*, is as follows:

"Meanwhile Vashishtha, due to the relationship between the king (Satyavrata's father) and himself, as a disciple and spiritual preceptor, governed the city of Ayodhya, the country, and the interior apartments of the royal palace. However, Satyavrata, whether due to folly or the force of destiny, continually harboured increasing indignation against Vashishtha, who, for a reason, had not intervened to prevent his exclusion from the royal power by his father. 'The formulas of the marriage ceremonies are only binding,' said Satyavrata, 'when the seventh step has been taken, and this had not been done when I seized the damsel; yet Vashishtha, who knows the precepts of the law, did not come to my aid.' Thus, Satyavrata was incensed in his mind against Vashishtha, who, however, had acted from a sense of rightcousness. Nor did Satyavrata understand the propriety of the silent penance imposed upon him by his father. When he had supported this arduous rite, he believed he had redeemed his family position. The venerable Muni Vashishtha did not, however, (as mentioned) prevent his father from setting him aside but resolved to install his son as king. After the powerful prince Satyavrata had endured the penance for twelve years, he beheld, when he was without flesh to eat, the milch cow of Vashishtha, which yielded all objects of desire. Under the influence of anger, delusion, and exhaustion, distressed by hunger and failing in the ten duties, he slew the cow and both partook of her flesh himself and gave it to Vishwamitra's sons to eat. Vashishtha, upon hearing this, became incensed against him and imposed upon him the name of Trishanku, as he had committed three sins. On his return home, Vishwamitra was gratified by the support which his wife had received, offered Trishanku the choice of a boon. When this proposal was made, Trishanku chose the boon of ascending bodily to heaven. All apprehension from the twelve years' drought being now at an end, the Muni Vishwamitra installed Trishanku in his father's kingdom and performed a sacrifice on his behalf. The mighty Kaushika then, despite of the resistance of the gods and Vashishtha, exalted the king alive to heaven."

As stated in the *Harivamsa*:

"In consequence of the wickedness that had been committed, Indra did not rain for twelve years. At that time, Vishwamitra had left his wife and children and gone to practise austerities on the seashore. His wife, driven to extremity by want, was on the point of selling her second son for a hundred cows to support the others. But this arrangement was stopped by the intervention of Satyavrata, who liberated the son when bound and maintained the family by providing them with the flesh of wild animals. According to his father's injunction, consecrated himself to perform a silent penance for twelve years." The next episode in which they appear on opposite sides is that of Harishchandra, the son of Trishanku. The story is told in the *Vishnu Purana* and the *Markendeya Purana*. This is how the story runs:

"On one occasion, while hunting, the king heard a sound of female lamentation which it appears, proceeded from the sciences who were becoming mastered by the austerely fervid sage Vishwamitra in a way they had never been before by anyone else and were consequently crying out in alarm at his superiority. In fulfilment of his duty as a Kshatriya to defend the weak, and inspired by the god Ganesha, who had entered into him, Harishchandra exclaimed, 'What sinner is this who is binding fire in the hem of his garment, while I, his lord, am present, resplendent with force and fiery vigour? He shall today enter on his long sleep, pierced in all his limbs by arrows, which, by their discharge from my bow, illuminate all the quarters of the firmament.' Vishwamitra was provoked by this address. In consequence of his wrath, the sciences instantly perished, and Harishchandra, trembling like the leaf of an

Ashvattha tree, submissively represented that he had merely done his duty as a king, which he defined as consisting in the bestowal of gifts on eminent Brahmins and other people of slender means, the protection of the timid, and war against enemies. Vishwamitra thereupon demanded a gift as a Brahmin intent upon receiving one. The king offered him whatever he might ask: gold, his son, wife, body, kingdom, or good fortune. The saint first required the present for the Rajasuya sacrifice. On this being promised, and still more offered, he asked for the empire of the whole earth, including everything but Harishchandra himself, his wife and son, and his virtue, which follows its possess or wherever he goes.' Harishchandra joyfully agreed. Vishwamitra then required him to strip off all his ornaments, clothe himself in the bark of trees, and quit the kingdom with his wife Shaivya (Taramati) and his son. As he was departing, the sage stopped him and demanded payment of his yet unpaid sacrificial fee. The king replied that he had only the possession of his wife his son, and himself left. Vishwamitra insisted that he must nevertheless pay and that 'unfulfilled promises of gifts to Brahmins bring destruction.' The unfortunate prince, after being threatened with a curse, agrees to make the payment in a month and commences his journey with a wife unaccustomed to such fatigues amid the universal lamentations of his subjects. While Harishchandra lingers, listening to his subjects' affectionate remonstrances against his desertion of his kingdom, Vishwamitra comes up and, being incensed by the delay and the king's apparent hesitation, strikes the queen with his staff as she is dragged along by her husband. Harishchandra then proceeds with his wife and little son to Banaras, imagining that this divine city, as the special property of Shiva, could not be possessed by any mortal. Here, he finds the relentless Vishwamitra waiting for him and ready to press his demand for the payment of his sacrificial gift, even before the expiration of the full period of grace. In this extremity, Shaivya, the queen, suggests with a sobbing voice that her husband should sell her. On hearing this proposal, Harishchandra swoons then recovers, utters lamentations, and swoons again, and his wife, seeing his sad condition, swoons. While they are in a state of unconsciousness, their famished child exclaims in distress, 'O father, father, give me bread; O mother, mother, give me food; hunger overpowers me, and my tongue is parched.' At this moment, Vishwamitra returns, and after recalling Harishchandra to consciousness by sprinkling water over him, again urges the payment of the present. The king again swoons and is again restored. The sage threatens to curse him if his engagement is not fulfilled by sunset. Being now pressed by his wife, the king agrees to sell her, adding, however, 'If my voice can utter such a wicked word, I do not know what the most inhuman wretches cannot perpetrate.' He then goes into the city and, in self-accusing language, offers his queen for sale as a slave. A rich old Brahmin offers to buy her at a price corresponding to her value to do his household work. Seeing his mother dragged away, the child ran after her, his eyes dimmed with tears, and cried 'Mother.' The Brahmin purchaser kicked him when he came up, but the child would not let his mother go and continued to cry 'Mother, mother'. The queen then said to the Brahmin, 'Be so kind, my master, as to buy also this child, for without him, I shall prove to thee but a useless purchase. Be thus merciful to me in my wretchedness, and unite me with my son, like a cow to her calf.' The Brahmin agrees, saying: 'Take this money and give me the boy.' After the Brahmin had gone out of sight with his purchases, Vishwamitra again appeared and renewed his demands. When the afflicted Harishchanda offered him the small sum he had obtained by the sale of his wife and son, he angrily replied, 'If, miserable Kshatriya, thou thinkest this a sacrificial gift befitting my deserts, thou shall soon behold the transcendent power of my ardent austere fervour, my spotless Brahmanhood, my terrible majesty, and my holy study. Harishchandra promises an additional gift, and Vishwamitra allows him the remaining quarter of the day for its liquidation. When the terrified and afflicted prince offers himself for sale to gain the means of meeting this cruel demand, Dharma (God of Righteousness) appears in the form of a hideous and offensive Chandala and agrees to buy him at his price, large or small. Harishchandra declines such a degrading servitude, declaring that he would rather be consumed by the fire of his persecutor's curse than submit to such a fate. Vishwamitra, however, again comes on the scene, asking why he does not accept the large sum offered by the Chandala. When Harishchandra pleads his descent from the solar race, Vishwamitra threatens to fulminate a curse against him if he does not accept that method of meeting his liability. Harishchandra implores that he be spared this extreme of degradation and offers to become Vishwamitra's slave in payment of the residue of his debt. Whereupon the sage rejoins, 'If thou art my slave, then I sell thee as such to the Chandala for a hundred millions of money.'

The Chandala, delighted, pays down the money and carries off Harishchandra, bound, beaten confused, and afflicted, to his for going place of abode. Harishchandra is sent by the Chandala to steal grave clothes in a cemetary and is told that he will receive two-sixths of the payment, with one-sixth going to the king. In this horrid spot and degrading occupation, he spent, in great misery, twelve months, which seemed to him like a hundred years. Harishchandra then falls asleep and has a series of dreams suggested by the life he had been leading. After he awoke, his wife came to the cemetary to perform the obsequies of their son, who had died from the bite of a serpent. At first, the husband and wife did not recognize each other due to the change in appearance brought upon them by their miseries. Harishchandra, however, soon discovers from the tenor of her lamentations that it is his wife and falls into a swoon, as does the queen when she recognizes her husband. When consciousness returns, they both break out into lamentations—the father bewailing in a touching strain the loss of his son and the wife at the degradation of the king. She then falls on his neck, embraces him, and asks, 'Whether all this is a dream, or reality, as she is utterly bewildered', and adds, 'if it is reality, then righteousness is unavailing to those who practise it.' After hesitating to devote himself to death on his son's funeral pyre without receiving his master's leave, Harishchandra resolves to do so, braving all the consequences, and consoling himself with the hopeful anticipation: 'If I have given gifts, offered sacrifices, and gratified my religious teachers, then may I be reunited with my son and with thee (my wife) in another world.' The queen determines to die in the same manner. When Harishchandra, after placing his son's body on the funeral pyre, is meditating on the Lord Shri Narayan Krishna, the supreme spirit, all the gods arrive, headed by Dharma (righteousness) and accompanied by Vishwamitra. Dharma entreats the king to desist from his rash intention, and Indra announces to him that he, his wife, and son have conquered heaven by their good works. Amrita, the antidote of death, and flowers are rained by the gods from the sky, and the king's son is restored to life and the bloom of youth. The king, adorned with celestial clothing and garlands, and the queen, embrace their son. Harishchandra, however, declares that he cannot go to heaven until he has received his master Chandala's permission and paid him a ransom. Dharma then reveals to the king that it was he himself who had miraculously assumed the form of a Chandala. The king than objects that he cannot depart unless his faithful subjects, who share in his merits, are allowed to acompany him to heaven, at least for one day. This request is granted by Indra, and after Vishwamitra has inaugurated Rohitashva the king's son, to be his successor, Harishchandra, his friends, and followers, all ascend in company to heaven. Even after this great consummation, however, Vashishtha, the family-priest of Harishchandra, hearing after a twelve-years abode in the waters of the Ganges an account of all that has occured, becomes vehemently incensed at the humiliation inflicted on the excellent monarch, whose virtues and devotion to the gods and Brahmins he celebrates. He declares that his indignation had not been so greatly roused even when his own hundred sons had been slain by Vishwamitra and, in the following words, dooms the latter to be transformed into a crane: 'Wherefore that wicked man, the enemy of the Brahmins, smitten by my curse, shall be expelled from the society of intelligent beings, and losing his understanding, shall be transformed into a Vaka.' Vishwamitra reciprocates the curse and changes Vashishtha into a bird of the species called Ari. In their new shapes, the two have a furious fight, the Ari being of the portentous height of two thousand yojanas (18,000 miles) and the Vaka of 3,090 yojanas.

They first assail each other with their wings; then the Vaka smites his antagonist in the same manner, while the Ari strikes with his talons. Falling mountains, overturned by the blasts of wind raised by the flapping of their wings, shake the whole earth. The waters of the ocean overflow, and the earth itself, thrown off its perpendicular, slopes downwards to Patala, the lower region. Many creatures perish by these various convulsions. Attracted by the dire disorder, Brahma arrives, attended by all the gods, on the spot and commands the combatants to desist from their fray. They are too fiercely infuriated to regard this injunction, but Brahma puts an end to the conflict by restoring them to their natural forms and counselling them to be reconciled.

The next episode in which they come in as opponents is connected with Ambarisha King of Ayodhya.

The story relates that Ambarisha was engaged in performing a sacrifice when Indra carried away the victim. The priest said that this ill-omened event had occurred owing to the king's poor administration and would call for a great expiation unless a human victim could be produced. After a long search, the Royal Rishi (Ambarisha) came upon the Brahmin-Rishi Richika, a descendent of Bhrigu, and asked him to sell one of his sons for a victim at the price of a hundred thousand cows. Richika answered that he would not sell his eldest son, and his wife added that she would not sell the youngest. 'Eldest sons,' she observed, 'being generally the favourites of their fathers and youngest sons of their mothers.' The second son, Shunahshepa, then said that in that case he regarded himself as the one who was to be sold and desired the king to remove him. The hundred thousand cows, with ten millions of gold pieces and heaps of jewels, were paid down, and Shunahshepa was carried away. As they were passing through Pushkar, Shunahshepa beheld his maternal uncle Vishwamitra, who was engaged in austerities there with other rishis and threw himself into his arms, imploring his assistance and urging his orphaned, friendless, and helpless state as claims on the sage's benevolence.

Vishwamitra soothed him and pressed his sons to offer themselves as victims in the room of Shunahshepa. This proposition met with no favour from Madhushyanda and the other sons of the royal hermit, who answered with haughtiness and derision: 'How is that thou sacrificest thine own sons and seekest to rescue those of others? We look upon this as wrong and like the eating of one's own flesh.' The sage was exceedingly wroth at this disregard of his injunction and doomed his sons to be born in the most degraded classes, like Vashishtha's sons, and to eat dog's flesh for a thousand years. He then said to Shunahshepa: 'When thou art bound with hallowed cords, decked with a red garland, and anointed with unguents, and fastened to the sacrificial post of Vishnu, then address thyself to Agni, and sing these two divine verses (gathas) at the sacrifice of Ambarisha; then shalt thou attain the fulfilment.' Being furnished with the two gathas, Shunahshepa proposed at once to king Ambarisha that they should set out for their destination. When bound at the stake to be immolated, dressed in a red garment, 'he celebrated the two gods, Indra and his younger brother (Vishnu), with the excellent verses. The thousand-eyed (Indra) was pleased with the secret hymn and bestowed long life on Shunahshepa.' The last episode recorded in which the two appear as opponents is connected with King Kalmashapada. The episode is recorded in the *Adi Parva* of the *Mahabharata*.

'Kalmashapada was a king of the race Ikshvaku. Vishwamitra wished to be employed by him as his officiating priest, but the king preferred Vashishtha.' It happened, however, that the king went out to hunt, and after having killed a large quantity of game, he became very much fatigued, as well as hungry and thirsty. Meeting Saktri, the eldest of Vashishtha's hundred sons, on the road, he ordered him to get out of his way. The priest civilly replied: 'The path is mine, O' King; this is the immemorial law; in all observances, the king must cede the way to the Brahmin.' Neither party would yield, and the dispute, waxing warmer, the king struck the muni with his whip. The muni, resorting to the usual expedient of offended sages by a curse, doomed the king to become a man-eater. 'It hapened that at that time, enmity existed between Vishwamitra and Vashishtha on account of their respective claims to be priests to Kalmashapada.' Vishwamitra had followed the king and approached him while he was disputing with Saktri. Perceiving, however, the son of his rival Vashishtha, Vishwamitra made himself invisible and passed them, watching his opportunity. The king began to implore Saktri's clemency, but Vishwamitra, wishing to prevent their reconciliation, commanded a Rakshasa (a man-devouring demon) to enter into the king. Owing to the conjoint influence of the Brahma-rishi's curse and Vishwamitra's command, the demon obeyed the injunction. Perceiving that his object was gained, Vishwamitra left things to take their course and absented himself from the country. The king, having happened to meet a hungry Brahmin, sent him, by the hand of his cook (who could procure nothing else), some human flesh to eat and was cursed by him too to the same effect as by Saktri. The curse, being now augmented in force, took effect, and Saktri himself was the first victim, being eaten up by the king. The same fate befell all the other sons of Vashishtha at the instigation of Vishwamitra. Perceiving Saktri to be dead, Vishwamitra again and again incited the Rakshasa against the sons of Vashishtha. Accordingly, the furious demon devoured those of his sons who were younger than Saktri as a lion ate the small beasts of the forest. On hearing of the destruction of his sons by Vishwamitra, Vashishtha supported his affliction as the great mountain sustains the earth. He meditated on his own destruction but never thought of exterminating the Kaushikas. This divine sage hurled himself from the summit of Meru but fell upon the rocks as if on a heap of cotton. Escaping alive from his fall, he entered a glowing fire in the forest. But the fire, though fiercely blazing, not only failed to burn him but seemed perfectly cool. He next threw himself into the sea with a heavy stone attached to his neck but was cast up by the waves on the dry land. He then went home to his hermitage. However, seeing it empty and desolate, he was again overcome by grief and went out. Seeing the river Vipasa, which was swollen by the recent rains and sweeping along many trees torn from its banks, he conceived the design of drowning himself in its water. He accordingly tied himself firmly with cords and threw himself in, but the river severing his bonds, deposited him unbound (vipasa) on dry land, whence the name of the stream, as imposed by the sage. He afterwards saw and threw himself into the dreadful Satadru (Sutlej), which was full of alligators, etc., and derived its name rushing away in a hundred directions on seeing the Brahmin brilliant as fire. In consequence of this, he was once more stranded, and seeing he could not kill himself, he went back to his hermitage." There are only particular instances of their general enmity towards each other. This general enmity was of a mortal kind, so much so that Vishwamitra wanted even to murder Vashishtha. It is mentioned in the *Shalaya Parva* of the *Mahabharata*. Says the author of the *Mahabharata*:

"There existed a great enmity, arising from rivalry in their austerities, between Vishwamitra and the Brahmin Rishi Vashishtha. Vashishtha had an extensive hermitage in Sthanutirtha, to the east of which was Vishwamitra's. These two great ascetics were every day exhibiting intense emulation regarding their respective austerities. But Vishwamitra, beholding the might of Vashishtha, was most chagrined and fell into deep thought. The idea of this sage, constant in duty, was the following: 'This river Saraswati will speedily bring to me on her current the austere Vashishtha, the most eminent of all mutterers of prayers. When that most excellent Brahmin has come, I shall most assuredly kill him.' Having thus determined, the divine sage Vishwamitra, his eyes reddened by anger, called to mind the chief of rivers. She, being thus the subject of his thoughts, became very anxious, as she knew him to be very powerful and irascible. Then, trembling, pale, and with joined hands, the Saraswati stood before the chief of munis. Like a woman whose husband has been slain, she was greatly distressed and said to him, 'What shall I do?' The incensed muni replied, 'Bring Vashishtha hither speedily so that I may slay him.' The lotus-eyed goddess, joining her hands, trembled in great fear like a creeping plant agitated by the wind. Vishwamitra, however, although he saw her condition, repeated his command.

The Saraswati, who knew how sinful his design was and that the might of Vashishtha was unequalled, went trembling and in great dread of being cursed by both the sages to Vashishtha and told him what his rival had said. Vashishtha, seeing her emaciated, pale, and anxious, spoke thus: 'Deliver thyself, O chief of rivers; carry me unhesitatingly to Vishwamitra, lest he curse thee.' Hearing these words of the merciful sage, the Saraswati considered how she could act most wisely. She reflected, 'Vashishtha has always shown me great kindness; I must seek his welfare.' Then, observing the Kaushik sage praying and sacrificing on her bank, she regarded that as a good opportunity and swept away the bank by the force of her current. In this way, the son of Mitra and Varuna (Vashishtha) was carried down. While he was being borne along, he celebrated the river: 'Thou, O Saraswati, issueth from the lake of Brahma and prevades the whole world with thy excellent streams. Residing in the sky, thou dischargest water into the clouds. Thou alone art all waters. By these, we study.' 'Thou art nourishment, radiance, fame, perfection, intellect, and light. Thou art speech; thou art Svaha; this world is subject to thee. Thou, in fourfold form, dwellest in all creatures.'

Beholding Vashishtha, brought near by the Saraswati, Vishwamitra searched for a weapon with which to make an end of him. Perceiving his anger and dreading lest Brahmanicide should ensue, the river promptly carried away Vashishtha in an easterly direction, thus fulfilling the commands of both sages but eluding Vishwamitra. Seeing Vashishtha so carried away, Vishwamitra, impatient and enraged by vexation, said to her: 'Since thou, O chief of rivers, hast eluded me, and hast receded, roll in waves of blood acceptable to the chief of demons" (which are fabled to gloat on blood). 'The Saraswati, being thus cursed, flowed for a year in a stream mingled with blood. Rakshasas came to the place of pilgrimage, where Vashishtha had been swept away and revelled in drinking to satiety the bloody stream in security, dancing and laughing as if they had conquered heaven."Some Rishis who arrived at the spot some time after were horrified to see the blood-stained water and the Rakshasas quaffing it and 'made the most strenuous efforts to rescue the Saraswati.'"

The foregoing cases relate to individual conflicts between a particular Brahmin and a particular Kshatriya. The cases which follow are cases of class or communal conflicts between Brahmins on the one hand and the Kshatriyas on the other. They are not mere conflicts. Nor is it correct to say that they were like communal riots. They were class wars undertaken by one community with the avowed intention of exterminating the other's root and branch. Two such class wars of extermination have been recorded in the *Mahabharata*. The first is a war between the Haihaya Kshatriyas and the Bhargava Brahmins. It occurred in the reign of the Haihaya King Kritavirya. The following is the description of this war in the *Adi Parva* of the *Mahabharata*.

"There was a king named Kritavirya, by whose liberality the Bhrigus, learned in the Vedas, who officiated as his priests had been greatly enriched with corn and money. After he had gone to heaven, his descendants were in want of money and came to beg for a supply from the Bhrigus, of whose wealth they were aware. Some of the latter hid their money under ground, and some bestowed it on Brahmins, being afraid of the Kshatriyas, while others again gave these last what they wanted. It happened, however, that a Kshatriya, while digging the ground, discovered some money buried in the house of a Bhrigu. The Kshatriyas then assembled and saw this treasure and, being incensed, slew all the Bhrigus, whom they regarded with contempt, down to the children in the womb. The widows, however, fled to the Himalayan mountains. One of them concealed her unborn child in her thigh. The Kshatriyas, hearing of its existence from a Brahmani informant, sought to kill it. But it issued forth from its mother's thigh with lustre and blinded the persecutors. After wandering about bewildered among the mountains for a time, they humbly supplicated the mother of the child for the restoration of their sight. But she referred them to her wonderful infant Aurva, into whom the whole Veda, with its six Vedangas, had entered, as the person who (in retaliation of the slaughter of his relatives) had robbed them of their eyesight and who alone could restore it. They accordingly had recourse to him, and their eyesight was restored. Aurva, however, meditated on the destruction of all living creatures in revenge for the slaughter of the Bhrigus and entered on a course of austerities which alarmed all: gods, asuras, and men. But his progenitors (Pitris) themselves appeared and sought to turn him from his purpose by saying that they had no desire to be revenged on the Kshatriyas: 'It was not from weakness that the devout Bhrigus overlooked the massacre perpetrated by the murderous Kshatriyas. When we became distressed by old age, we ourselves desired to be slaughtered by them. The money which was buried by someone in a Bhrigu's house was placed there for the purpose of exciting hatred by those who wished to provoke the Kshatriyas. For what had we, who were desiring heaven, to do with money?' They add that they hit upon this device because they did not wish to be guilty of suicide and concluded by calling upon Aurva to restrain his wrath and abstain from the sin he was meditating. 'Destroy not the Kshatriyas, O son, nor the seven worlds. Suppress thy kindled anger which nullifies the power of austerefervour.' Aurva, however, replies that he cannot allow his threat to remain unexecuted. His anger, unless wreaked upon some other object, will, he says, consume himself. He argues on grounds of justice, expediency, and duty against the clemency which his progenitors recommend. He is, however, persuaded by the Pitris to throw the fire of his anger into the sea, where they say it will find exercise in assailing the watery element, and in this way, his threat will be fulfilled.' The second class war, which was also a war of extermination, was declared by the Bhargava Brahmins on the Haihaya Kshatriyas. The leader of the Bhargava Brahmins in this conflict was Parashurama. The story of the birth of Parashurama is described in the *Vishnu Purana* in the following terms:

"Gadhi's daughter Satyavati had been given in marriage to an old Brahmin called Richika, of the family of Bhrigu. So that his wife might bear a son with the qualities of a Brahmin, Richika had prepared for her a dish of Charu (rice, barley, and pulse, with butter and milk) for her to eat and a similar mess for her mother, calculated to make her conceive a son with the character of a warrior. Satyavati's mother, however, persuaded her to exchange messes. She was blamed by her husband on her return home for what she had done. I quote the words of the original:

"Sinful woman, what improper deed is this that thou has done? I beheld thy body of a very terrible appearance. Thou hast certainly eaten the Charu prepared for thy mother. It was wrong. For into that Charu I had infused all the endowments of heroism, vigour, and grace, whilst into thine I had introduced all these qualities of quietude, knowledge, and patience which constitute the perfection of a Brahmin. Since thou hast acted in contravention of my design, a son shall be born to thee who shall live the dreadful, martial, and murderous life of a Kshatriya, and thy mother's offspring shall exhibit the peaceful disposition and conduct of a Brahmin." As soon as she had heard this, Satyavati fell down and seized her husband's feet, and said, 'My lord, I have acted from ignorance; show kindness to me, let me not have a son of the sort thou hast described; if thou pleasest, let me have a grandson of that description.' Subsequently, she bore Jamadagni, and her mother gave birth to Vishwamitra. Satyavati became the river called Kaushiki. Jamadagni wedded Renuka, the daughter of Renu, of the family of Ikshvaku, and on her he begot a son called Parashurama." The following additional details about Parashurama's family history are given in the *Vena Parva* of the *Mahabharata*:

"Jamadagni and Renuka had five sons, the youngest of whom was the repubtable Parashurama. By his father's command, he kills his mother (who, by the indulgence of impure desire, had fallen from her previous sanctity) after the four elder sons had refused this matricidal offence, and had, in consequence, been deprived of reason by their father's curse. At Parashurama's desire, however, his mother is restored by his father to life and his brothers to reason. He himself is absolved from all the guilt of murder and obtains the boon of invincibility and long life from his father." This second class war took place in the reign of the Haihaya King Arjuna, the son of King Kritavirya. To understand it correctly, it is necessary to divide it into two parts, for there are two stages in it. The trouble began with the Brahmins claiming certain prerogatives and powers exclusively for themselves and King Arjuna scouting them in the most contemptuous terms. As the *Anushasana* Parva of the *Mahabharata* puts it.

"Then, ascending his chariot, glorious as the resplendent sun, he exclaimed in the intoxication of his prowess, 'Who is like me in fortitude, courage, fame, heroism, energy, and vigour?' At the end of this speech, a bodiless voice from the sky addressed him: 'Thou knowest not, O fool, that a Brahmin is better than a Kshatriya. It is with the help of the Brahmin that the Kshatriya rules his subjects.' Arjuna answers: 'If I am pleased, I can create, or, if displeased, annihilate living beings; and no Brahmin is superior to me in act, thought, or word. The first proposition is that the Brahmins are superior; the second is that the Kshatriyas are superior: both of these thou hast stated with their grounds, but there is a difference between them. The Brahmins are dependent on the Kshatriyas and not the Kshatriyas on the Brahmins. The Kshatriyas are not eaten up by the Brahmins, who wait upon them and only make the Vedas a pretence. Justice, the protection of the people, has its seat in the Kshatriyas. From them, the Brahmins derive their livelihood; how then can the latter be superior? I always keep in subjection to myself those Brahmins, the chief of all beings, who subsist on alms and have a high opinion of themselves. For truth was apoken by that female, the Gayatri, in the sky. I shall subdue all those unruly Brahmins clad in hides. No one in the three worlds, god or man, can hurl me from my royal authority. Wherefore, I am superior to any Brahmin." On hearing, this, Vayu comes and says to Arjuna:

"Abandon this sinful disposition and give obeisance to the Brahmins. If thou shalt do them wrong, thy kingdom shall be convulsed. They will subdue thee; those powerful men will humble thee and expel thee from thy country." The king asks him, Who art thou? Vayu replies, I am Vayu, the messenger of the gods, and I tell thee what is for thy benefit.' Arjuna rejoins, "Oh, thou displayest today a great warmth of devotion to the Brahmins. But say that a Brahmin is like any other earth-born creature. Or say that this most excellent Brahmin is something like the wind. But fire is like the waters, the sun, or the sky." Vayu then adduces various instances in which the superiority of the Brahmins has been manifested. Arjuna then drops his hostility against the Brahmins and becomes their friend. In the *Anushasana Parva,* he is reported to have said:

"I live altogether and always for the sake of the Brahmins. I am devoted to the Brahmins and do obeisance to them continually. And it is through the favour of Dattatreya (a Brahmin) that I have obtained all this power and high renown and that I have practised righteousness."

It is in the second stage that Parashurama comes on the scene and exterminates the Kshatriyas. The story is told in the *Shanti Parva* in the following terms:

"Being of a meek, pious, kind, and charitable turn of mind, the valiant Arjuna thought nothing of the curse. But his sons, who were of an arrogant and barbarous disposition, became the cause of it, resulting in his death. Without their father's knowledge, they took away Jamadagni's calf. In consequence, Parashurama attacked Arjuna and cut off his arms. His sons retaliated by killing Jamadagni. Parashurama, incensed at the slaughter of his father, having vowed in consequence to sweep away all Kshatriyas from the earth, seized his weapons and, slaying all the sons and grandsons of Arjuna, along with thousands of the Haihayas, turned the earth into a mass of ensanguined mud. Having thus cleared the earth of Kshatriyas, he became penetrated by deep compassion and retired to the forest. After some thousands of years had elapsed, the hero, naturally irascible, was taunted by Paravasu, the son of Raibhya and grandson of Vishwamitra, in a public assembly with these words: 'Are not these virtuous men, Pratardana and the others, who are assembled at the sacrifice in the city of Yayati—are they not Kshatriyas? Thou hast failed to execute thy threat and vainly boasted in the assembly. Thou has withdrawn to the mountain from fear of those valiant Kshatriyas while the earth has again become overrrun by hundreds of their race.' Hearing these words, Rama seized his weapons. The hundreds of Kshatriyas who had previously been spared had now grown into powerful kings. These, however, Parashurama now slew, along with their children and all the numerous infants then unborn as they came into the world. Some, however, were preserved by their mothers." Those who are curious to know the subsequent history of the Kshatriyas might be interested in the following extract from the *Adi Parva*.

"Having, twenty-one times, swept away all the Kshatriyas from the earth, the son of Jamadagni engaged in austerities on Mahendra, the most excellent of mountains. After he had cleared the world of Kshatriyas, their widows came to the Brahmins, praying for offspring. The religious Brahmins, free from any impulse of lust, cohabited at the proper seasons with these women, who, in consequence, became pregnant and brought forth valiant Kshatriya boys and girls to continue the Kshatriya stock. Thus, the Kshatriya race was virtuously begotten by Brahmins on Kshatriya women and became multiplied and long-lived. Thence arose four castes inferior to the Brahmins." These instances of enmity were accompanied by challenges from one side to the other, showing how high tempers were running on both sides. The conduct of King Nimi, who yoked the Brahmins to his chariot and made them drag it like horses, demonstrates how determined the Kshatriyas were to humiliate the Brahmins. The challenges uttered by Kartavirya Arjuna against the Brahmins indicate his determination to bring them down. The Brahmins, on their side, were quick to take up this challenge and issued counter-challenges to the Kshatriyas, warming them not to provoke the Brahmins. It is very clear from the way Vayu, the messenger or ambassador of the Brahmins, speaks to Kartivirya Arjuna after he had issued his challenge to the Brahmins. Vayu tells Arjuna how the Brahmins Atri made sea water salty by urinating in it, how Dandakas were overthrown by the Brahmins, how the Kshatriyas of the Talajaughas were destroyed by a single Brahmin, Aurva. The striking power of the Brahmins, Vayu asserts, is not only superior to that of the Kshatriyas but also superior to that of the Devas. Vayu then proceed to tell Arjuna some of the victories achieved by the Brahmins over the Devas. He tells him how Varuna ran away with Bhadra, the daughter of Soma and wife of the Brahmin Utathya of the Angiras race. Utathya, through his curse, caused the earth to dry up, and as a consequence, Varuna submitted to Utathya and returned his wife. Vayu also tells him how the Devas were once conquered by the Asuras and the Danavas, deprived of all oblations and stripped of their dignity. The Devas came to earth and sought protection from the Brahmin Agastya, who scorched the Danavas from heaven and earth, and made them fly to the South, and reinstated the Devas in their dominion. He tells Arjuna how once the Adityas were performing a sacrifice and, while engaged in it, were attacked by Danavas called Khalims, who came in thousands to slay them. The being Adityas went to Indra but Indra himself, attacked by the Daityas and unable to help the Adityas, went to the Brahmin Vashishtha for help. Vashishtha, taking mercy on the Adityas, saved them by burning the Danavas alive. He next tells Arjuna how the Danavas once fought with the Devas, how by enveloping them in dreadful darkness, the Danavas slaughtered the Devas, and how the Devas implored the Brahmin Atri to become the moon and dispel the gloom around the sun. Atri did so, thereby saving the Devas from the Danavas. The last episode of Brahmin prowess that Vayu recounts to Arjuna is how the Brahmin Chyavana compelled Indra to admit the Ashwins to equal rank and drink Soma with them as a token of equality. When Indra refused, Chyavana took away both the earth and heaven from him, named created a demon Mada, and put the Devas, including Indra, into his mouth. He then compelled Indra to admit the Ashwins to equal rank and drink Soma with them. Ultimately, Indra surrendered to Chyavana.

Vayu did not merely recount these exploits of the Brahmins. He did something more. Every time he gave Arjuna an instance of the power of the Brahmins, he ended by asking Arjuna pointed questions such as, "Can you tell me of any Kshatriya who was superior to him (i.e., the Brahmins' hero of the story) "Declare, if you can, any Kshatriya who has been superior to him. Tell me of any Kshatriya superior to Atri."

This class war between the Brahmins and the Kshatriyas must have gone on for ages. In light of this, the attitude of Manu towards this class war seems very strange. Consider the following verses from the *Manusmriti*:

IV. 135. "Let him who desires prosperity, indeed, never despise a Kshatriya, a snake, and a learned Brahmin, be they ever so feeble."

IV. 136. "Because these three, when treated with disrespect, may utterly destroy him; hence, a wise man must never despise them."

X. 322. "Kshatriyas prosper not without Brahmins, Brahmins prosper not without Kshatriyas; Brahmins and Kshatriyas, being closely united, prosper in this world and the next." Here, there is a clear attempt on the part of Manu to close the ranks. Against whom did Manu want the Brahmins and the Kshatriyas to close their ranks? Was this an attempt to forgive, and forget or was the motive to combine them in a conspiracy to achieve some unholy purpose? What were the circumstances that forced Manu to advise the Brahmins to forget their age-old enmity with the Kshatriyas and seek a helping hand? The circumstances must have been very hard and pressing, for there was no room left for rapproachment between the two. The Brahmins had hurled a terrible insult at the Kshatriyas and had wounded their pride by saying quite openly that the Kshatriyas were the illegitimate children of Brahmins, begotten by them on Kshatriya widows. The next offensive thing that the Brahmins had done to wound the feelings of the Kshatriyas was to extract from the latter a confession that the Brahmins were superior to the Kshatriyas in military prowess and had made Bhishma say:

"The prowess of the Brahmins can destroy even the gods. Those wise beings behold all these worlds. To them, it is indifferent whether they are perfumed with sandalwood or deformed with mire, whether they eat or fast, whether they are clad in silk or in sackcloth or skins. They can turn what is not divine into what is divine, and the converse; in their anger, they can create other worlds with their guardians. They are the gods of the gods and the cause of the cause. The ignorant Brahmin is a god, whilst a learned Brahmin is yet more a god, like the full ocean."

All this makes the sudden surrender by the Brahmins to win over the Kshatriyas very mysterious. What can be the key to this mystery?

❑

Chapter 12

The Shudras and the Counter-Revolution

This is a 21-page foolscap typed manuscript. The cover page has the title 'Shudras and the Counter-Revolution', and the text on next page starts with the same title. All these pages were loose and tagged together. Unfortunately, only 21 pages are available, and the latter pages seem to be lost.

–Editors

The laws of Manu relating to the status of the Shudra make for very interesting reading for the simple reason that they have moulded the psychology of the Hindus and determined their attitude towards the Shudras, who form at present and have always formed the most numerous part of Hindu society. They are set out below under separate heads so that the reader may have a complete idea of the status given by Manu to the community of Shudras.

Manu asks the householders of the Brahmin, Kshatriya, and Vaishya Class:

IV. 61. Let him not dwell in a country where the rulers are Shudra.

A Shudra is not to be deemed a respectable person. For Manu enacts that:

XI. 24. A Brahmin shall never beg from a Shudra property for performing a sacrifice, i.e., for religious purpose. All marriage ties with the Shudra were proscribed. Marriage with a woman belonging to any of the three other classes was forbidden. A Shudra was not to have any connection with a woman of the higher classes, and an act of adultery committed by a Shudra with her was declared by Manu to be an offence involving capital punishment.

VIII. 374. A Shudra who has intercourse with a woman of a higher caste guarded or unguarded, shall be punished in the following manner:

If she was unguarded, he lost the offending part. If she was guarded, then he should be put to death and his property confiscated.

As to office, Manu prescribes:

VIII. 20. A Brahmin who is only a Brahmin by decent, i.e., one who has neither studied nor performed any other act required by the Vedas, may, at the king's pleasure, interpret the law to him, i.e., act as the judge, but never a Shudra (however learned he may be).

VIII. 21. The kingdom of that monarch who looks on while a Shudra settles the law will sink low like a cow in a morass.

VIII. 272. If a Shudra arrogantly presumes to preach religion to Brahmins, the king shall have burning oil poured in his mouth and ears.

In the matter of acquiring learning, Manu ordains as follows:

III. 156. He who instructs Shudra pupils, and he whose teacher is a Shudra, shall become disqualified for being invited to a Shudra.

IV. 99. He must never read the Vedas in the presece of Shudras.

Manu's successors went much beyond him in the cruelty of their punishment of the Shudra for studying the Veda. For instance, Katyayana lays down that if a Shudra overheard the Veda or ventured to utter a word of the Veda, the king shall cut his tongue in twain and pour hot molten lead in his ears.

As to the right to property by the Shudra, Manu enjoins as follows:

X. 129. No superfluous collection of wealth must be made by a Shudra, even though he has power to make it, since a servile man who has amassed riches becomes proud and, by his insolence or neglect, gives pain to Brahmins.

VIII. 417. A Brahmin may seize without hesitation, if he is in distress for his subsistence, the goods of his Shudra.

The Shudra can have only one occupation. It is one of the inexhorable Laws of Manu. Says Manu:

I. 91. One occupation only, the Lord prescribed to the Shudra: to serve meekly these other three castes, namely Brahmin, Kshatriya, and Vaishyas.

X. 121. If a Shudra, unable to subsist by serving Brahmins, seeks a livelihood, he may serve Kshatriyas, or he may also seek to maintain himself by attending a wealthy Vaishya.

X. 122. But let a Shudra serve Brahmins, either for the sake of heaven or with a view to both this life and the next; for he who is called the servant of a Brahmin thereby gains all his ends.

X. 123. The service of Brahmins alone is declared to be an excellent occupation for a Shudra, for whatever else besides this he may perform will bear him no fruit. Service by Shudra is not left by Manu to be regulated as a free contract.

If the Shudra refuses to serve, there is a provision for conscription, which runs as follows:

VIII. 413. A Brahmin may compel a Shudra, whether bought or unbought, to do servile work. He is created by the Creator to be the slave of a Brahmin.

X. 124. They must allot to him out of their own family property a suitable maintenance after considering his ability, his industry, and the number of those whom he is bound to suport.

X. 125. The remnants of their food must be given to him, as well as their old household furniture.

A Shudra is required by Manu to be servile in his speech and manner towards the other classes.

VIII. 270. A Shudra who insults a twice-born man with gross invective shall have his tongue cut out, for he is of low origin.

VIII. 271. If he mentions the names and castes of the twice-born with contumely, an iron nail, ten fingers long, shall be thrust red hot into his mouth.

Manu is not satisfied with this. He wants this servile status of the Shudra to be expressed in the names and surnames of persons belonging to that community. Manu says:

II. 31. Let the first part of a Brahmin's name denote something auspicious, a Kshatriya's be connected with power, and a Vaishya's with wealth, but a Shudra's express something contemptible.

II. 32. The second part of a Brahmin's name shall be a word implying happiness; of a Kshatriya's, word implying protection; of a Vaishya's, a term expressive of thriving; and of a Shudra's, an expression denoting services.

What was the position of the Shudra before Manu? Manu treats the Shudra as though he is an alien, a Non-Aryan not entitled to the social and religious privileges of the Aryan. Unfortunately, the view that the Shudra was a Non-Aryan is too readily accepted by the generality of the people. However, there can be no doubt that this view has not the slightest foundation in the literature of the ancient Aryans.

Reading the religious literature of the ancient Aryans, one comes across the names of various communities and groups of people. There were, first of all, the Aryans with their fourfold divisions of Brahmins, Kshatriyas, Vaishyas, and Shudras. Besides them, and apart from them, there were *(i)* Asuras, *(ii)* Suras or Devas, (iii)Yakshas, *(iv)* Gandharvas, *(v)* Kinnars, *(vi)* Charanas, *(vii)* Ashvins, and *(viii)* Nishadas. The Nishadas were a jungle people, primitive and uncivilized. The Gandharvas, Yakshas, Kinnars, Charanas, and Ashvins were professional classes and not communities. The word *Asura* is generic name given to various tribes known by their tribal names of Daityas, Danavas, Dasyus, Kalananjas, Kaleyyas, Kalins, Nagas, Nivata-Kavachas, Paulomas, Pishachas, and Rakshasas. We do not know if the Suras and Devas were composed of various tribes as the Asuras were. We only know the leaders of the Deva Community. The well-known among them were Brahma, Vishnu, Rudra, Surya, Indra, Varuna, Soma, etc.

Due mostly to the ignorant interpretations of Sayanacharya, some very curious beliefs prevail even among the best-informed people about these communities, namely the Aryans, the Asuras and the Devas, and their inter-relation and consanguinity. It is believed that the Asuras were not a human species at all. They are held to have been ghosts and goblins who plagued the Aryans with their nocturnal visitations. The Suras or Devas are understood to be poetic deifications of nature's forces. About the Aryans, the belief is that they were a fair race with sharp nose and had a great deal of colour prejudice. As to the Dasyus, it is asserted that a Dasyu is only another name for a Shudra. The Shudras, it is said, formed the aboriginals of India. They were dark and flat-nosed. The Aryans, who invaded India, conquered them and made them slaves, and as a badge of slavery, gave them the name Dasyu, which, it is said, comes from the word Das, which means a slave.

Every one of these beliefs is unfounded. The Asuras and Suras were communities of human beings, as the Aryans were. The Asuras and Suras were descended from a common father, Kashyapa. The story is that Daksha Prajapati had 60 daughters, of whom 13 were given in marriage to Kashyapa. Diti and Aditi were two among the 13 of Kashyapa's wives. Those born to Diti were called Asuras, and those born to Aditi were called Suras or Devas.

The two fought a long and bloody battle for the sovereignty of the world. This no doubt is mythology, and mythology, though it is history in hyperbole, is still history.

The Aryans were not a race. The Aryans were a collection of people. The cement that held them together was their interest in the maintenance of a type of culture called Aryan culture. Anyone who accepted the Aryan culture was an Aryan. Not being a race, there was no fixed type of colour and physiognomy, which could be called Aryan. There was no dark and flat-nosed people for the Aryans to distinguish themselves from. The whole of this edifice of colour prejudice as being factors for division and antagonism between Aryans and the Dasyus is based upon a wrong meaning given to the two words *Varna* and *Anas,* which are used concerning the Dasyus. The word *Varna* is taken to mean colour, and the word *Anas* is taken to mean without nose. Both these meanings are erroneous. *Varna* means caste or group, and *Anas,* if read as *An-As*, means uncultivated speech. That statement that the Aryans had a colour prejudice which determined their social order is arrant nonsense. If any people were devoid of colour prejudice, it was the Aryans, and that is because there was no dominant colour to distinguish them.

It is wrong to say that the Dasyus were non-Aryans by race. The Dasyus were not a pre-Aryan race of aboriginals of India. The Dasyus were members of the Aryan community who were deprived of the title of Arya for opposing some belief or cult, which was an essential part of the Aryan culture. How this belief that the Dasyus were non-Aryans by race could have arisen is difficult to understand. In the *Rig Veda* (X. 49) Indra says: "I (Indra) have killed with my thuderbolt for the good of the man, known as Kavi. I have protected Kupa by adopting means of protection. I took up the thunderbolt for killing Susna. I have deprived the Dasyus of the appellation of Arya."

Nothing can be more positive and definite than this statement of Indra that the Dasyus were Aryans. Further and better proof of this fact can be had in the impeachment of Indra for the various atrocities he had committed. Among the charges, there was one, namely the killing of Vratra. Vratra was the leader of the Dasyus. It is unthinkable that such a charge could be framed against Indra if the Dasyus were not Aryans.

It is erroneous to believe that the Shudras were conquered by the Aryan invaders. In the first place, the story that the Aryans came from outside India and invaded the natives has no evidence to support it. There is a large body of evidence that India is the home of the Aryans. In the second place, there is no evidence anywhere of any warfare having taken place between Aryans and Dasyus, and the Dasyus have nothing to do with the Shudras. In the third place, it is difficult to believe that the Aryans were powerful people capable of much military prowess. Anyone who reads the history of the Aryans in India in their relation to the Devas will be reminded of the relationship that subsisted between the Villeins and their lords during the feudal times. The Devas were the feudal lords, and the Aryans were the Villeins. The innumerable sacrifices the Aryans performed have the look of fudal dues paid to the Deva. This servility of the Aryans to the Devas was due to the fact that, without the help and the protection of the Devas, they could not withstand the assualts of the Asuras. It is too much to presume that so effete people could have conquered the Shudras. Lastly, there was no necessity to conquer the Shudra. They were Aryans in the only sense in which the word Aryan is used, namely, the upholders of the Aryans culture. Two things are clear about the Shudras. Nobody has ever contended that they were dark and flat-nosed. Nobody has contended that they were defeated or enslaved by the Aryans. It is wrong to treat the Dasyus and Shudras as the same. As people, they may be the same. But culturally, they were quite different. The Dasyus were non-Aryans in the sense that they had fallen away and rebelled against the Aryan culture. The Shudras on the other hand, were Aryans, i.e., they were believers in the Aryan way of life. The Shudra was accepted as an Aryan, and as late as Kautilya's *Arthashastra*, he was addressed as Arya.

That the Shudra was an intergral, natural, and valued member of the Aryan society is proved by a prayer found in the *Yajur Veda* and offered by the sacrificer. It runs as follows:" O Gods, give lustre to our holy priests, set lustre in our ruling chiefs, lustre to Vaishyas, Shudras: give, through lustre, lustre unto me." It is a remarkable prayer. Remarkable because it shows that the Shudra was a member of the Aryan community and was also a respected member of it.

That the Shudras were invited to be present at the coronation of the king along with Brahmins, Kshatriyas, and Vaishyas is proved by the description given in the *Mahabharata* of the coronation of Yudhishthira, the eldest brother of the Pandavas. The Shudra took part in the consecration of the king. According to ancient writer named Nilkantha, speaking of the coronation ceremony, expressly says: "that the four chief Ministers, Brahmin, Kshatriya, Vaishya, and Shudra consecrated the new king. Then the leaders of each Varna and by the Castes lower still consecrated him with the holy water. Then followed acclamation by the twice-born." In the post-Vedic period preceding Manu, there was a group of representatives of the people called the Ratnis. The Ratnis played a significant part in the investiture of the king. The Ratnis were so called because they held the Ratna (jewel), which was a symbol of sovereignty. The king received his sovereignty only when the Ratnis handed over to him the jewel of sovereignty, and on receiving his sovereignty, the king went to the house of each of the Ratnis and made an offering to him. It is a significant fact that the Shudra was one of the Ratnis.

Shudras were members of the two political assemblies of ancient times, namely the Janapada and Paura, and as a member of this, he was entitled to special respect even from a Brahmin. That the Shudra in the ancient Aryan society had reached a high political status is indisputable. They could become ministers of state. The *Mahabharata* bears testimony to this. Enumerating the different classes of ministers within his memory, the writer of the *Mahabharata* mentions a list of 37 ministers, of whom four are

Brahmins, eight Kshatriyas, twenty-one Vaishyas, three Shudras, and one Suta.

Shudras did not stop with being ministers of state. They even became kings. The story of Shudras, as given in the *Rig Veda,* stands in cruel contrast to the views expressed by Manu regarding the eligibility of the Shudra to be a king. The reign of Sudas, if referred to at all, is mentioned only in connection with the terrible contest between Vasishtha and Vishwamitra as to who should become the purohit or royal priest of King Sudas. The issue involved in the contest was the right to officiate as the Purohit of the king. Vasishtha, who was a Brahmin and already the officiating priest of Sudas, claimed that a Brahmin alone could become the Purohit of a king, while Vishwamitra, who was a Kshatriya, contended that a Kshatriya was competent for that office. Vishwamitra succeeded, and, in turn, became the Purohit of Sudas. The contest is indeed memorable because the issue involved is very crucial, although the result has permanently deprived the Brahmins. However, there can be no doubt that the story is probably the best piece of social history found in the ancient literature. Unfortunately, nobody has taken serious notice of it. Nobody has even asked who this king was. Sudas was the son of Paijavana, and Paijavana was the son of Devodas, who was the King of Kashi, i.e., Banaras. What was the Varna of Sudas? Few would believe if they were told that King Sudas was a Shudra. But that is a fact, and it can be proved by the testimony of the *Mahabharata*, where, in the Santipurva, a reference is made to *Paijavana.* It is stated that Paijavana was a Shudra. In light of this, the story of Sudas sheds new light on the status of the Shudra in the Aryan society. It shows that a Shudra could be a reigning monarch. It also shows that both the Brahmins and the Kshatriyas not only saw no humiliation in serving a Shudra king but vied with each other to secure his patronage and were ready to perform Vedic ceremonies at his house.

It cannot be said that there were no Shudra kings in later times. On the contrary, history shows that the two dynasties that preceded Manu were dynasties of Shudras kings. The Nandas, who ruled from 413 B.C. to 322 B.C., were Shudras. The Mauryas, who succeded the Nandas and ruled from 322 B.C., to 183 B.C., were also Shudras. What more glaring piece of evidence can there be to show the high dignity enjoyed by the Shudra than to point to the case of Ashoka who was not merely the Emperor of India but a Shudra and whose empire was built by the Shudras.

On the question of the right of the Shudra to study the Vedas, a reference may be made to the *Chandogya Upanishad* (V.1.2). It relates the story of one Janasruti, to whom Veda Vidya was taught by the preceptor Raikva. This Janasruti was a Shudra. This story, if it is genuine, leaves no doubt that there was a time when there was no bar against the Shudra in the matter of studying the Vedas.

Not only was the Shudra free to study the Vedas, but there were Shudras who had reached the status of Rishis and had been composers of the hymns of the Vedas. The story of the Rishi Kavasha Ailusha is very illuminating. He was a Rishi and the author of several hymns of the Tenth Book of the *Rig-Veda*.

On the question of the spiritual eligibility of the Shudra to perform the Vedic ceremonies and sacrifices, the following data may be presented. Jaimin, the author of the *Purva Mimamsa,* mentions an ancient teacher by the name of Badari—whose work is lost—as an exponent of the view that even Shudras could perform Vedic sacrifices. The *Bharadvaja Srauta Sutra* (V.28) admits that there exists another school of thought which holds that a Shudras can consecrate the three sacred fires necessary for performing a Vedic sacrifice. Similarly, the commentator of the *Katyayana Srauta Sutra* (I & 5) admits that certain Vedic texts lead to the inference that the Shudra was eligible to perform Vedic rites. In the Satapatha Brahmana (1.1.4.12), there is a rule of etiquette enunciated that the priest officiating at the performance of a sacrifice is required to observe. It relates to how the priest should address the *Haviskut* (the person celebrating the sacrifice) when calling upon him to begin the ceremony. The rule says:

"Now there are four different forms of this call: 'Come hither' (Ehi) in the case of a Brahmin; 'Approach' (Agahi) and 'Hasten hither' (Adarva) in the case of a Vaishya and a member of the military caste and 'Run hither' (Adhava) in that of a Shudra." In the Satapatha Brahmana, there is evidence to show that the Shudra was eligible to perform the Soma Yaga and partake in the divine drink Soma. It says that in the Soma Yaga, in place of a 'payovrata' (vow to drink milk only), *Mastu* (whey) is prescirbed for the Shudra. In another place, the same Satapatha Brahmana says:

"There are four classes: the Brahmin, Rajanya, Vaishya, and Shudra. No one of these dislikes Soma. If any one of them, however, should do so, let there be an atonment." This means that the drinking of Soma was not only permissible but also compulsory on all, including the Shudra. In the story of the Ashvins, there is definite evidence that the Shudra had a right to the divine drink of Soma. The Ashvins, as the story goes, once happened to behold Sukanya when she had just bathed and her person was bare. She was a young girl married to a Rishi by the name of Chyavana, who, at the time of marriage, was so old as to be dying almost any day. The Ashvins were captivated by the beauty of Sukanya and said, "Accept one of us for your husband; it behooveth thee not to spend thy youth fruitlessly."

She refused, saying, "I am devoted to my husband." They spoke to her again and, this time, proposed a bargain: "We two are celestial physicians of note. We will make thy husband young and graceful. Do thou then select one of us as thy husband?" She went to her husband and communicated to him the terms of the bargain. Chyavana said to Sukanya, "Do thou so", and the bargain was carried out. Chyavana was made a young man by the Ashwins. Subsequently, a question arose as to whether the Ashwins were entitled to Soma, which was the drink of the gods. Indra objected, saying that the Ashwins were Shudras and, therefore, not entitled to Soma. Chyavana, who had received perpetual youth from the Ashwins, set aside the contention and compelled Indra to give them Soma.

All these provisions can have no meaning unless the Shudra was performing the Vedic ceremonies to which they relate. There is evidence to show that a Shudra woman took part in the Vedic sacrifice known as the Ashwamedha.

Regarding the Upanayana ceremony and the right to wear the sacred thread, there is nowhere an express prohibition against the Shudra. On the other hand, in the *Sanskara Ganapati,* there is an express provision declaring the Shudra eligible for Upanayana. The Shudra, though belonging to a lower class, was nonetheless a free citizen in the days before Manu. This cannot be gainsaid. Consider the following provisions in Kautilya's *Arthashastra*:

"The selling or mortgaging by kinsmen of the life of a Shudra who is not a born slave and has not attained majority, but is an Arya by birth, shall be punished with a fine of 2 panas."

"Deceiving a slave of his money or depriving him of the privileges he can exercise as an Arya (*Aryabhava*) shall be punished with half the fine levied for enslaving the life of an Arya."

"Failure to set a slave at liberty on the receipt of a required amount of ransom shall be punished with a fine of 12 panas; putting a slave under confinement for no reason (*samrodhaschakaranat*) shall likewise be punished."

"The offspring of a man who has sold himself as a slave shall be an Arya. A slave shall be entitled, without prejudice to his master's work, to the inheritance he has received from his father."

Why did Manu suppress the Shudra?

This riddle of the Shudra is not a simple one. It is a complex one. The Aryans were forever attempting to Aryanize the non-Aryans, i.e., bringing them within the pale of the Aryan culture. So keen were the Aryans on Aryanization that they developed a religious ceremony for the mass conversion of the non-Aryans.

The ceremony was called *Vratya-stoma.* Speaking of the Vratya-stoma, Mahamahopadhyaya Haraprasad Shastri says:

"The ceremony by which these Vratyas were purified, and which is described in the *Pancavimsa-Brahmana,* differed at least in one particular from other great ceremonies of the Vedic times, namely, while other ceremonies had only one sacrificer and his wife in the hall of sacrifice, this ceremony had thousands of sacrificers. One of them, the wisest, the richest, or the most powerful, acted as Grahapati or Patriarch, and the rest simply followed him. The Grahapati had to pay a higher dakshina or fee than the rest."

"I consider this to be a device by which thousands of Vratyas were admitted to the society of the Rishis by one ceremony, and such ceremonies were of frequent occurrence, thus admitting hordes of nomadic Aryans into settled habits. The purified Vratyas were not allowed to bring their possessions from Vratya life with them into settled life. They had to leave them to those who remained Vratyas or to the so-called Brahmins of the Magadha-desa, which, as I have elsewhere shown, was mostly inhabited by men whom the Rishis looked down upon."

"But when the Vratyas were admitted to settled life, they were admitted as full—equals. The Rishis used to eat food cooked by them, and they used to eat food cooked by the Rishis. They were taught all the three Vidyas Sama, Rk, and Yajus—and they were allowed to study the Vedas and teach them and to sacrifice for themselves and for others; that is, they were considered as full equals. Not only were they treated as full equals, but they also attained the highest proficiency of a Rishis. *Samans* were revealed to them, and even *Rks*. One of the purified Vratyas, Kausitaki, was allowed to collect Brahmins of the *Rig Veda*, which collection still goes under his name."

The Aryans were not only converting willing non-Aryans to their way of life, but they were also attempting to make converts from among the unwilling Asuras, who were opposed to the

Aryans, their cult of sacrifice, their theory of *Chaturvarna,* and even their Vedas, which, according to the mythology, the Asuras stole from the Aryas. The story of Vishnu rescuing Prahlada by killing his father, the Asura called Hiranyakashipu, because Prahlada was willing to be converted to the Aryan culture while Hiranyakashipu was opposed to it, is an illustration in point. Here are instances of non-Aryans being naturalized and enfranchised. Why was an opposite attitude taken against the Shudra? Why was the Shudra, who had been fully naturalized and fully enfranchised, later denaturalized and disfranchised?

The treatment given to the *Nishadas* adds another layer to this riddle, which should not be overlooked. Ancient Sanskrit literature is full of references to the five tribes. They are described under various appellations such as Panch-Krishtayah, Panch-Kshitayah, Panch-Kshityas Manushyah, Panch-Charshanayah, Panch-Janah, and Panchi-Janya, viz., Pancha-Bhuma, and Panchajata. There is a difference of opinion regarding what these terms denote. Sayanacharya, the commentator of *Rig Veda,* says that these expressions refer to the four Varnas and the Nishadas. The *Vishnu Purana* gives the following story about the Nishadas:

7. The Maiden named Sunitha, who was the first born of Mrityu (Death), was given as wife to Anga, and of her, Vena was born.

8. This son of Mrityu's daughter, infected with the taint of his maternal grandfather, was born corrupt, as if by nature.

9. When Vena was inaugurated as king by the eminent Rishis, he caused this proclamation to be made on the earth; "Men must not sacrifice, give gifts, or present oblations. Who else but myself is the enjoyer of sacrifices? I am forever the lord of offerings."

10. Then all the Rishis, approaching the king with respectful salutations, said to him in a gentle and conciliatory tone:

11. Hear, O King, what we have to say:

12. We shall worship Hari, the monarch of the gods and the lord of all sacrifices, with a *Dirghasattra* (prolonged sacrifice), from which the highest benefits will accrue to your kingdom, your person, and your subjects. May blessing rest upon you. You shall have a share in the ceremony.

13. Vishnu, the Lord of Sacrifices being propitiated by us with this rite, will grant all the objects of your desire. Hari, the Lord of Sacrifices, bestows on those kings in whose country he is honoured with oblation everything that they wish." Vena replied: "What other being is superior to me? Who else but I should be adored? Who is this person called Hari, whom you regard as the Lord of Sacrifices? Brahma, Janardana, Rudra, Indra, Vayu, Yama, Ravi (the Sun), Agni, Varuna, Dhatri, Pushan, Earth, and the Moon,—these and the other gods who curse and bless are all present in king's person: for he is composed of all the gods. Knowing this, ye must act in conformity with my commands. Brahmins, ye must neither give gifts, nor present oblations, nor sacrifices.

14. As obedience to their husbands is esteemed the highest duty of women, so is the observance of my orders incumbent upon you." The Rishis answered, 'Give permission, great king; let not religion perish: this whole world is but a modified form of oblations.

15. When religion perishes, the whole world is destroyed with it. "When Vena, although thus admonished and repeatedly addressed by the eminent Rishis, did not give his permission, then all the Munis, filled with wrath and indignation, cried out to one another, "Slay, slay the sinner."

16. "This man of degraded life, who blasphemes the Sacrificial Male, the God, the Lord without beginning or end, is not fit to be lord of the earth." So saying, the Munis smote with blades of *kusa* (grass), consecrated by texts, this king, who had already been smitten by his blasphemy of the divine being and his other offences. The Munis afterwards beheld

dust all around and asked the people who were standing near what that was.

17. They were informed: "In this country which has no king, the people being distressed, have become robbers and have begun to seize the property of others.

18. It is from these robbers, rushing impetuously and plundering other men's goods, that this great dust is seen." Then all the Munis, consulting together, rubbed with force the thigh of the king, who was childless, to produce a son. From his thigh, when rubbed, there was produced a man like a charred log, with flat face and extremely short stature.

19. "What shall I do?" cried the man in distress to the Brahmins. They said to him, "Sit down (Nishida)," and from, this he became a Nishada.

20. From him sprang the Nishadas, dwelling in the Vindhya mountains, distinguished by their wicked deeds.

21. By this means, the sin of the king departed from him; and so were the Nishadas produced, the offspring of the wickedness of Vena.

It is a mythological origin of the Nishadas. But it contains historical facts. It proves that the Nishadas were a low, primitive jungle tribe living in the forests of the Vindhya mountains and that they were wicked people, i.e., opposed to the Aryan culture. The Aryans invented a mythology to explain their origin and connect them with the Aryan society. All this was done to support the inclusion of the Nishadas into the Aryan fold though not fully into the Aryan society. Nowhere were there any sort of disabilities imposed upon Nishadas, a low, uncivilized, and foreign tribe. The question remains: why were disabilities imposed upon the Shudra, who was civilized and an Arya?

❑

Chapter 13

The Women and the Counter-Revolution

There is one copy with the title 'The Woman and the Counter-Revolution.' There is another copy of the same text with the title, 'The Riddle of the Woman.' The Editorial Board felt this essay would be more appropriate in this Volume rather than in the Volume of 'Riddles in Hinduism.'

–Editors

Manu can hardly be said to be more tender to women than he was to the Shudra. He starts with a low opinion of women. Manu proclaims:

II. 213. It is the nature of women to seduce men in this world; for that reason, the wise are never unguarded in the company of females.

III. 214. Women can lead astray in this world, not only fools but even learned men, and make them slave of desire and anger.

IV. 215. One should not sit in a lonely place with one's mother, sister, or daughter. For the senses are powerful and can master even a learned man.

IX. 14. Women do not care for beauty, nor their attention is fixed on age; thinking that is enough that he is a man,' they give themselves to the handsome and the ugly.

X. 15. Through their passion for men, through their mutable temper, through their natural heartlessness, they become disloyal towards their husbands, however carefully they may be guarded in this world.

XI. 16. Knowing their disposition, which the Lord of Creatures laid in them at the creation to be such, every man should most strenuously exert himself to guard them.

XII. 17. When creating them, Manu allotted to women a love of their bed, their seat, and their ornament, impure desires, wrath, dishonesty, malice, and bad conduct.

The laws of Manu against women are of a piece with this view. Women are not to be free under any circumstances. In the opinion of Manu:

XIII. 2. Day and night, women must be kept dependent by the males of their families, and if they attach themselves to sexual enjoyment, they must be kept under one's control.

XIV. 3. Her father protects her in childhood, her husband protects her in youth, and her sons protect her in old age; a woman is never fit for independence.

XV. 5. Women must especially be guarded against evil inclinations, however trifling they may appear. For if they are not guarded, they will bring sorrow on two families.

XVI. 6. Considering that the highest duty of all castes, even weak husbands must strive to guard their wives.

XVII. 147. By a girl, by a young woman, or even by an aged one, nothing must be done independently, even in her own house.

XVIII. 148. In childhood, a female must be subject to her father, in youth to her husband, when her husband is dead to her sons. A women must never be independent.

XIX. 149. She must not seek to separate herself from her father, husband, or sons; by leaving them, she would make both her own and her husband's families contemptible. Women do not have a right to divorce.

XX. 45. The husband is declared to be one with the wife, which means that there could be no separation once a woman is married. Many Hindus stop here as though this is the whole story regarding Manu's law of divorce and keep on idolizing it by comforting their conscience by holding out the view that Manu regarded marriage as sacrament and, therefore, did not allow divorce. This, of course, is far from the truth. His law against divorce had a very different motive. It was not to tie up a man to a woman but to tie up the woman to a man and to leave the man free.

Manu does not prevent a man from giving up his wife. Indeed, he not only allows him to abandon his wife, but he also permits him to sell her. But what he does is to prevent the wife from becoming free. See what Manu says:

XXI. 46. Neither by sale nor by repudiation is a wife released from her husband.

The meaning is that a wife, sold or repudiated by her husband, can never become the legitimate wife of another who may have bought or received her after she was repudiated. If this is not monstrous, nothing can be. But Manu was not worried by considerations of justice or injustice in his law. He wanted to deprive women of the freedom they had under the Buddhist regime. Manu knew that by her misuse of her liberty, by her willingness to marry the Shudra, the system of the gradation of the Varna had been destroyed. Manu was outraged by her license, and in putting a stop to it, he deprived her of her liberty.

A wife was reduced by Manu to the level of a slave in the matter of property.

XXII. 416. A wife, a son, and a slave are declared to have no property; the wealth which they earn is acquired for him to whom they belong.

When she becomes a widow, Manu allows her maintenance if her husband was joint and a widow's estate on the property of her husband if he was separate from his family. But Manu never allows her to have any dominion over property.

A woman, under the laws of Manu, is subject to corporal punishment, and Manu allows the husband the right to beat his wife.

VIII. 299. A wife, a son, a slave, a pupil, and a younger brother of blood who have committed faults may be beaten with a rope or split bamboo. In other matters, the woman was reduced by Manu to the same position as the Shudra.

The study of the Veda was forbidden to her by Manu, as it was to the Shudra.

11.66. Even for a woman, the performance of the *Sanskaras* is necessary, and they should be performed. But they should be performed without uttering the Veda Mantras.

IX. 18. Women have no right to study the Vedas. That is why their Sanskaras are performed without Veda Mantras. Women do not know about religion because they have no right to know the Vedas. The uttering of the Veda Mantras is useful for removing sin. As women cannot utter the Veda Mantras, they are as unclean as untruth is.

Offering sacrifices, according to Brahmanism, formed the very soul of religion. Yet Manu will not allow women to perform them. Manu ordains that:

XI. 36. A woman shall not perform the daily sacrifices prescribed by the Vedas.

XI. 37, If she does it, she will go to hell.

To disable her from performing such sacrifices, Manu prevents her from getting the aid and services of a Brahmin priest.

IV. 205. A Brahmin must never eat food given at a sacrifice performed by a woman.

V. 206. Sacrifices performed by women are inauspicious and not acceptable to God. They should, therefore, be avoided. Women were not to have any intellectual pursuits free will, or freedom of thought. She was not to join any heretical sect such as Buddhism. If she continues to adhere to it till death, she is not to be given the libation of water as is done in the case of all dead.

Finally, a word regarding the ideal of life Manu has sought to place before a woman. It is better to state in his own words:

VI. 151. Him to whom her father may give her or her brother with the father's permission, she shall obey as long as he lives, and when he is dead, she must not insult his memory.

VII. 154. Though destitute or virtue, or seeking pleasure elsewhere, or devoid of good qualities, a husband must be constantly worshipped as a god by a faithful wife.

VIII. 155. No sacrifice, no vow, no fast must be performed by women apart from their husbands; if a wife obeys her husband, she will, for that reason alone, be exalted in heaven. Then comes the choicest text, which forms the pith and marrow of this ideal that Manu prescribes for women:

IX. 153. The husband who wedded her with sacred Mantras is always a source of happiness to his wife, both in season and out of season, in this world and the next.

X. 150. She must always be cheerful, clever in the management of her household affairs, careful in cleaning her utensils, and economical in expenditure.

This, the Hindus regard as a very lofty ideal for a woman! Compare this with the position of the woman before the days of Manu.

That a woman was entitled to *Upanayan* is clear from the *Atharva Veda,* where a girl is spoken of as being eligible for marriage having finished her *Brahmacharya*. From the *Shrauta Sutras,* it is clear that women could repeat the Mantras of the

Vedas and that women were taught to read the Vedas. Panini's *Ashtaadhyai* bears testimony to the fact that women attended *Gurukul* and studied the various Shakhas of the Veda and became expert in *Mimansa*. Patanjali's *Mahabhasya* shows that women were teachers and taught the Vedas to girl students. The stories of women entering into public discussions with men on the most abstruse subjects of religion, philosophy, and metaphysics are by no means few. The story of public disputation between Janaka and Sulbha, between Yajnavalkya and Gargi, between Yajnavalkya and Maitrei, and between Shankaracharya and Vidyadhari shows that Indian women in pre-Manu times could rise to the highest pinnacle of learning and education.

That women in pre-Manu days were highly respected cannot be disputed. Among the *Ratnis* who played so prominent a part in the coronation of the king in ancient India, was the queen, and the king made her an offering, as he did to the others. Not only the king-elect do homage to the queen, but he also worshipped his other wives of lower castes. In the same way, the king offers salutations after the coronation ceremony to the ladies of the chiefs of the shremes (guides).

In the days of Kautilya, women were deemed to have attained their age of majority at 12 and men at 16. The age of majority was, in all probability, the age of marriage. That the marriages were post-puberty marriages is clear from Baudhayana's *Grihya Sutras*, where an expiatory ceremony is specially prescribed in the case of a bride passing her menses on the occasion of her marriage.

In Kautilya, there is no law as to the age of consent. That is because marriages were post-puberty marriages, and Kautilya is more concerned with cases in which a bride or a bridegroom is married without disclosing the fact of his or her having had sexual intercouse before marriage with another person or a maiden in menses having had sexual intercouse. In the former case, Kautilya says:

"Any person who has given a girl in marriage without announcing her guilt of having laid with another shall not only be punished with a fine but also be made to return the *Sulka* and *Stridhana.* Any person receiving a girl in marriage without announcing the blemishes of the bridegroom shall not only pay double the above fine but also forfeit the *Sulka* and *Stridhana* he paid for the bride." Regarding the latter case, the rule in Kautilya is:

"It is no offence for a man of equal caste and rank to have connection with a maiden who has been unmarried three years after her first menses. Nor is it an offence for a man, even of different caste, to have connection with a maiden who has spent more than three years after her first menses and has no jewellery on her person."

Unlike Manu, Kautilya's idea is monogamy. A man can marry more than one wife only under certain conditions. They are given by Kautilya in the following terms:

"If a woman either brings forth no (live) children, or has no male issue, or is barren, her husband shall wait for eight years before marrying another. If she bears only a dead child, he has to wait for ten years. If she brings forth only females, he has to wait for twelve years. Then if he is desirious to have sons, he may marry another. In case of violating this rule, he shall be made to pay her not only *Sulka*, her property (*Stridhana*) and an adequate monetary compensation (*adhivedanika martham*), but also a fine of 24 *panas* to the government. Having given the necessary amount of *Sulka* and property (*Stridhana*) even to those women who have not received such things on the occasion of their marriage with him, and also having given his wives the proportionate compensation and an adequate subsistence (*vrutti*), he may marry any number of women; for women are created for the sake of sons."

Unlike Manu, in Kautilya's time, women could claim divorce on the grounds of mutual enmity and hatred.

"A woman, hating her husband, cannot dissolve her marriage with him against his will. Nor can a man dissolve his marriage with his wife against her will. But from mutual enmity, divorce may be obtained (*parasparam dveshanmokshah*). If a man, apprehending danger from his wife, desires divorce (*mokshamichchhet*), he shall return to her whatever she was given on the occasion of her marriage. If a woman, under the apprehension of danger from her husband, desires divorce, she shall forfeit her claim to her property." A wife can abandon her husband if he is of bad character.

"A woman who has a right to claim maintenance for an unlimited period of time shall be given as much food and clothing (*grasacchadana*) as necessary for her, or more than is neessary in proportion to the income of the maintainer (*yathapurushapari-vapam va*). If the period for which such things are to be given to her with one-tenth of the amount in addition) is limited, then a certain amount of money, fixed in proportion to the income of the maintainer, shall be given to her; so also if she has not been given her *Sulka*, property, and compensation (due to her for allowing her husband to re-marry). If she places herself under the protection of anyone belonging to her father-in-law's family (*Svasurakula*), or if she begins to live independently, then her husband shall not be sued for her maintenance. Thus, the determination of maintenance is dealt with."

In the days of Kautilya, there was no ban on a woman or a widow remarrying:

"On the death of her husband, a woman desirous of leading a pious life shall at once receive not only her endowment and jewellery (*sthapyabharanam*) but also the balance of *Sulka* due to her. If, after obtaining these two things, she remarries another, she shall be caused to pay them back together with interest (on their value). If she is desirous of a second marriage (*kutumbarkama*), she shall be given, on the occasion of her remarriage (*nivesakale*) whatever either her father-in-law or her husband or both had given to her. The time at which women can remarry shall be explained in connection with the subject of long sojourn of husbands."

"If a widow marries any man other than one of her father-in-law's selection (*svasurapratilomyenanivishta*), she shall forfeit whatever had been given to her by her father-in-law and her deceased husband."

"The kinsmen (*gnatis*) of a woman shall return to her old father-in-law whatever property of her own she had taken with her while remarrying a kinsman. Whoever justly takes a woman under his protection shall equally protect her property. No woman shall succeed in her attempt to establish her title to the property of her deceased husband after she remarries."

"If she lives a pious life, she may enjoy it (*dharmaKarna bhunjita*). No woman with a son or sons shall (after remarriage) be at liberty to make free use of her own property (*Stridhana*); for that property of hers, her sons shall receive." If a woman after re-marriage, attempts to take possession of her own property under the plea of maintaining her sons by her former husband, she shall be made to endow it in their name. If a woman has many male children by many husbands, then she shall conserve her property in the same condition as she had received from her husbands. Even that property which has been given her with full powers of enjoyment and disposal, a remarried woman shall endow in the name of her sons.

"A barren widow who is faithful to the bed of her dead husband may, under the protection of her teacher, enjoy her property as long as she lives. As it is to ward off calamities that women are endowed with property. Upon her death, her property shall pass into the hands of her kinsman (Dayada). If the husband is alive and the wife is dead, then her sons and daughters shall divide her property among themselves. If there are no sons, her daughters shall inherit it. In their absence, her husband shall take that amount of money (*Sulka*) that he had given her, and her relatives shall reclaim whatever in the shape of gift or dowry they had presented to her. Thus, the determination of the property of a woman is dealt with."

"Wives who belong to the Shudra, Vaishya, Kshatriya or Brahmin caste and who have not given birth to children should wait for one, two, three, and four years, respectively, for their husbands who have gone abroad for a short time. If they have given birth to children, they should wait for their absent husbands for more than a year. If they are provided with maintenance, they should wait for twice the period just mentioned. If they are not so provided for, their well-to-do *gnatis* should maintain them for four or eight years. Then, the gnatis should allow them to marry, after taking what was presented to them on the occasion of their marriages. If the husband is a Brahmin, studying abroad, his wife with no children should wait for him for ten years; if she has given birth to children, she should wait for twelve years. If the husband is a servant of the king, his wife should wait for him until her death. However, if she bears children to a *savarna* husband (i.e., a second husband belonging to the same *gotra* as that of the former husband) to avoid the extinction of her lineage, she shall not be liable to contempt (*savarnatascha prajata na 'pavadam labheta*). If the wife of an absent husband lacks maintenance and is deserted by well-to-do *gnatis*, she may remarry one whom she likes and who is in a position to maintian her and relieve her misery."

Unlike Manu, every precaution was taken to guarantee economic independence for a married woman. This is clear from the following provisions in Kautilya's *Arthashastra* relating to wife's endowment and maintenance:

"Means of subsistence (*vruti*) or jewellery (*abadhya*) constitute what is called the property of a woman. Means of subsistence valued above two thousand shall be endowed (in her name). There is no limit to jewellery. It is not a sin for the wife to make use of this property in maintaining her son, her daughter-in-law, or herself whenever her absent husband has made no provision for her maintenance. In times of calamities, disease and famine, warding off dangers, and charitable acts, the husband, too, may make use of this property. There shall no complaint against the enjoyment of this property by mutual consent between a couple who have brought forth a twin. Nor shall there be any complaint if this property has been enjoyed for three years by those wedded according to the customs of the first four kinds of marriage. However, the enjoyment of this property in the cases of Gandharva and Asura marriages shall be liable to be restored together with interest. In the case of marriages such as Rakshasa and Paisacha, the use of this property shall be treated as theft. Thus, the duty of marriage is dealt with."

"A woman who has the right to claim maintenance for an unlimited time shall be given as much food and clothing (grasachhadan) as is necessary for her, or more if necessary in proportion to the income of the maintainer (yatha-purushaparivapam va). If the maintenance period is limited, then a certain amount of money, fixed in proportion to the income of the maintainer, shall be given to her, along with one tenth of the amount in addition. It also applies if she has not received her sulka, property, and compensation due to her allowing her husband to remarry. If she places herself under the protection of someone belonging to her father-in-law's family (*svasurkula*), or if she begins to live independently, then her husband shall not for her maintenance. Thus, the determination of maintenance is dealt with." Surprising as it may appear, in Kautilya's time, a wife could bring an action in a court of law against her husband for assault and defamation.

In short, in pre-Manu days, a woman was free and equal partner of a man. Why did Manu degrade her?

❑